Black Americans
in the Roosevelt Era

Twentieth-Century America Series

Black Americans in the Roosevelt Era

LIBERALISM AND RACE

John B. Kirby

THE UNIVERSITY OF TENNESSEE PRESS

KNOXVILLE

ℬ *Twentieth-Century America Series*

DEWEY W. GRANTHAM, GENERAL EDITOR

Publication of this book was assisted by a grant from the American Council of Learned Societies.

Clothbound editions of University of Tennessee Press books are printed on paper designed for an effective life of at least 300 years, and binding materials are chosen for strength and durability.

Library of Congress Cataloging in Publication Data

Kirby, John B   1938-
    Black Americans in the Roosevelt era.

    (Twentieth-century America Series)
    Bibliography: p.
    Includes index.
    1. Afro-Americans—History—1877-1964. 2. United States—Politics and government—1933-1945. 3. Afro-Americans—Civil rights. 4. United States—Race relations. I. Title.
    E185.6.DK548   973'.04'96073   79-10315
    ISBN 0-87049-279-9

To my family—past and present

Contents

Preface

This is a twofold story. In part, it chronicles the ideas and activities of a small group of white liberal interracialists who took up the cause of race equality during the 1930s and 1940s and helped to make the solving of the "Negro problem" part of the concern of New Deal reform and a central consideration of reform liberalism. It is also a story of black Americans and how they, particularly a number of their leaders and spokespersons, responded to the events of the Great Depression, the New Deal, and World War II and to the philosophy of racial liberalism. That these two strands of the Roosevelt era's history are distinct yet joined should not be surprising, since the experience of black and white in this country has always been one of separateness and interdependence.

It was, however, the theme of interdependence, of common interest and mutual endeavor, especially of an economic and class nature, which established the dominant tone of the 1930s and 1940s and shaped the thought and action of both black and white reformers. That tone was determined, of course, by the combined force of economic depression, New Deal reform and recovery, and World War II. Historian Richard Pells writes that "the key word in the vocabulary of the Roosevelt Administration was 'balance.' New Dealers were especially disturbed by the *chaos* of private capitalism; in their view, American life needed a greater sense of order and control if the nation was to survive the depression." Thus New Dealers were led, Pells concludes, to a "desire to create a harmony of interests among all classes without destroying the profit system at the same time. To them, national unity was more compelling than class struggle."[1]

For those New Dealers and supporters of the New Deal who were acknowledged "friends" of black America during the thirties and forties, among them Harold L. Ickes, Eleanor Roosevelt, Will W. Alexander, and Edwin R. Embree, "order," "control," and, most important, "harmony of interests" were essential components of the racial liberalism they espoused and of their conception of the New Deal welfare state as a change which promised to lighten some of the

1. Richard H. Pells, *Radical Visions and American Dreams: Culture and Social Thought in the Depression Years* (New York, 1973), 79.

burdens on black people. Because these liberals were a minority within the Roosevelt administration and their friendship came at a time when few liberals concerned themselves nationally with civil rights matters, their views and actions were important to Afro-Americans and to their leaders. Responding to the needs and demands of their own people, black spokespersons, moderates and radicals, activists and intellectuals, found it necessary to formulate ideas and strategies within a context that was established in part by the proposals of their liberal white sympathizers.

This study is not intended to be a comprehensive view of the black and white experience during the "Age of Roosevelt." Many things have drawn me to analyze liberal and black thought during this time, but it was Gunnar Myrdal's comment in his monumental work *An American Dilemma* that the Roosevelt administration had "changed the whole configuration of the Negro problem" which sparked my most intense interest.[2] Thus, this book is an attempt to understand just what the new "configuration" signified in altering the conditions of black life in America, in defining the relationship of Negroes to the federal government, and in effecting different relations between black and white people. Myrdal clearly implied that the changes which came with the 1930s and 1940s were positive from the perspective of blacks, and I am in general agreement. Yet the "configuration" was extremely complex, and new problems and difficulties emerged that were of a serious nature—problems that relate directly to the influence of white race liberals and to the response of black leaders and organizations.

A word about the term *white race liberal*. Throughout, I have used that label interchangeably with *white liberal, race liberal*, and *liberal interracialist*. I realize fully the limitations of such an approach, when even a definition of *liberal* can mean almost anything. But I have in mind those individual whites who during the 1930s were strong advocates of the New Deal's style of reform and who saw in that reform a means for achieving racial progress in this country. There were, of course, some liberals and leftists during this time who supported efforts to improve the Negro's situation but who did not see the New Deal as a legitimate mechanism for attaining that goal. Likewise, there were many liberals—and others—who backed the Roosevelt administration throughout the thirties and forties but

2. Gunnar Myrdal, *An American Dilemma: The Negro Problem and Modern Democracy*, 2 vols. (2d ed., New York, 1962), I, 74.

who cared little about the welfare of blacks. Yet there were only a few, within and outside the government, who combined a passionate championing of New Deal reform and black rights and who perceived the success of both as being fundamentally linked. It is that group I have called *white race liberals* or *liberal interracialists*.

Though the major emphasis of this study is on the 1930s, I have referred to the entire period as the "Roosevelt era" rather than the "New Deal era," since my telling of both the black and white stories carries over to the war years of the 1940s, where many ideas and actions that took root in the thirties underwent certain modification and change. I have begun by giving a brief background to the Depression and New Deal years, suggesting some of the difficulties black Americans faced during the twenties but giving primary attention to the dilemma of the white interracialist who struggled to find both a meaningful voice and an audience for his cause. The race liberal's political and social isolation during the New Era of the 1920s made him especially receptive to the reform programs of the New Deal. The link between reform liberalism and race liberalism was therefore established early in the Roosevelt administration, particularly through the efforts of Harold L. Ickes and Clark Foreman, who are discussed in Chapter 2. Their interracial experiences and the positions of power they held in the government during the 1930s allowed them to determine the New Deal's racial priorities and justify government policy on behalf of Negro Americans.

Southern interracialists, especially the dean of southern race liberalism, Will W. Alexander, whose importance is noted in Chapter 3, strongly influenced Ickes and Foreman, who was from Georgia. Men like Alexander carried considerable weight in shaping the Roosevelt administration's racial attitudes, and in many respects the strength and weakness of New Deal interracial activity reflected the southern liberal perspective. One important critic of that perspective was the southern novelist Lillian Smith, whose ideas are analyzed at the end of Chapter 3.

In pulling together a number of the threads which combined to make up the evolving liberal racial ideology of the thirties and forties, I have focused on the thought of Eleanor Roosevelt, the New Deal's most important symbol of its commitment to black America. Mrs. Roosevelt's growth as a defender of Negro rights was shaped by her asssociation with liberal interracialists like Ickes and Alexander, her friendship with blacks like Mary McLeod Bethune and Walter White, and her interpretation of those events that affected race relations in America. The concluding section in Chapter 4 assesses the broad dimensions of white race liberalism, exemplified in part by Mrs. Roosevelt, as it developed during the 1930s and the war years.

The second half of the book turns to an examination of how the New Deal and the war shaped black thought and action and of the differences and similarities that existed among black and white points of view. Given the already difficult conditions blacks faced in the 1920s, the Depression's impact on their lives was immediate and often overwhelming. By the end of the Hoover years, black leaders and organizations were desperately searching for ways to help their people simply survive the devastation brought on by the economic collapse that began in 1929. Chapter 5 briefly indicates some of the problems they confronted and suggests why, under such circumstances, many blacks were eager to embrace Franklin D. Roosevelt and his New Deal after 1932. Those who chose to serve their people by also serving the New Deal were faced directly with the racial and reform priorities established by administration liberals. Chapter 6 analyzes the experiences of four of these individuals—Mary McLeod Bethune, Robert C. Weaver, Robert L. Vann, and Forrester B. Washington—and the different conclusions they reached as to the significance of the New Deal welfare state for blacks. The attitudes of black New Dealers were often determined by their personal circumstances in government and their sense of how an expanding federal state might enhance the status of their people.

Whatever views they held, the activities of New Deal blacks and blacks outside the government were closely linked; administration reform and recovery programs affected not only the lives of individual Negro Americans but also the political strategies and leadership priorities of black organizations. This is apparent in the following chapter, where I examine the efforts of three black activists—John P. Davis, who was involved on many political fronts in the 1930s and 1940s; A. Philip Randolph, labor leader and organizer of the March on Washington; and Walter White, national secretary of the National Association for the Advancement of Colored People. Like other black leaders of the time, they responded differently to the Great Depression, the New Deal, World War II, and white race liberalism, and they proposed distinctive strategies for Negro people to follow. What often exacerbated divisions among them and between black and white spokespersons were the different emphases they gave to race and class as priorities in determining government policy and black strategy. The tension between race and

xii

class was particularly acute in the thought of a number of black intellectuals who sought to influence white and black reformers. Chapter 8 looks at three prominent thinkers, W.E.B. Du Bois, Charles S. Johnson, and Ralph J. Bunche, who symbolized this tension in their critiques of the "Negro problem" and the proposals they offered for racial change.

Finally, I have attempted to bring together the white liberal and black perspectives by analyzing some of the main features of the "changed configuration" produced by the events of the 1930s and early 1940s—and by the separate yet collective struggle of black and white.

Acknowledgments

Without the considerable aid and guidance provided me by countless library staffs, this book would not exist. The same applies also to those friends, colleagues, and former teachers who over the years offered both suggestions and encouragement. Thomas A. Krueger, Frederick Cople Jaher, Robert A. Waller, August Meier, and Dewey W. Grantham all read the manuscript in its dissertation form. Tom Krueger, my friend and former mentor at the University of Illinois, was the most important source of support for the project in its initial stage. Later on, Dewey W. Grantham provided the kind of thoughtful criticism and scholarly wisdom one often dreams of but frequently finds lacking in the academic profession. Bill Nichols, a long-time friend, gifted writer, and teacher of English at Denison University, took time off from his summer retreat in Oregon to peruse the entire book and make it more readable. Whatever infelicities remain, of course, are my responsibility, as are all errors of fact and interpretation.

Both the University of Illinois and Denison University made available valuable financial assistance through summer research grants and Denison helped in other ways to support my efforts. During my sabbatical year in Arizona, where the writing was completed, I was fortunate that Maggi Jones of Tempe, Arizona, not only found the time to type the final draft but blessed me with her patience and her joyful personality. My thanks also to Ms. Carol Orr and her editorial staff at the University of Tennessee Press for their cooperation and assistance.

Finally, my family. Undoubtedly, this book could have been completed earlier if, beyond my responsibilities as a teacher in a liberal arts college, I were not also a husband and father of four active children. Yet whatever the volume's merit, I am most proud that my family did not have to suffer unduly because of "Daddy's book." My family instead offered me the wonderful distractions of living in this world with the daily challenges of school and play. I love them for that, and for the countless other ways in which they have enriched my life. My wife, Sara, not only typed the original manuscript and offered her "lay person's" opinion, but during our year in Arizona, while I took care of the home, she found work as a teacher and managed to keep us financially solvent. Her encouragement, along with that of other members of my family, is hardly compensated for by a simple dedication. Nevertheless, I think they know how much they have meant to me and how much this book is a product of their endeavors too.

January 15, 1979

List of Commonly Used Abbreviations

AAA: Agricultural Adjustment Administration
CCC: Civilian Conservation Corps
CIC: Commission on Interracial Cooperation
CIO: Congress of Industrial Organizations
FEPC: Fair Employment Practices Committee
FERA: Federal Emergency Relief Administration
FSA: Farm Security Administration
KKK: Ku Klux Klan
MOWM: March on Washington Movement
NAACP: National Association for the Advancement of
        Colored People
NNC: National Negro Congress
NRA: National Recovery Administration
NUL: National Urban League
NYA: National Youth Administration
PWA: Public Works Administration
SCHW: Southern Conference for Human Welfare
SRC: Southern Regional Council
USHA: United States Housing Authority
WPA: Works Progress Administration

Black Americans
in the Roosevelt Era

ONE

Prelude
to the Thirties

THE STRUGGLE FOR SURVIVAL

Black Americans and white racial liberals shared a common dilemma in the 1920s—they were both beleaguered minorities. The status of white reformers, of course, followed largely from their decision to support the unpopular cause of race justice; in the case of blacks, there was no choice at all.

For the Negro, the decade began ominously in the aftermath of race rioting in Chicago, Washington, D.C., Omaha, and a score of other cities, North and South. The decade closed with the arrest and speedy conviction in 1931 of nine black youths accused of raping two white women, an incident famous in the 1930s as the "Scottsboro case." Between 1919 and 1931, blacks found little comfort in the New Era. The most encouraging actions taken on their behalf were perhaps the United States Supreme Court decisions of 1927 declaring unconstitutional a Texas law restricting Negro participation in the Democratic party primary and overturning a New Orleans segregation ordinance.[1]

But the fruits of the Court's action would be a long time coming, and in the meantime, black people were deriving few benefits from the general prosperity which characterized American life in the 1920s. In the South, where the vast majority of Negroes still lived in 1930, agricultural problems exacerbated the already brutal existence of the average sharecropper and tenant farmer. As a result, the twenties witnessed another million southern rural blacks making their way north in search of the "promised land." Yet for the new migrants and those who had come earlier, lured in part by the editorial urgings of black newspapers like the Chicago *Defender,* conditions were not much better. Many of the gains won by black workers during World War I were canceled out in the years after 1919. A combination of

1. For a general discussion of the riots and the Scottsboro incident, see Arthur L. Waskow, *From Race Riot to Sit-In, 1919 and the 1960s: A Study in the Connections Between Conflict and Violence* (Garden City, N.Y., 1966), 12-120, 304-7; William M. Tuttle, Jr., *Race Riot: Chicago in the Red Summer of 1919* (New York, 1972); and Dan T. Carter, *Scottsboro: A Tragedy of the American South* (Baton Rouge, 1969).

factors—persistent labor union discrimination, decline in the number of semiskilled jobs, and the general fluctuation of American industry during the 1920s—seriously restricted black America's share in the increased standard of living.[2]

In some black urban centers, like Harlem and Chicago's South Side, black businessmen capitalized on the race market and expanded their financial interests along with their personal fortunes. But the limited data available suggest that "black capitalism" made only modest gains, as the total number of black-owned and -operated enterprises constituted a small percentage of the growing national economy. As interracial organizations like the National Association for the Advancement of Colored People and the National Urban League knew from experience, economic power was firmly controlled by the white corporate and financial establishment.

The anxiety and uncertainty that characterized many Americans in the 1920s did not breed a sympathetic appreciation of black people's problems. Disillusionment over the recent war and over attempts at progressive reform helped determine the general tone of the New Era. So also did the upheaval in individual and societal customs and values which, in part, was produced by technological and industrial expansion. Labor strife, religious fundamentalism, and anti-foreign and anti-radical paranoia frequently established the context for public discussion of important issues. For blacks and liberal whites concerned about racial matters, the most menacing feature of the twenties was the revival and growth of the Ku Klux Klan. Abetted by the many insecurities of the postwar years, the KKK provided a convenient vehicle for venting frustrations. These led too often to violent assaults against not only blacks but the foreign-born, labor organizers, political radicals, Catholics, Jews—all who struck the Klan as not quite "100 percent American." Extending its activities beyond the South, the KKK by the mid-twenties was a powerful force in a number of northern communities. In 1924, its influence was so strong that attempts made to censor the Klan at the National Democratic Convention met with dismal failure. The Republican presidential candidate, Calvin Coolidge, similarly did not consider it wise to make the KKK a political issue in his successful campaign for election. Although Coolidge criticized the Klan in 1925, after he was safely in the White House, he did nothing to discourage its attacks on Negroes or other minorities.

2. Theodore Kornweibel, Jr., "An Economic Profile of Black Life in the Twenties," *Journal of Black Studies* 6 (June 1976), 307-20; Irving Bernstein, *The Lean Years: A History of the American Worker, 1920-1933* (Boston, 1970); Nancy J. Weiss, *The National Urban League, 1910-1940* (New York, 1974), 141-215.

The Klan's own excesses finally contributed to its decline in the late 1920s.[3]

President Coolidge's unwillingness to brave the wrath of Klan supporters indicated the general insensitivity shown by Republican leaders toward the concerns of minority people. Blacks hoped that the party of Lincoln would be more attentive to their needs than Woodrow Wilson and his recently departed Democratic administration, but the events of the twenties suggested otherwise. Presidents Harding, Coolidge, and Hoover were either oblivious to minority rights or indisposed to invest their own political fortunes in support of minority causes. Republicans had little need for the still small black vote in the 1920s to assure their own political power. Few efforts were made, therefore, to reverse racist trends in government—for example, civil service segregation, which had increased under Wilson's direction. Nor were many blacks appointed to federal posts during the decade, although some black Republicans, such as Robert L. Vann, the editor and publisher of the Pittsburgh *Courier,* sought such appointments and worked hard for the election of Republican office seekers. When Herbert Hoover assumed the presidency in 1929, only a handful of Negroes held presidential appointments, and the total of black federal employees numbered only a hundred more than at the start of the Harding administration.[4]

Republicans did not display any greater enthusiasm for civil rights issues raised by others. Harding and Coolidge both professed an abhorrence for lynching but gave little assistance to the NAACP's attempts to secure passage of a federal law prohibiting the practice. When the Dyer anti-lynching bill passed the House of Representatives in 1922, President Harding showed limited concern as the bill was destroyed by a southern filibuster in the Senate. With the Democrats deeply divided, radicalism under attack, and progressivism either in decline or restricted to questionable reform efforts like prohibition and immigration restriction, little opposition

3. Discussion of the Klan's resurgence after World War I can be found in David M. Chalmers, *Hooded Americanism: The History of the Ku Klux Klan* (Garden City, N.Y., 1965); Kenneth T. Jackson, *The Ku Klux in the City, 1915-1930* (New York, 1967); and George B. Tindall, *The Emergence of the New South, 1913-1945* (Baton Rouge, 1967), ch. 5.

4. Richard B. Sherman, "Republicans and Negroes: The Lessons of Normalcy," *Phylon* 27 (First Quarter 1966), 63-79; Sherman, "The Harding Administration and the Negro: An Opportunity Lost," *Journal of Negro History* 49 (July 1964), 145-68; John L. Blair, "A Time For Parting: The Negro During the Coolidge Years," *Journal of American Studies* 3 (Dec. 1969), 177-79; Andrew Buni, *Robert L. Vann of the Pittsburgh Courier* (Pittsburgh, 1974), 174-87.

existed to the complacent conservatism pursued by the Republican party. Harding, Coolidge, and Hoover may have represented the confused political and cultural currents of the time, the popular acceptance of "normalcy," but that precluded their representing the needs of blacks and other minorities or encouraging black participation in American life. The failure of Republican leaders to use their political power to further the cause of racial justice paved the way for black political disaffection in the 1930s. Such failure also encouraged separatist sentiment in the black community during the 1920s, symbolized by the appeal of Marcus Garvey, who owed his success in part to the continued presence of racism. Reform, racial or otherwise, was, in short, a low-priority item in New Era politics.[5]

For the majority of white Americans, given their national love affair with economic growth and consumption, there was simply little interest in black rights. But that remained the case even for those whites dissatisfied with "normalcy." Certainly reformers were on the defensive during the twenties; yet in spite of the practical obstacles working against change, the "reform spirit," Richard H. Pells recently reminded us, "managed to remain alive after 1920."[6] In the final analysis, however, that "spirit" demonstrated scant appreciation for the problems of black Americans.

Liberals devoted their efforts primarily toward discovering a program of reform which might address the new circumstances of the twenties. Since few of them were in positions of political influence, their concern was naturally directed to speculation about the future. Although most critics of the period attacked the materialistic and competitive nature of modern society, they did not always agree about what should replace it. Those who expressed themselves in journals like the *New Republic* and the *Nation* emphasized a cooperative order which would bring together the interests of government, labor, and progressive business concerns. For the more radically inclined, however, that view was too reminiscent of a rejected prewar progressivism, and it did not address their need for a major overhaul of American political and economic institutions. Many writers and artists of the twenties, on the other hand, dismissed politics and economics altogether, arguing that what America required was a redefinition of its social attitudes and cultural priorities. Joseph Wood Krutch's *The*

5. See E. David Cronon, *Black Moses: The Story of Marcus Garvey and the Universal Negro Improvement Association* (Madison, Wis., 1955), for analysis of Garvey's appeal and activities in the 1920s.

6. Pells, *Radical Visions and American Dreams*, 12, and ch. 1, "Prologue — Progressivism and the 1920s."

Modern Temper, written in 1929, summed up the feelings of many intellectuals and writers: they believed it futile to pursue political action without first attacking the crisis in modern human values.[7]

Whatever their personal preferences, New Era dissidents seldom gave attention to the race question in their analyses. With the exception of the Communists in the late 1920s, reform activists and white intellectuals did not appear to consider the "Negro problem" a problem. Although activists might make reference to the Negro's plight, those most concerned with attacking the failures inherent in contemporary society displayed the same narrow appreciation for race issues as did the progressives earlier. At best, black concerns were assumed to be no different from those of other Americans; at worst, they simply went unrecognized.[8] In 1929, when a number of prominent liberal intellectuals joined together to form the League for Independent Political Action, the noted black scholar and editor of the NAACP's journal, the *Crisis,* W.E.B. Du Bois, was listed as one of the organization's vice chairmen. But Du Bois soon left the League because of its obliviousness to the political problems confronting black people. Responding to a pamphlet written by Paul Douglas, one of the League's founders, detailing the need for a new political alignment, Du Bois argued that "nowhere in this pamphlet, and more particularly in the program for a new party, is any mention made of political rights for Negroes or for other disfranchised classes." Noting that he had previously voiced the same concern, he concluded that the IPA's "tendency to forget or ignore the place of the Negro in American democracy puts me in an extraordinarily difficult position."[9]

There were, of course, a handful of white liberals in the 1920s who had not forgotten the "Negro in American democracy." Both the NAACP and the National Urban League had been founded with

7. *Ibid.,* 13-21; Krutch, *The Modern Temper* (New York, 1929). For the views of other intellectuals during the period, sees Harold Stearns, ed., *Civilization in the United States* (New York, 1922), and Charles A. Beard, ed., *Whither Mankind* (New York, 1928).

8. Some white intellectuals and writers, of course, found in Harlem and black life of the 1920s an alternative "culture" to the American culture they often attacked. Such a romanticized view of black life, however, did little to help them appreciate the oppressive conditions faced by many black Americans. See, in this regard, Nathan Irvin Huggins, *Harlem Renaissance* (New York, 1971).

9. Du Bois to Douglas, Feb. 21, 1930, in Herbert Aptheker, ed., *The Correspondence of W.E.B. Du Bois,* I (Boston 1973), 419. For a discussion of the League's ideas and its early hopes, see R. Alan Lawson, *The Failure of Independent Liberalism, 1930-1941* (New York, 1971), 39-46.

considerable help from liberal and left-wing white reformers, and both organizations continued to rely on these groups for their philosophical and financial support. Increasingly, however, the leadership of the National Association and the NUL was assumed by blacks themselves. Writing on the activities of the NAACP, Joyce Ross has noted that by the mid-1920s, the "coalition of white liberal leadership" which had organized the association and led it during its first decade and a half "had been narrowed to Mary White Ovington and Arthur Spingarn, who held posts of Board Chairman and Chairman of the Legal Committee, respectively."[10] Joel E. Spingarn, who had devoted much of his energy to the NAACP prior to World War I (and would again do so in the 1930s), had withdrawn from active involvement in the twenties because of his disillusionment with the political and social climate in America.[11] Whites who remained committed to the cause of race justice seldom linked their racial concerns to the larger questions which troubled intellectuals and theorists like Paul Douglas, John Dewey, and Lewis Mumford. There was, in effect, little connection between race liberalism and philosophical and political liberalism. For those ideologically inclined, race was a minor matter; for those worried about race relations, ideological speculation was of secondary interest.

What generally motivated whites who did concern themselves with the "Negro problem" in the years following the war was the impulse to aid the disadvantaged, inspired largely by strong religious, primarily Christian, convictions. That was especially true for those instrumental in founding the Commission on Interracial Cooperation in the midst of the race riots of 1919. The commission was directed throughout the 1920s and early 1930s by Will W. Alexander, a white Methodist minister and later head of the New Deal's Farm Security Administration. The best-known of the interracial organizations of the period, the CIC confined its activities primarily to the South, where it endeavored to ease racial friction which had increased after the war and the resurgence of the Ku Klux Klan. By 1923, there were over 800 CIC-sponsored committees scattered throughout the region, and the organization received strong financial backing from northern philanthropists like John D. Rockefeller, Jr., who approved of its program of interracial education and moderation. Operating within a hostile environment, the commission worked to avert lynching, investigate health problems

---

10. B. Joyce Ross, *J. E. Spingarn and the Rise of the NAACP* (New York, 1972), 100.

11. *Ibid.*, 104-24.

and other social needs in the black community, and improve dialog between the races. Despite its name, the Interracial Commission was essentially composed of white liberals; by 1934, there was only one paid black in the CIC and none in the organization's national office in Atlanta.[12]

Will Alexander later noted that he had no "creed about race, I never had any. I have no doctrine, no ideology about it. I believe in the essential unity of the human race and that the black man may be as important as the white man."[13] That attitude led Alexander and others like him to address race relations issues on a pragmatic basis. In the south, reformers were an even smaller minority than in other regions, and that virtually dictated their refusal to challenge the segregation question or even to support federal anti-lynching legislation, despite the fact that lynching was one of their foremost concerns. Education among blacks and whites, research into social issues, and an appeal to public officials for better understanding of minority needs constituted their basic program.[14] During the late 1920s, the Commission on Interracial Cooperation joined the newly formed Race Relations Department of the Federal Council of Churches, the American Friends Service Committee, the National Federation of Settlements, foundations like the Phelps-Stokes and Rosenwald Funds, and occasionally the NAACP and the National Urban League, in sponsoring a series of national conferences designed to formulate policies and goals for improving minority toleration. Meeting in Cincinnati in 1927, representatives declared that the "causes of racial antagonism" arose "fundamentally from social conditions" and "as such they are remediable through social changes." But other than their traditional appeal to education, they proposed little to bring about the desired social change. They urged government to grant Negroes "educational facilities and opportunities equal to those of white students" even "where separate schools existed" and asked "leaders of the colored people" to provide encouragement and other "legitimate means . . . to induce the

12. A recent analysis of the commission's background and activities through the early 1930s can be found in Morton Sosna, *In Search of the Silent South* (New York, 1977) 20-41. Also see Tindall, *Emergence of the New South*, 175-99, and for an earlier discussion, Paul E. Baker, *Negro-White Adjustments: An Investigation and Analysis of Methods in the Interracial Movement in the United States* (New York, 1934), 18-19, 211-25.

13. "The Reminiscences of Will W. Alexander" (Columbia Univ. Oral History Collection, 1952), 259-60.

14. Sosna, *In Search of the Silent South*, 23-41; David M. Reimers, *White Protestantism and the Negro* (New York, 1965), 87.

9

Negro people everywhere to avail themselves of the maximum educational opportunity, to the end that the difference in the cultural level between the two races be reduced as rapidly as possible."[15]

As important as it no doubt was for liberals and blacks to join one another in the 1920s to exchange ideas and information, established civil rights organizations like the NAACP and the Urban League clearly recognized that far more was required to improve the status of Negro Americans. *Opportunity,* the National Urban League's official publication, suggested after a conference in Washington, D.C., in 1928, in which the NUL had been a major participant, that it was time for discussions on race to be "lifted out of the realm of the academicians and placed into the stream of actual life and living. . . ." Social research, it concluded, "must be made to live through organized social efforts designed to meet the problems which research reveals."[16]

An organized social struggle, urged by the Urban League and pursued to some degree by the NAACP in the New Era decade, was not the essential strategy of white race liberals. Militant blacks, who urged a direct assault against race oppression, were viewed with suspicion and even fear by liberals, especially those connected with the southern interracial movement. So when the American Communist party late in the 1920s developed an interest in the Negro cause and made race equality part of its revolutionary attack on the established order, the CIC and other interracial groups denounced the party's activities. Communists were "making a very determined drive to reach Negro labor in the South," Will Alexander wrote to the Urban League's T. Arnold Hill in 1931, and "in this they are logical and consistent." He was certain, however, that Communist "agitation among Negroes will do serious harm to Negro workers and the whole interracial situation."[17]

The "harm," Alexander and others envisioned was that the already precarious liberal voice in the South and elsewhere would be undermined by the linking of civil rights with radical politics. Race liberals were not only a minority among Americans in the 1920s, they were an extremely isolated minority, and they knew it. They received little or no encouragement for their views from the national

15. Monroe N. Work, ed., *Negro Year Book: An Annual Encyclopedia of the Negro, 1931-32.* (Tuskegee, Ala., 1931), 5-6, 31-32; Guichard Parris and Lester Brooks, *Blacks in the City: A History of the National Urban League* (Boston, 1971), 199-201.

16. *Opportunity* 7 (Feb. 1929), 36.

17. Alexander to Hill, June 23, 1931, quoted in Baker, *Negro-White Adjustment,* 114. Also see Sosna, *In Search of the Silent South,* 36-38.

liberal community; they were ignored by the leadership of the two major political parties; they were suspect, often condemned, by a majority of whites in the South for their endeavors. Even if race liberals had possessed a broader philosophy (beyond Christian goodwill and a belief in the "unity of the human race"), the New Era's political and social environment posed major obstacles for them. To get around those obstacles, they pursued the cause of equal rights gingerly, emphasizing educational and spiritual reform and eschewing both political agitation and militant ideological pronouncements. Communist pressure upset their cautious strategy and threatened their future effectiveness as moderate defenders of black progress.

Nevertheless, it was clear that if either blacks or whites were to follow the liberal approach on race matters, they would have to find additional support and create an expanded platform in order to pursue their objectives. The Great Depression provided them with that opportunity. Although the effect was not immediate, in the long run the economic devastation that began in 1929 with the collapse of the stock market forced many Americans to rethink assumptions held without question during the years of Republican prosperity. The opportunity resulted partly from the Depression's disruption of normal life patterns and institutions and partly from the sweeping nature of its impact. Though minorities such as blacks were particularly hard hit by the economic fallout, the Depression affected millions of Americans, often ignoring racial, ethnic, and class distinctions. As a consequence, some people who had been deeply troubled by the course of events in the 1920s saw in the midst of adversity new possibilities for change. Since race liberals had stressed the need to alter old ideas and attitudes in order to improve the American racial climate and increase opportunities for Negroes, they viewed the Depression as expediting that process.

What really gave them encouragement, however, was the election of Franklin D. Roosevelt in 1932 and the inauguration of the New Deal. Blacks, as will be noted later, were more cautious than white liberals in their initial response to Roosevelt and his reforms. But as the administration's program emerged, most race liberals became enthusiastic. Despite the new President's lack of any previous commitment to black Americans, FDR's vague reference in his campaign to social and economic planning based upon the "forgotten" and the "unorganized" heightened their optimism. Adding to it was Roosevelt's selection of many reformers for positions within the federal government. Harold Ickes, former president of the local NAACP chapter in Chicago, and Will Alexander, head of the Com-

11

mission on Interracial Cooperation, were only two who had been active during the 1920s on behalf of blacks and who were to hold important posts in the Roosevelt administration during the 1930s and 1940s.

The New Deal, in effect, provided what most race liberals had needed so desperately in the twenties—a reform program to which they might attach their concern for Negro rights. As they began to interpret the meaning of the New Deal and its relevance to the racial situation of the 1930s and early 1940s, they gained confidence in their—and others'—ability to alter the "Negro problem." And now, having some authority, they were able to formulate certain guidelines for changing the nature of American race relations. Of fundamental importance was the link they established between reform liberalism and racial liberalism in determining some of the priorities of the emerging welfare state.

TWO

Reform and the Black American

DEFINING THE PRIORITIES

I.

The "capital of the nation has again moved to Washington," wrote Edwin R. Embree, president of the Julius Rosenwald Fund, in June 1933 to his friend and associate Clark H. Foreman; "and the economy of the whole country is being planned from that center."[1] Embree found particular delight in the possibility of "an opportunity as never before to see to it that the Negro gets a fair share of attention in economic development."[2] Shortly after receiving Embree's encouraging letter, Foreman, then on vacation in Europe, returned to the United States; in August 1933 he was chosen as the Roosevelt administration's "Adviser on the Economic Status of the Negro."

Edwin Embree's own concern for the Negro went back to his early childhood and to a long involvement in the field of philanthropy. Born in Nebraska in 1883, the son of a Union Pacific Railroad employee, he was raised in the Berea, Kentucky, home of his mother's grandfather, John G. Fee, a well-known preacher and abolitionist. Another relative on his father's side, Elihu Embree, was founder of the first Tennessee abolitionist newspaper and a militant foe of slavery. Embree attended interracial Berea College, went on to Yale University, and there received a degree in philosophy and an exposure to a different social class. After a brief try as a journalist, he returned to Yale, where he worked for six years in the alumni office.

Subsequently Embree was hired by the Rockefeller Foundation when George Vincent, whom he had met at Yale, became its president. For a decade he served the organization in a number of roles, becoming a vice president in 1927. The following year, Julius Rosenwald, head of Sears, Roebuck and Company of Chicago, reor-

---

1. Edwin R. Embree to Clark Foreman, June 19, 1933, Julius Rosenwald Fund Archives, Fisk Univ. Box 412.
2. *Ibid.*

ganized his philanthropic interests and selected Embree as president of the Rosenwald Fund, a position Embree held until the fund was terminated in 1948.[3] Impressed with the work of Booker T. Washington, Rosenwald directed a major portion of his wealth toward improving the "welfare of Negroes"; and through Embree's influence, the Rosenwald Fund became active as a financial provider and adviser to many blacks and interracial causes. W.E.B. Du Bois, who knew at first hand of white philanthropic activity, considered Embree one of the most sensitive of foundation leaders in his concern for the Afro-American.[4]

Embree's racial sensitivity was strengthened by a friendship developed in the late 1920s with Will Alexander and Charles S. Johnson, a prominent black sociologist, former National Urban League official, and later president of Fisk University. During the 1930s and 1940s, Alexander and Johnson became associated with numerous Rosenwald projects and, with Embree, deeply involved in racial affairs.[5]

The immediate and forceful action of the Roosevelt administration in responding to the Depression favorably impressed Embree and his friends. In writing to Foreman, who had joined the Rosenwald staff in 1928, Embree noted that under FDR's capable leadership "things are moving in this country with breathless speed." Will Alexander was even more excited, seeing Roosevelt as "a sort of messiah." He had a "hunch," he recalled later, that "Washington was going to become the center of this country and . . . perhaps the next stage in race relations would sort of center around what happened in Washington in the period while this strange fella was there."[6]

3. John A. Garraty and Edward T. James, eds., *Dictionary of American Biography, Supplement 4, 1946-1950* (New York, 1974), 250-51; Edwin R. Embree and Julia Waxman, *Investment in People: The Story of the Julius Rosenwald Fund* (New York, 1949), 5-36.

4. Embree and Waxman, *Investment in People*, 25; Weiss, *National Urban League*, 82. Du Bois' comment is in Raymond Wolters, *Negroes and the Great Depression: The Problem of Economic Recovery* (Westport, Conn., 1970), 64.

5. The close relationship of Embree, Johnson, and Alexander is noted in a number of secondary references. See Sosna, *In Search of the Silent South;* Wilma Dykeman and James Stokely, *Seeds of Southern Change: The Life of Will Alexander* (Chicago, 1962); and Embree and Waxman, *Investment in People*. Also illuminating is the correspondence of the three men in the Rosenwald Fund Archives and the Charles S. Johnson Papers, Fisk University. Alexander comments on the relationship in "Reminiscences of Will Alexander," Columbia Oral History, 362.

6. Embree to Foreman, June 19, 1933, Rosenwald Fund Archives, Box 412; "Reminiscences of Will Alexander," Columbia Oral History, 368.

Aware that Roosevelt and the Democratic party had shown little concern in the past for black Americans, racial liberals nevertheless sensed that national power was being redirected from conservative business interests and state and local politics to the federal government. By the spring of 1933, they had become convinced of the Roosevelt administration's commitment to reform; and they were confident of the President's ability to persuade Congress, even reactionary southerners, to accept his recovery program. Now their goal was to convince Roosevelt of the special problems of blacks and to ensure a place for the Negro in the New Deal.

That need was on the minds of many who participated in a number of conferences in mid-1933 to assess the critical issues facing Afro-American people. A meeting in May, held in Washington, D.C., was sponsored by the Rosenwald Fund to discuss the "Economic Status of the Negro." In June, members of the NAACP at their annual convention gave considerable attention to the activities of the New Deal. And in the following month, the previously postponed Second Amenia Conference continued the discussion of black economic conditions and the Roosevelt administration at the home of NAACP president Joel E. Spingarn.[7]

Although they differed in purpose and membership, the three gatherings agreed that New Deal policies were of primary importance. Of the eight recommendations set forth by the Rosenwald Conference's "Findings and Action Committee," chaired by Charles S. Johnson, six addressed recently enacted or pending federal legislation.[8] And at all meetings, the problem of how black needs might be met by administration reforms was a fundamental question.

7. On the "Conference on the Economic Status of the Negro," see Will Alexander to Walter White, June 6, 1933; White to Alexander, June 9, 1933; and Charles S. Johnson to White, June 19, 1933, which includes the "Findings Committee" report, NAACP Papers, Manuscript Div., Library of Congress (LC), File C-230. Other members of the committee were Kelly Miller, T. Arnold Hill, Will Alexander, Robert R. Moton, Bishop George C. Clement, Broadus Mitchell, and Walter White. See also William E. Hill to White, June 4, 1933, and White to Hill, June 9, 1933, NAACP Papers, File C-230. The New York *Times*, May 12-14, 1933, Pittsburgh *Courier*, May 20, 1933, and *Crisis* 40 (July 1933), 156-57, covered the Rosenwald conference. On the NAACP convention, see "Memorandum from the National Office to Members of the Resolutions Committee," June 24, 1933, NAACP Papers, File C-73; "Resolutions to the 24th Annual Conference of the NAACP, Chicago, June 29-July 2, 1933," *ibid.*, File B-10. The Amenia Conference is discussed in "Youth and Age at Amenia," *Crisis* 40 (Oct. 1933), 226; Wolters, *Negroes and the Great Depression*, 219-29; and Ross, *J.E. Spingarn, passim,* but esp. 169-85.

8. Johnson to Walter White, June 19, 1933, NAACP Papers, File C-230.

Edwin Embree and Will Alexander were convinced that it could be answered only by Negroes gaining a direct voice in the federal government, and their pursuit of that objective during the summer of 1933 led to the appointment in August of Clark Foreman.

The creation of a special adviser concerned with the "economic status of the Negro" suggests the early strategy of liberals seeking to make the New Deal more responsive to racial considerations. Harold L. Ickes, Secretary of the Interior and long considered a friend of blacks, was finally responsible for establishing the race advisory post under his jurisdiction and for selecting Foreman. But it was Labor Secretary Frances Perkins, because of her key role in the government, whom Embree and Alexander thought first of approaching with the racial adviser idea.

In June, however, Perkins had named Lawrence A. Oxley, a young North Carolina Negro and former director of black Unemployment Relief for the North Carolina Welfare Department, as her assistant. Oxley's appointment was a great disappointment to Embree and Alexander and led to their seeking out Ickes instead of the Secretary of Labor. Alexander questioned Oxley's ability to represent the black perspective to Perkins or to others in the administration. "He was a 'white man's nigger' if there ever was one," Alexander remembered; he "knew how to talk with white folks," but that was all. Race liberals also questioned Perkins' own reasons for bringing a Negro into the Labor Department, believing that the secretary was responding more out of fear than sensitivity to blacks.[9]

What Alexander and Embree had in mind was a "generalissimo of Negro welfare" who would "look after the Negro's interests in all phases of the recovery."[10] That kind of responsibility could not be satisfied by officials' anxiety or black patronage. There were other considerations, too. Although it was never directly stated, Alexander and Embree clearly wanted an adviser with whom they could maintain close communication and who shared their point of view. In Foreman, they had someone who not only was on "loan" to the

9. For the role of Edwin Embree and Will Alexander in securing the "Negro Adviser" position and their relationship with Ickes, see Embree to Harold Ickes, July 21, 1933; Ickes to Embree, July 27, 1933; Embree to Ickes, Aug. 11, 1933; Will Alexander to Embree, Aug. 23, 1933; Embree to William Rosenwald, Sept. 5, 1933; and Embree to Major R.R. Moton, Sept. 6, 1933, Rosenwald Fund Archives, Box 152; Embree to T. Arnold Hill, Aug. 14, 1933, *ibid.*, Box 306; and Dykeman and Stokely, *Seeds of Southern Change*, 194-96. On the Frances Perkins and Lawrence Oxley matter, see "Reminiscences of Will Alexander," Columbia Oral History, 369.

10. Embree to Clark Foreman, June 19, 1933, Rosenwald Fund Archives, Box 412.

administration from the Rosenwald Fund but whose salary was paid by the fund.

Foreman was also white, and from the perspective of race liberals that was another crucial consideration. "This is not a question simply of a political job, for which Negroes are naturally hungry," Embree wrote William Rosenwald in September 1933. "It is an attempt to work out in the most strategic fashion a method of keeping the welfare of the whole race effectively before the persons responsible for the national recovery." Blacks who were consulted on the matter were in agreement that "only a white man could carry the kind of influence that is necessary for results." To Robert R. Moton, president of Tuskegee Institute, Embree added that the "peculiar influence which we hope to bring into play in this particular post can . . . be exercised only by a white man, and best of all, by a white person from the South." No "thoughtful person can believe than any Negro, however capable," Embree concluded in a letter to the black intellectual Kelly Miller, who had supported Foreman, "can accomplish as much as a white man—assuming, of course, that the white man is of the right sort."[11]

Despite black protests, Embree and Alexander never doubted that Clark Foreman was the "right sort." White paternalism, nourished by a southern racial experience and a traditional progressive faith in "government by experts," shaped their beliefs. As the New Deal evolved, as some difficulties emerged in the relationship of the welfare state to black Americans, and as Negroes exerted their own pressure on the federal government, there was some change in white liberal attitudes. Yet in the early 1930s, with little national liberal or left agitation for civil rights and a social climate still hostile to race opportunity, the contributions of interracialists like Embree, Alexander, Foreman, and Ickes were crucial. Whatever their faults, they struggled to bring the New Deal to blacks; in so doing, men like Ickes and Foreman, who assumed an early responsibility in this area, established a racial posture within the administration for others to follow—an attitude that black and white reformers outside the government had to acknowledge in their own thought and activity.

II.

If Edwin Embree felt it necessary to justify the selection of a southern white as "Negro Adviser," the man who made the ap-

---

11. Embree to William Rosenwald, Sept. 5, 1933, Embree to Moton, Sept. 6, 1933; and Embree to Miller, Sept. 14, 1933, *ibid.*, Box 152.

pointment did not. Harold L. Ickes was one of the few New Dealers who, prior to taking up residence in Washington, had been engaged in racial matters. Chosen Interior Secretary by FDR in 1933, he retained the position until 1946. Egotistical and arrogant, a political activist and former Bull Moose Progressive, he was a central figure in the formulation and execution of many Roosevelt programs. He also considered himself a prominent articulator of New Deal philosophy. As the New Deal progressed, he assumed responsibilities beyond the Interior, and the most significant from the standpoint of black Americans was his selection by FDR to head the Public Works Administration.[12]

From late 1922 until 1924, Ickes had been president of the Chicago chapter of the National Association for the Advancement of Colored People. At that time, the Chicago NAACP was weak and disorganized, and there is evidence in Ickes' papers which suggests that his presidency was not a happy one. Writing to his friend Jane Addams in 1922, he noted that, as far as he could find out, "there is really no such organization as the Chicago branch" of the NAACP. Had he known the chapter was simply a "paper organization," he doubted he could have been "convinced" that it was his "duty to accept this office." Shortly after leaving the presidency, he wrote Robert Bagnall, NAACP local branch director, that he was "not the right person" for the job and had accepted it only because he had been persuaded by local leaders that his "name would be helpful."[13]

It is not clear what lasting impression this involvement had on Ickes, though he used the NAACP connection on numerous occasions to impress upon blacks his long commitment to their welfare. It certainly must have given him added confidence in responding to the criticism which he received from Negroes, including the NAACP, when the Foreman appointment was made public. Both the Pittsburgh *Courier* and the Chicago *Defender* sharply rebuked him, while W.E.B. Du Bois, then editor of the *Crisis*, considered it simply

12. Arthur M. Schlesinger, Jr., *The Age of Roosevelt: The Politics of Upheaval* (Boston, 1960), 358-60, 422; Judd M. Harmon, "Some Contributions of Harold L. Ickes," *Western Political Quarterly* 7 (June 1954), 238-52. For Ickes' writings on New Deal philosophy, see Ickes, "Is the Roosevelt 'New Deal' Proving Successful? Pro or Con," *Congressional Digest* 13 (June-July 1934), 170-72; "The Social Implications of the Roosevelt Administration," *Survey Graphic* 23 (March 1934), 111-13, 143-44, and most important, *The New Democracy* (New York, 1934). Also see Joan E. Curlee, "Some Aspects of the New Deal Rationale: The Pre-1936 Writings of Six of Roosevelt's Advisors" (Ph.D. diss., Vanderbilt Univ., 1957), 140-70, 341-47.

13. Ickes to Jane Addams, Nov. 1, 1922; Ickes to Robert W. Bagnall, Nov. 6, 1924, Harold L. Ickes Papers, Ms. Div., LC, File "NAACP, 1922-1924," Box 3.

an "outrage" that blacks should "again', through the efforts of some
of our best friends . . . be compelled to have our wants and aspirations interpreted by one who does not know them and our ideas and
ambitions expressed by a person who cannot understand them."[14]

Roy Wilkins expressed the official view of the NAACP and cap-
tured the spirit of much black resentment in 1933 when he informed
Ickes that objections were not to Foreman's personal qualities but
"to the idea of a white adviser for Negroes." The "age of paternalism" was over, and black people bitterly resented "having a white
man officially designated by the government to advise on their
welfare." Wilkins argued that there were a number of blacks who had
"as great training [as] . . . and far richer experience" than Foreman,
and he concluded that Ickes' appointment would "be regarded as
most unfortunate by colored citizens of every section and station in
life." Elaborating on the NAACP protest, Walter White told William
Rosenwald that the "self-respecting Negro, especially the younger
one, is exceedingly dissatisfied with the continuation of the appointment of white spokesmen for the Negro. . . . [M]oney which
has been expended on education and training of the Negro would
have been wasted had there not by this time been produced enough
trained Negroes who could do the job as well as and better than Mr.
Foreman."[15]

Ickes was not impressed, and his reaction to his critics provides
some insight into his personal approach to race concerns. Replying
to Wilkins, he stated that he could not see "how any fair-minded
individual, either white or colored," could expect to "advance the
interests of the Negro if mutuality of contact is not established
through the efforts of both races." His appointment of Foreman,
who had devoted "his life to establishing opportunities for a more
propitious outlook for the Negro in our economic and social system," was designed to facilitate such contacts. Blacks might call this
"paternalism," but to Ickes it reflected "recognition of an injustice
that a sympathetic government" was trying to correct. Like Embree,
he believed not only that it was unimportant to have a black as
adviser to ensure the Negro's well-being but also that it was advan-
tageous, if real changes were to be made, for a white man to hold the
position. Foreman later recalled that when he told Ickes he himself

14. Pittsburgh *Courier*, Sept. 6, 1933; Chicago *Defender*, Sept. 16, 1933; W.E.B.
Du Bois, "Postscript: NRA and Appointments," *Crisis* 40 (Oct. 1933), 237.

15. Wilkins telegram to Ickes reprinted in the Pittsburgh *Courier*, Sept. 2, 1933;
also Wolters, *Negroes and the Great Depression*, 142; White to William Rosenwald,
Sept. 6, 1933, NAACP Papers, Box C-78.

felt a Negro should have the job, Ickes responded that if Foreman refused the appointment, "he would offer it to another white man." The secretary was convinced that Foreman would provide blacks with "better service than a Negro in his position."[16]

Ickes was also certain that he and Foreman understood the problems of black Americans; they were, he told Wilkins, men "honestly interested in the Negro."[17] Therefore, he could not agree with the charge that only a black might comprehend the "difficulties of American Negroes." Assuming there was no problem in this respect, it was, from Ickes' perspective, better to have a sympathetic white man available to deal with white governmental administrators and predominantly white business and labor interests in the country. Significantly, he implied—and later explained more fully—that he saw little fundamental difference between the conditions confronting blacks and those faced by whites. The central mission was to see that Negroes were included in reform policies and that they were not discriminated against because they were black; once this was achieved, the matter would cease being racial and become a question of Negroes themselves capitalizing on the efforts of a "sympathetic government."

The Foreman appointment marked the low point in Ickes' relationship with the black community. Once Foreman became more acceptable to blacks and with the appointment of Negro economist Robert C. Weaver as his assistant, little criticism was voiced over Ickes' activities. Indeed, throughout the Roosevelt years, there was much praise for his outspoken friendship. From the start, the black press commented favorably on his selection by FDR. Walter White telegraphed his personal congratulations, which brought from Ickes a reply reaffirming his ties to the NAACP and pledging "every citizen regardless of race or creed" a "square deal" while he headed the Interior.[18] Arthur M. Schlesinger, Jr., has written that during the thirties Ickes functioned in effect as an "informal Secretary of Negro

---

16. Ickes' reply to Wilkins, included in a note which Ickes sent to President Roosevelt's personal secretary Louis Howe, Oct. 12, 1933, FDR Papers, FDR Library, Hyde Park, N.Y., President's Personal File (PPF), File 93. Foreman's observation in *South Today* 7 (Spring 1942), 51.

17. Ickes to Howe, Oct. 12, 1933, FDR Papers, PPF, File 93.

18. The Pittsburgh *Courier*, Mar. 4, 1933, noted that Ickes' selection demonstrated again the "wisdom of the NAACP in identifying with the organization in its official capacity white people of ability and prominence." White's telegram and Ickes' reply printed in Pittsburgh *Courier*, Mar. 11, 1933.

relations" and that, with characteristic immodesty, Ickes claimed he was "the one man in the Administration who had a real standing" with the Negro.[19]

In a sense, both assessments were correct. Ickes symbolized for black (and many white) Americans the engaged, moral reformer, committed to the cause of assuring the underdog an elevated status in the American system. In 1936 he told a gathering of black Americans that he had "always felt it to be my privilege, no less than my duty, to do everything in my power to see that the Negro was given that degree of justice and fair play to which he is entitled."[20] It was his sense of "fair play" which led him to support Marian Anderson in her celebrated conflict with the Daughters of the American Revolution in 1939 and to introduce her to a huge throng massed before the statue of Abraham Lincoln. The *Journal of Negro Education* remarked that the "brevity and force" of Ickes' speech that day was "destined to rival Lincoln's Gettysburg address."[21] Due largely to Ickes' efforts, a number of prominent blacks were brought into the administration during the thirties and forties to serve as race relations advisers in New Deal departments and agencies. After Clark Foreman resigned in 1934 to take a job with the PWA's Power Division, Ickes elevated the Harvard-educated Weaver to Foreman's position. About the same time, he chose another young black, William H. Hastie, as assistant solicitor in the Interior Department. Some years later, he was instrumental in persuading Roosevelt to make Hastie, an NAACP attorney, a federal judge in the Virgin Islands.[22] The secretary was also known for his willingness to hire Negro professionals and clerical workers in both Interior and the PWA, and under his direc-

19. Schlesinger, *Politics of Upheaval*, 434; Harold L. Ickes, *The Secret Diary of Harold L. Ickes*, I (New York, 1954), 680.

20. Speech, Harold L. Ickes to the Chicago Urban League, Feb. 26, 1936, FDR Papers, Official File (OF) 6.

21. "Address of Secretary Harold L. Ickes Introducing Marian Anderson,"*Journal of Negro Education* 8 (Apr. 1939), 260.

22. Ralph J. Bunche, "The Political Status of the Negro" (unpub. memorandum for the Carnegie-Myrdal Study, 1940, New York Public Library (NYPL), 1411-19; Robert C. Weaver, *Negro Labor: A National Problem* (New York, 1946); *The Negro Ghetto* (New York, 1948); Chicago *Defender*, Dec. 23, 1933; "The Presidency," *Time* 29 (Feb. 15, 1937), 15. For Ickes' own statement on his role in appointing Hastie and supporting his candidacy for federal judge, see Harold L. Ickes, "My Twelve Years with F.D.R.,"*Saturday Evening Post* 220 (June 26, 1948), 79, 81-82, and*Secret Diary*, I, 416, and II, 94-95.

tion the Interior Department lunchroom facilities were finally desegregated.[23]

These activities won him warm support, but Ickes' policies as head of PWA were important for the more tangible effects they had on black masses. On September 1, 1933, he issued an order prohibiting discrimination on all PWA projects, and he made sure that a nondiscrimination clause was included in every PWA contract. The difficulty in enforcing such a clause, however, was considerable. Thus, in 1934, with the help of Foreman and Weaver, he devised a program to guarantee Negro employment on Public Works building projects by instituting a labor quota system. Under this plan, based on the 1930 occupational census, local contractors were required to employ a fixed percentage of available skilled black workers. The importance of this action, as one recent study has noted, was that it "shifted the burden of proof from the PWA to the contractor."[24]

As the program showed some success, Ickes and his associates expanded its scope to include unskilled black workers. And despite opposition from the white building trade unions, as well as from some black construction workers who feared a quota might restrict their employment on other jobs, Ickes personally saw that the program was put into effect. The Bureau of Labor Statistics negotiated the contracts, Ickes, Weaver, and others approved them, and the PWA's Inspection Division guaranteed their implementation; as a result, the labor quota plan brought benefits to black workers that otherwise would not have been possible. In 1937, when Robert Weaver went to the United States Housing Authority as race relations adviser, he established a similar system there.

Of course, there were limitations. The quota idea did not affect a large percentage of Negro workers; it did not increase the number of skilled black construction workers or encourage black membership in craft unions, and it was conceived as only a temporary device. But it showed the possibilities that existed if there was willingness to use

23. Samuel Krislov, *The Negro in Federal Employment: The Quest for Equal Opportunity* (Minneapolis, 1967), 23; Walter White, *How Far the Promised Land* (New York, 1955), 180; Allen F. Kifer, "The Negro Under the New Deal, 1933-1941" (Ph.D. diss., Univ. of Wisconsin, 1961), 230-31, Ickes, *Secret Diary*, III, 641.

24. Marc W. Kruman, "Quotas for Blacks: The Public Works Administration and the Black Construction Worker," *Labor History* 16 (Winter, 1975) 40-41. See also Robert C. Weaver, "An Experiment in Negro Labor," *Opportunity* 14(Oct. 1936), 296-97; "Federal Aid, Local Control and Negro Participation," *Journal of Negro Education* 11 (Jan. 1942), 47-59; Wolters, *Negroes and the Great Depression*, 200-203.

the power of the federal government to ensure some protections for black laborers.[25]

Ickes also made certain that blacks were included in PWA's low-income housing program. According to Richard Sterner, of the forty-nine projects built by the PWA between 1933 and 1937, fourteen were constructed for blacks alone and another seventeen for joint black and white occupancy. A little more than a third of the total housing units built under PWA were occupied by black people in 1940.[26] In October 1934 the first low-cost housing project constructed for Negroes near Atlanta University was dedicated personally by Ickes. The Atlanta project, he informed his predominantly black audience, reflected the spirit and the purpose of the New Deal. "We have learned that it is for the economic benefit of the whole country for all divisions of it to be prosperous; that discrimination against a section, a race, a religion or an occupation is harmful to the people as a whole and disturbing to any attempts to work out a balanced economy." Even Robert Abbott, publisher of the Chicago *Defender*, who was not very happy with the Roosevelt administration by 1934, was pleased with Ickes. "To those who know him," the *Defender* remarked, "his attitude in Atlanta typifies his rugged character, his high regard of fair dealing and the honesty of purpose which has always characterized his life in the performance of his responsibilities, whether public or private."[27]

The Atlanta speech exemplified a central theme propounded by Ickes. In contrast to its predecessors, he argued, the Roosevelt administration was dedicated to assuring equal opportunity for all; and with persons like himself in authority, blacks could feel certain that they would gain from the government's reforms. Moreover, Ickes clearly believed that his special abilities and liberal racial commitments should be exerted within almost every area of New Deal activity. Supporters of the Interior Secretary, like Edwin Embree, originally had hoped Ickes would use his influence to see that the Negro advisory post was expanded to oversee activities throughout the administration. Embree felt it might even be necessary to establish a "national advisory council on Negro welfare," appointed by the President, to act as a watchdog in the interest of blacks. In December 1933, Robert R. Moton directly proposed to

25. Kruman, "Quotas for Blacks," 47-49.
26. Sterner, *The Negro's Share* (New York, 1943), 317.
27. Ickes' speech in Pittsburgh *Courier*, Oct. 6, 1934; Chicago *Defender*, Oct. 13, 1934.

Ickes the formation of just such a committee "to advise with the government as to the needs of the colored people and the best ways in which the provisions of the Recovery Acts can be applied to them." But Ickes rejected the idea; to create a committee representing "different races, nationalities or other groups," he told Moton, would be a bad precedent.[28]

However, it would not be a bad precedent for the Interior Secretary and his adviser, Clark Foreman, to establish within the government, under their authority, a body to represent blacks. With the approval of Roosevelt (and under Foreman's supervision), Ickes created in 1934 the "Interdepartmental Group Concerned with Special Problems of Negroes."[29] The Group met for the first time on February 7, 1934. Its obvious purpose was to provide Ickes and Foreman with the opportunity to press the cause of Negro participation in the National Recovery Administration and the Agricultural Adjustment Administration, in agencies such as the Civilian Conservation Corps and the Federal Emergency Relief Administration, and in administrative departments where the two had little influence. At its first meeting both black and white representatives from a broad cross section of New Deal agencies and departments were included.[30] By June 1934, however, when they met for the fourth time, the membership had been reduced considerably. The theory behind Ickes' interdepartmental approach, as Allen Kifer has noted, was that if no one else in the administration "cared about the Negro's special economic problems, then Interior would have to remind them of their responsibilities."[31] Even before the Group was formed, correspondence between Ickes and Foreman indicated their con-

28. Edwin Embree to T. Arnold Hill, Aug. 14, 1933, Rosenwald Fund Archives, Box 306; Robert Moton to Harold L. Ickes, Dec. 19, 1933; Ickes to Moton, Jan. 2, 1934, Department of Interior, National Archives (NA), Record Group (RG) 48.

29. Kifer, "The Negro Under the New Deal," 220-21; Wolters, *Negroes and the Great Depression*, 143-45; "Minutes of the Interdepartmental Group concerned with the Special Problems of Negroes," Feb. 7, 1934, NARG 48.

30. Whites in attendance at the early Group meetings besides Clark Foreman were W.D. Searle from the War Department's Civilian Personnel Division and William D. Bergman from the Navy Department. Blacks included Henry A. Hunt, representing the Farm Credit Administration, Eugene Kinckle Jones, Department of Commerce, Forrester B. Washington, Federal Emergency Relief Administration, and Robert L. Vann, Justice Department, "Minutes of the Interdepartmental Group Concerned with Special Problems of Negroes," Feb. 7, Mar. 21, Mar. 30, 1934, NARG 48. Representatives from departments and agencies other than those normally present at Group meetings might sit in on one or more sessions or be asked to address the Group.

31. Kifer, "The Negro Under the New Deal," 230.

cern over the situation confronting blacks in other governmental areas. During the Group's brief life, studies were made which dealt with the status of Negroes in many New Deal agencies; on occasion, such studies were sent to administrators like Harry L. Hopkins of the Civil Works Administration, with a request that something be done to increase black employment.[32] When Ickes discovered that Robert Fechner of the CCC was limiting the number of black applications on the grounds that there was a lack of available camp locations, he offered the National Parks and National Forests as future sites.[33]

But Fechner and other New Dealers did not share the Interior Department's zeal in the cause of black equal opportunity. Agriculture Secretary Henry A. Wallace, addressing the third Interdepartmental Group meeting, cautioned the participants to go slow and avoid "making trouble for other groups." Too much concern for one "underprivileged" segment of the population, Wallace argued, could cause harm for others. Since officials like Wallace did not share the same commitment as Ickes for the "special problems of Negroes" and, more importantly, because they feared encroachments by the Interior Secretary in their own fiefdoms, it is not surprising that the interdepartmental concept ultimately failed.[34]

Yet Ickes no doubt influenced other New Dealers. Although it is impossible to tell how much he was personally responsible, the appointment of black advisers became a widely accepted practice during the 1930s and the war years. By 1939, there were only a few federal departments that did not have a "Negro adviser," though their responsibilities varied considerably.[35]

With the exception of Eleanor Roosevelt, Ickes was the New Dealer with the most direct personal tie to Negroes, a relationship he spent considerable time and effort cultivating. It was to Ickes that the NAACP and National Urban League often took their problems. Throughout the 1930s, despite his other involvements, he could

32. Memos, Ickes to Foreman, Oct. 16, Oct. 23, Nov. 11, Nov. 22, 1933, NARG 48; Harold L. Ickes to Harry Hopkins, Feb. 3, 1934, Civil Works Administration, NARG 69, Box 83.

33. Kifer, "The Negro Under the New Deal," 32.

34. "Minutes of the Interdepartmental Group . . . ," Mar. 30, 1934, NARG 48; Kifer, "The Negro Under the New Deal," 218-33; Wolters, *Negroes and the Great Depression*, 133; Buni, *Robert L. Vann*, 209-11. Some of the blacks who attended Group meetings later formed what became known as the "Black Cabinet," discussed in Ch. 6.

35. For general discussion, see Bunche, "Political Status of the Negro," 1444-52, and Henry Lee Moon, "Racial Aspects of Federal Public Relations Programs," *Phylon* 4 (First Quarter, 1943), 66-67.

usually be counted on to address NAACP and Urban League conventions or send them a message, make a commencement talk to a black college or university, or write an essay for some Negro periodical.[36] In election years, when he was particularly valuable to Democrats and the President, he campaigned in the black community for the New Deal. "No previous administration," he told NAACP supporters in June 1936, "has provided employment in the various departments and agencies for so many Negroes."[37] At Howard University, in one of President Roosevelt's infrequent public appearances before a black audience, Ickes claimed that not only had the PWA furnished funds for institutions like Howard but it had "sought to increase educational equipment to Negroes in all sections of the nation from elementary schools to colleges."[38] Relief, federal farm aid, low-income housing, employment of black laborers and white-collar workers, rural resettlement, and social security were stressed in the 1930s as evidence of the New Deal's efforts on behalf of black Americans. During World War II, when he was less active and domestic reform was less a reality, he emphasized the Fair Employment Practices Committee, defense employment, and the addition of black officers to the armed forces. In Harlem during the 1944 election, he maintained that since FDR had taken office, the government had "pressed steadily toward the goal of a democratic Army where there will be no segregation or discrimination."[39]

In these and other activities, Harold Ickes symbolized some of the changes which occurred in the general liberal perspective on civil rights during the Roosevelt years. The political and ideological

36. Ickes' ties to the NAACP have already been noted; correspondence between Walter White and Ickes can be found in the NAACP Papers, LC, Administrative and Personal Correspondence files. For the Urban League's friendship with the Interior Secretary, see Weiss, *National Urban League*, 272; Parris and Brooks, *Blacks in the City*, 227-28; Arvarh E. Strickland, *History of the Chicago Urban League* (Urbana, Ill., 1966), 117-18. Also, for the correspondence of various black leaders to Ickes, "Miscellaneous Correspondence to the Negroes," Department of Interior, NARG 48. A list of Ickes' speeches to racial and interracial organizations in the thirties and forties can be found in the introduction to the Ickes Papers, LC. Two representative Ickes talks are the previously cited Chicago Urban League speech, Feb. 26, 1936, and his 1936 NAACP address, reprinted as "The Negro As Citizen," *Crisis* 18 (Aug. 1936), 230-31, 242, 253. Also see Ickes, "Will Fair Employment Be Demobilized," *Negro Digest* 2 (Aug. 1944), 3-5 and "To Have Jobs or To Have Not," *Negro Digest* 4 (Jan. 1946), 73-75.

37. Ickes, "Negro As Citizen," 242.

38. New York *Times*, Nov. 2, 1944.

39. New York *Times*, Feb. 27, Oct. 27, 1936; John Van Deusen, *Black Man in White America* (Washington, D.C., 1944). On the 1944 election, see the New York *Times*, Nov. 2, 1944.

isolation felt by many liberals in the 1920s was abruptly altered by the impact of the Depression and New Deal reform. Many now found themselves "in," and some, like Edwin Embree and Will Alexander, quickly perceived the opportunity not only for restructuring American institutions through the Roosevelt administration but for doing so in a manner that would enhance the possibilities for racial justice. That a man like Ickes, with his liberal racial attitudes, was now a power in Washington was extremely encouraging; even better, Ickes and others were seeking counsel from racial "experts" and even hiring some of them to serve in the government.

Thus, in view of Ickes' position as a supporter of New Deal liberalism and minority opportunity, his ideas and activities are crucial in understanding the link that developed gradually between economic and social reform and Negro rights. Running through most of his public statements were a number of themes: the historic plight of black people, the effect of the Depression and the New Deal on Negro life, and the future of black progress. What in turn structured these themes was Ickes' conviction that the thirties afforded blacks special opportunities and that fulfillment of these opportunities rested on the success of the New Deal itself. The fate of the Negro, then, was inextricably tied to the fate of the Roosevelt administration; and, one might say, so was that of many white liberals.

Ickes' historical analysis of the black experience usually began with the post– Civil War period. To him, the era of Reconstruction was significant as the period during which black people were fundamentally assigned their low economic and political status. "The Negroes of America had scarcely been set free," he noted, "before they became the general object of economic as well as political exploitation."[40] Since emancipation, the Afro-American had been forced to exist "for generations on the very fringes" of American life.[41] He had been systematically excluded from the best jobs, consigned to the most unsanitary living conditions, and stripped of a political voice to express his discontent. Ickes assigned primary responsibility for segregation to the political dependence of Negroes on the Republican party. "Taught to believe that it was the Republican party that by its unaided efforts had manumitted him from slavery, the Negro not only felt grateful to that party, he

40. Ickes, "The Negro Holds His Fate in His Own Hands," speech intended for delivery at Wilberforce Univ., Oct. 10, 1936, FDR Papers, OF 6.
41. Ickes, "Negro As Citizen," 231.

27

thought he was duty bound to express that gratitude."[42] Republicans, however, entertained no reciprocal feeling of gratitude for black political support, according to Ickes. "From the time of the Civil War until 1932 the Republican party deliberately and in cold blood exploited the Negro. During the political campaigns Republican candidates were the solicitous and protesting friends of the Negro race," but between campaigns, the situation was quite different; "then the economic exploiter could have his will of the Negro who seemed to have no friends except when his votes were wanted."[43]

For Ickes, Republican failure to provide strong and progressive leadership helped explain the low economic and social position of blacks in the American system. Economic exploitation would "not have been possible," he argued, "without the political exploitation that preceded and accompanied it." Unfortunately, as he frequently told Negro audiences, black people must also be held responsible since it was their "willing acquiescence" in Republican domination which helped to create the horrors of their past. "This meek submission to political exploitation," he explained to the Chicago Urban League, "which foreran and was the cause of economic exploitation brings into relief one of the great virtues of the Negro race as well as one of its great faults."[44] The black man's "virtue" was his ability to endure decades of oppression. As Ickes put it, it was black people's "saving sense of humor and their optimism" that had "brought them smiling through hardships which would have meant disaster to lesser people."[45]

Yet if endurance and optimism were virtues, they could also be liabilities; the failure of blacks realistically to confront their past dependence on the Republican party had led to their forced separation from the American mainstream. Fortunately, Ickes believed, the times were changing. A new and better educated generation of Negroes had begun to add up the cost of their political debt and were questioning "whether political slavery, even if voluntarily assumed, was any more desirable than the physical slavery which their ances-

42. Speech, Chicago Urban League, Feb. 26, 1936; speech, Wilberforce Univ., Oct. 10, 1936, FDR Papers, OF 6.
43. Speech, Wilberforce Univ., Oct. 10, 1936.
44. *Ibid*.
45. Ickes, "Welcome Address," *The National Conference on Fundamental Problems in the Education of Negroes, Washington, D.C., May 9-12, 1934* (U.S. Dept. of Interior, Office of Education, 1935), 7.

tors had endured."[46] By 1932, many black voters concluded that they had long ago paid whatever debt they owed the Republicans; they decided "that they owed something to themselves and to their children."[47]

The bonds tying blacks to the Republican party could not be broken overnight. Ickes recognized the force of tradition in shaping a people's attitudes; he also recognized that up to the 1930s, the Democratic party had failed to offer the Negro a political alternative. Thus he considered the Depression and the New Deal's response to it critically important in opening up new avenues for racial advancement. The Depression, he argued, had two major consequences for blacks. First, the economic collapse had destroyed the ideological justification which had sanctioned the old order's economic and political exploitation. Laissez-faire principles were exposed as the rationales by which the rich and powerful had exploited the poor and the weak; both black and white Americans were now forced to reevaluate their attitudes and to "rediscover some of the simpler happinesses of life." Second, the New Deal made possible the creation of a new "modern economic and industrial" society; and such a society, based on equal opportunity for all people, gave fresh hope for black progress.[48]

If the Depression had taught Americans nothing else, Ickes wrote in 1934, the "terrible period through which we are passing . . . has made us realize our interdependence."[49] This new American sense of "interdependence" formed the basis for his belief that black people had "profited more from this depression than any other class of citizens." The benefit to the Negro was not, of course, material but lay "in the understanding and sympathy which have drawn him into closer bond with those of the white race." Such understanding and sympathy between blacks and whites led in turn to Ickes' optimistic assertion that "in the future there will not be the mistrust, the misunderstanding or the antipathy which has existed in the past between certain members of these two races." Of major significance was his thesis that "when the members of one race, whatever they may have felt in the past, have come to regard those of another as

46. Speech, Chicago Urban League, Feb. 26, 1936.
47. Speech, Wilberforce Univ., Oct. 10, 1936.
48. Speech, Chicago Urban League, Feb. 26, 1936; Ickes, "Welcome Address"; "Negro As Citizen," 242. Also see Ickes, *New Democracy*, 62-69, 74-75, 120-21.
49. *New Democracy*, 74; "Is the Roosevelt 'New Deal' Proving Successful?", 170; Harmon, "Some Contributions of Harold L. Ickes," 240.

members of the same human family, possessing the same weaknesses, capable of the same sacrifices and endowed with the same aspirations, it becomes very difficult indeed for them to retain prejudices that were based entirely upon race, color, or religion."[50]

For Ickes, then, the Depression created conditions which bound people together; old ideas and values which had previously perpetuated class, racial, and religious divisions would be discarded through the need for mutual assistance. The implication, as his use of such terms as "mistrust," "misunderstanding," and "antipathy" indicated, was that racial and religious conflicts, among others, were not deeply ingrained in American society but resulted from the past failure of groups to understand and empathize with one another's common predicament. The Depression now provided the occasion for these groups to join together, and it would be up to the federal government to capitalize on the opportunity by bringing into common cause the varied elements of the American populace. This, as Ickes saw it, was the mission and purpose of the New Deal; it was this mission and purpose which he believed would ultimately carry the black man into the mainstream of American life.

To Ickes, the New Deal was a complete departure from the past; Roosevelt's election signified a "bloodless revolution."[51] The President's reference to the "forgotten man" was not simply a campaign slogan but an "expression of a profound conviction, of a mature social purpose."[52] It would now be the responsibility of government, Ickes wrote in *The New Democracy*, to build a "new social order," to protect the weak against the strong; to curb "over-reaching and ruthless power"; and to reaffirm "that equality of opportunity . . . is the cornerstone of our American civilization."[53] In its "simplest terms," the "social revolution" of 1932 consisted "in turning out from the seats of power the representatives of wealth and privilege and exploiting ruthlessness and substituting for them a man whose purpose it is to make this country of ours a better place to live in for the average man and woman."[54]

Ickes never questioned that a "better place to live in for the average man and woman" meant a better place to live in for the Negroes. The New Deal responded to the demands of all the

50. Speech, Chicago Urban League, Feb. 26, 1936.
51. Ickes, "Is the Roosevelt 'New Deal' Proving Successful?" 170; "Social Implications of the Roosevelt Administration," 111.
52. "Social Implications of the Roosevelt Administration," 111.
53. *New Democracy*, 73-74.
54. "Social Implications of the Roosevelt Administration," 112.

people, blacks as well as whites. Relief, public housing, employment, education, and social security would be provided irrespective
of race, creed, or color. The administration was "seeking the greatest
good for the greatest number," and, as Ickes told the NAACP in 1936,
under the New Deal's "new conception of democracy, the Negro
will be given the chance to which he is entitled—not because he will
be singled out for special consideration but because he preeminently
belongs to the class that the new democracy is designed especially to
aid."[55]

This briefly was Ickes' message to blacks. Freed of his "political
slavery" and aided by the New Deal, the Negro held, as the title of
one of Ickes' speeches put it, "His Fate in His Own Hands." If he
would use his political independence to win his "economic freedom," if he took advantage of the administrative programs aimed at
assuring him "equal opportunity" and a "square deal," if he utilized
the increased educational facilities being offered him to prepare for
"the modified social and economic foundation upon which the new
democracy" was being built, then Ickes foresaw a bright future and a
time when "we can cease to think of any race as a problem and
instead, begin to take delight in its achievements."[56]

Like many liberals in the early thirties, Ickes thus viewed the
Depression as a blessing, a turning point in the national experience—the uprooting of the "old order," the beginning of an era of
interdependence and cooperation. Unlike liberal and radical critics
of the Roosevelt administration, the former Bull Moose Progressive
never doubted the critical role the New Deal was playing in achieving that transformation. He was equally certain that the result of
such a transformation would be beneficial to Negro people; the New
Deal "revolution" clearly signified a revolution in race relations.
Through the efforts of unprejudiced public servants like himself, the
national government had become a symbol to blacks and whites that
race discrimination and injustice would no longer be tolerated at the
highest political levels. His personal activity on behalf of blacks, his
appearance before Negro groups, and his appointment of race advisers were all examples, especially to white America, proving that
racism had no place in a democratic nation. Americans, he believed,
had in the past "deceived" themselves that they were "more right-
eous and social-minded than in fact" they were. "We have talked so
much about our sense of justice, about equal opportunity under the

55. "Negro As Citizen," 231.
56. "Welcome Address," 8; also "Negro As Citizen," 230-31.

law, regardless of race, or color, or creed, that we have actually blinded our moral perception to the gross exploitation of weaker groups that has been going on under our very eyes."[57]

Initially, Ickes believed it necessary to establish certain guarantees, such as the PWA's quota plan, to ensure blacks equal opportunity under reform measures. But beyond this, any special reference to race needed to be minimized; government should not sanction any policy which affirmed race differences or perceived black needs as distinct from the needs of other Americans. Ickes felt that it was equally important for blacks and whites to understand that whatever the past significance of race in defining the "Negro problem," it need not interfere with the present solution of that problem. The New Deal was designed to aid every American; jobs, housing, and education transcended race. He consistently held, as he wrote in *Negro Digest* in 1946, that the "Negro problem merges into and becomes inseparable from the greater problem of American citizens generally, who are at or below the line in decency and comfort from those who are not."[58]

Therefore, the New Deal's most important contribution in eliminating racial antagonism stemmed from its commitment to incorporate the Negro into its economic reform program. If blacks and whites were brought together by the New Deal in a common endeavor to improve their lot, their previous antagonism would dissipate; the "Negro problem" would then be "recognized to be individual and not racial," and to the degree that the Negro trained his mind through education, he would "be able to compete on more equal terms with the educated whites among whom he dwells."[59]

As Ickes defined them, administration priorities rested primarily on the federal government's willingness to provide necessary aid to assist black people in improving their own class status. Responsibility in utilizing the opportunities for economic and political advancement depended, as Ickes told black groups, upon Negroes themselves.[60] In the 1930s, the advantages resulted from the domestic programs of the PWA, the WPA, social security, and aid to education; during the war years, he maintained that "new opportunities" were being provided blacks through federal defense spending; and by 1946 he was saying, in language similar to that of the 1930s, that

57. Speech, Wilberforce Univ., Oct. 10, 1936.
58. "To Have Jobs," 73.
59. "Welcome Address," 9; speech, Chicago Urban League, Feb. 26, 1936.
60. See, for instance, "Negro As Citizen" and speech, Chicago Urban League, Feb. 26, 1936.

once "the full employment program was brought to its full fruition, Negroes would be given opportunities to which they are entitled, not because they would be singled out for special considerations but because a great majority of Negroes belong to the class that the program is designed especially to benefit."[61]

Whatever was advocated, the emphasis remained the same; but so did the limits of the mandate to confront racial problems. When in 1937, for example, Ickes was accused by Senators Josiah W. Bailey of North Carolina and Carter Glass of Virginia of supporting FDR's court-packing scheme in order to overthrow their beloved Jim Crow restrictions in the South, he emphatically denied the charge. He felt compelled, moreover, to write Bailey and disavow any such intention.[62] Commenting on the controversy in his diary, he stated that it was

> up to the states to work out their own social problems if possible and while I have been interested in seeing that the Negro has a square deal, I have never dissipated my strength against the particular stone wall of segregation. I believe that wall will crumble when the Negro has brought himself to a higher educational and economic status. After all, we can't force people on each other who do not like each other, even when no question of color is involved. Moreover, while there are no segregation laws in the North, there is segregation in fact and we might as well recognize this.[63]

The statement indicated a major dilemma inherent in his and the New Deal's approach to racial matters in the 1930s and 1940s. For Ickes, the key to altering the pattern of race relations in America lay in the "educational and economic status" of blacks. Once that status was raised, essentially as blacks capitalized on New Deal reform and recovery efforts and, later, on measures such as "full employment," the "stone wall of segregation" would "crumble." Ickes assumed that white racial values and beliefs were predicated on the continued low level of black American existence. Remove the source which nourished these attitudes by elevating the economic and social class status of blacks, and there no longer would exist any rational basis for

---

61. "To Have Jobs," 74, and "Will Fair Employment Be Demobilized?" 4.

62. Frank Freidel, *F.D.R. and the South* (Baton Rouge, 1965), 93-94, discusses Carter Glass's attack on Ickes regarding the Supreme Court and the race question. See also New York *Times*, Mar. 13, 1937, for excerpts from Ickes' speech in Raleigh, N.C., which originally set off the Glass and Bailey attacks. The New York *Times*, Mar. 30, 1937, includes the full text of Glass's nationally broadcast speech opposing Roosevelt's court plan and referring to Ickes.

63. Ickes, *Secret Diary*, II, 115.

white prejudice and bigotry; then all Americans, black and white, would see that they belonged to the "same human family," possessed the "same weaknesses," and were "capable of the same sacrifices and endowed with the same aspirations."

Such a view, though consistent with Ickes' understanding of the black experience, his vision of the New Deal, and his personal sense of moral duty, was not always consistent with the reality of the Roosevelt years. Nor was it consistent with the manner in which New Deal economic and social assistance often came to black Americans. When Ickes assumed personal responsibility for federal policies, as he did in the case of PWA labor programs, blacks made some gains; but that was the exception rather than the rule. For the most part, recovery and reform programs were decentralized, i.e., administered and implemented at state and local levels, and they had limited impact on the uprooting of traditional attitudes. As a result, existing racial practices frequently compromised the noble goals of federal officials like Ickes; in order to secure acceptance of assistance measures, a price had to be paid—namely, acceptance of local racial custom.

In the North, almost all the housing projects inspired by the PWA and later the USHA were built in all-black neighborhoods.[64] Robert Weaver noted later that "public housing prior to World War II attempted to avoid the problems of residential segregation in the North by concentrating on slum cities and giving preference in tenant selection to the racial groups previously in the site and the surrounding neighborhood."[65] A recent analysis of Negro housing and work projects developed for Cleveland blacks during the 1930s concludes that "although the New Deal public housing and emergency work programs played an important part in alleviating the problems generated by the Depression, they also contributed to the preservation of perhaps the two salient components which combine to produce a caste-like Negro social structure—residential segregation and a distinctly racial occupational pattern."[66] In the South there was little pretense to do otherwise; the tradition of

64. Weaver, *Negro Ghetto*, 15, 179-80; Sterner, *The Negro's Share*, 319-21. On the implications of decentralized administration, see also B. Joyce Ross, "Mary McLeod Bethune and the National Youth Administration: A Case Study of Power Relationships in the Black Cabinet of Franklin D. Roosevelt," *Journal of Negro History* 60 (Jan. 1975). 20-28, and Christopher G. Wye, "The New Deal and the Negro Community: Toward a Broader Conceptualization," *Journal of American History* 59 (Dec. 1972), 636-38.

65. Weaver, *Negro Ghetto*, 75, 179.

66. Wye, "The New Deal and the Negro Community," 639.

separating the races was simply preserved by constructing separate black and white facilities, as was the case in the Atlanta project which Ickes personally dedicated to New Deal idealism.[67]

Since economic uplift was the avowed priority of Ickes and the New Deal, capitulation to local racial customs was inevitable, especially in view of the force of those customs. FDR's unwillingness to support publicly a federal anti-lynching law, which he personally favored, was one indication of the strength of such attitudes. But that was the point. How would blacks bring themselves to a "higher educational and economic status" if racism remained essentially unchallenged and unchanged? Even if the Negro standard of living were raised by their inclusion in federal reform, would white hostility to black Americans therefore diminish? The difficulty of implementing New Deal programs when race became the issue, almost always the case when federal assistance involved the Negro, suggests the persistence rather than the lessening of such hostility. Faith that racism would lose its grip on the American mind was based more on hope than reality.

New Deal racial liberals, and Ickes in particular, never fully confronted these problems, although there is evidence that at times they were aware of their existence. Certainly the problems were complex, and one could not expect a handful of liberals in the government (even someone as confident of himself as Harold Ickes) to eradicate what had taken centuries to bring about. But the problem was complicated by Ickes' and others' confidence in the New Deal's ability to affect social change and by their interpretation of the "Negro problem." In maintaining that the solution to America's racial dilemma was predicated on altering the economic position of black Americans, New Dealers like Ickes simply rationalized their own assumptions and the limits of the administration's response to Negro needs.

III

During the critical first years of the New Deal, much of the burden of convincing blacks and whites that America's race problem could be ameliorated through New Deal reformism rested with Clark Foreman. Foreman's southern background and his position with the Commission for Interracial Cooperation no doubt persuaded Ickes that he was the man for the task. By 1933, despite the continued

67. Weaver, *Negro Ghetto*, 179; Sterner, *The Negro's Share*, 320.

flight of Negroes northward, the majority of black people remained south of the Mason-Dixon line. As a native Georgian, with strong southern roots, Foreman could be expected to provide a perspective different from that of the northern-bred Ickes.

Although Ickes exaggerated Foreman's race relations experience (he was just thirty when Roosevelt was elected in 1932), it was true that the southerner was no novice in the field. His first personal contact with race hostility came as an undergraduate at the University of Georgia, when he witnessed what he later recalled was "one of the most cruel and sordid lynchings that has ever taken place in the South." Shocked by the incident, he concluded that lynchings were a manifestation of the deeper dilemma of "race prejudice and oppression," and, unlike some of his liberal elders in the South, he was inclined to perceive race within a broad social and economic framework.[68]

In the 1920s, he combined a number of pursuits: studies at the London School of Economics, where he came across James H. Oldham's *Christianity and the Race Problem*, a book which gave him a "comprehensive idea of the race problem throughout the world"; three years with Alexander's Interracial Commission, where he received practical experience in dealing with racial issues; and, in the late twenties and early thirties, graduate work in political science at Columbia University, where he wrote a master's thesis on the southern interracial struggle and a doctoral dissertation, later published as *The Environmental Factors in Negro Elementary Education*. His concern with black education led him in 1928 to accept a position with the Rosenwald Fund, on the recommendation of Will Alexander, despite a strong attraction for the academic life.[69]

Foreman remained with the fund until 1937, and during his brief time as Ickes' chief assistant on race matters, he kept in close touch with his friends at Rosenwald. With Foreman's help, George S. Mitchell and Horace Cayton, two Rosenwald fellows, secured em-

---

68. *South Today* (Spring 1942), 52. *South Today* was coedited by the southern novelist Lillian Smith. This particular issue was devoted in part to biographical sketches of Foreman and other leaders of the Southern Conference for Human Welfare. Smith is discussed in the following chapter.

69. *South Today*, 51-52; *Current Biography: Who's News and Why* (New York, 1942), 218-20; Dykeman and Stokely, *Seeds of Southern Change*, 157-58; Edwin Embree to Clark Foreman, Oct. 17, Oct. 23, 1928, Rosenwald Fund Archives, Box 105; Foreman to Embree, Oct. 19, 1928, *ibid.*, Box 121.

ployment in the Interior Department and carried on an analysis of Negro industrial conditions which they published in 1939 as *Black Workers and the New Unions*. Edwin Embree and Alexander often relied on information furnished them by Foreman to stay abreast of New Deal policies; and the three liberals conversed frequently on ways to engage the administration more directly in racial concerns.[70]

After two years as adviser, Foreman decided it was time for the position to be assumed by a black representative, and with Ickes' support Robert Weaver was given the responsibility. But Foreman did not leave the New Deal. At the urging of Ickes, he accepted the directorship of the Power Division within the Public Works Administration, and during the early war years he worked on defense housing under John Carmody of the Federal Works Agency. In the spring of 1942, he was abruptly dismissed from the FWA for his involvement in a racial conflict at Detroit's Sojourner Truth Housing project.[71]

Foreman's support of black occupancy in the project, at a time when the federal government's policy vacillated from one extreme to another on the issue, won him the admiration of many black leaders, including Mary McLeod Bethune of the National Youth Administration, the NAACP's Walter White, and Dr. Channing H. Tobias, director of the Colored YMCA. Writing to Roosevelt in the aftermath of his dismissal, the three claimed that Foreman had been "blacklisted" from the government because he had taken the "position— and stuck to it despite terrific pressure upon him—that Negro

70. Mitchell and Cayton, *Black Workers and the New Unions* (Chapel Hill, 1939). Foreman's role in helping Mitchell and Cayton to find government employment is noted in Charles S. Johnson to Will Alexander, June 4, 1934; Edwin Embree to Johnson, Apr. 18, 1934, Charles S. Johnson Papers, Box 78; Embree to Foreman, June 7, 1934, Rosenwald Fund Archives, Box 309. Also see "Reminiscences of Will Alexander," Columbia Oral History, 372-75. After a discussion with Foreman, Alexander wrote Embree that what "we need to hit upon, as I see it, are some major projects which will bring Negroes in a big way into the efforts at economic reconstruction," Alexander to Embree, Oct. 12, 18, 1933, Rosenwald Fund Archives, Box 94. Later, in reflecting on Foreman's early career with the New Deal, Alexander noted that Foreman "had a rather rough time but that made it interesting for him. He always liked to have a rough time. He was getting something done, I suppose, and he gave us information that was useful to us in one way or another. That seemed all we could do." "Reminiscences of Will Alexander," 371-72.

71. New York *Times*, Mar. 1, 2, 3, 10, 1942; *Crisis* 49 (Apr. 1942), 112. See also Gunnar Myrdal, *An American Dilemma: The Negro Problem and Modern Democracy*, 2 vols. (2d ed., New York, 1962), II, 568, 678, and Weaver, *Negro Ghetto*, 94-95.

37

citizens were as entitled as whites to enjoy the benefits of housing made possible by taxation of all the people, Negro and white."[72]

Foreman did not return to the government after the Sojourner Truth episode. From 1942 on, he turned his attention to building the Southern Conference for Human Welfare, an organization he helped to establish in 1938 and chaired until its demise in 1948.[73] But the backing he received from the Negro community in 1942 was a testimony to how black Americans had come to respect him in contrast to their initial reaction 1933.[74] Foreman's hiring of the young economist Robert Weaver in October 1933 no doubt quieted some of his critics. Although Weaver was not well known at the time, his association with the Joint Committee on National Recovery, an organization supported by the NAACP and militant in its advocacy of black economic rights, made him a popular choice. The Pittsburgh *Courier*, critical of Foreman's nomination, considered the appointments of Weaver and other blacks "far more beneficial to the Negro masses than any previously made."[75]

But more important in changing black attitudes toward him were Foreman's ideas on black progress. On November 14, 1933, he made a major address to a Conference of Presidents of Negro Land Grant Colleges in Chicago. His speech included an analysis of what Foreman conceived the role of the New Deal to be in aiding Negro Americans and won loud praise from the Chicago *Defender*, which two months previously had vociferously condemned him. In a

---

72. Mary McLeod Bethune, Walter White, and Channing H. Tobias to FDR, June 17, 1942, FDR Papers, OF 4947. Also Edwin Embree to Will Alexander, Jan. 22, 1942, Rosenwald Fund Archives, Box 94. Alexander believed that Harry Hopkins was responsible for Foreman's dismissal because he disliked Foreman's pressing the cause of blacks. "Reminiscences of Will Alexander," Columbia Oral History, 371.

73. Thomas A. Krueger, *And Promises to Keep: The Southern Conference for Human Welfare, 1938–1948* (Nashville, 1967), 103-104; *South Today*, 51-52. Morton Sosna discusses Foreman's work with the SCHW during the 1940s in *In Search of the Silent South*, 141-47.

74. Hostile response to Foreman's appointment has already been noted, but see Chicago *Defender*, Sept. 16, 23, 1933; Pittsburgh *Courier*, Sept. 19, 1933. Both the *Courier* and *Defender* gave coverage (Nov. 4, 1933) to the demands by the National Equal Rights League that Foreman be immediately dismissed. William Monroe Trotter served as secretary of the Rights League.

75. Pittsburgh *Courier*, Nov. 11, 1933. Foreman stated in a letter to the Joint Committee on National Recovery that he had "consulted with several of the most important Negro leaders and . . . had their unanimous and enthusiastic approval for Dr. Weaver." The Pittsburgh *Courier*, Nov. 18, 1933, published the full text of Foreman's letter. Just who Foreman consulted is not clear, but he did include a letter from black insurance executive C.C. Spaulding endorsing both himself and Weaver.

"Close-Up of Clark Foreman," the *Defender* observed that his "recent address . . . placed him in a new light as a national figure"; after studying his ideas, they "were of the opinion that he deserves to be given free and unhampered opportunity to carry out his program." As Ickes had done earlier, the *Defender* now argued that Foreman should not be dismissed by blacks "solely on grounds that he is a Southern man"; in fact, since he had the "confidence of his own race" it would be of "great benefit in bringing to the [whites] a more enlightened view of many questions which still await a satisfactory solution."[76]

In most respects, Foreman's "program" was similar to that of Ickes. He had, of course, collaborated with the Interior Secretary in his book *The New Democracy*, Ickes' most extensive philosophical treatment of the New Deal's importance and of the social, political, and economic changes he perceived taking place in American life.[77] Foreman recalled some years later that as a result of his experiences in the 1920s, he had come to believe that the "greatest contribution" a political scientist could make to civilization was in developing "methods and instruments whereby group could cooperate with group, race with race, country with country throughout the world."[78] Ickes' stress on the cooperative spirit, on class and racial interdependency, fitted in nicely with these concerns. So also did Ickes' conception of the "methods and instruments" required to achieve a more democratic order; for both Foreman and the Interior Secretary, the expansion of federal power based upon rational social and economic planning was the key to the "New Democracy." Increased centralization was essential not only in building a more coordinated and humane economic system but in developing greater social unity.

Commitment to federal planning in the areas of social and economic reconstruction was given added force by Foreman's southern perspective. He knew firsthand the sense of impotence and isolation felt by those who carried on the lonely struggle for equal rights in the South. Historian Morton Sosna notes that most southern liberals strongly championed the New Deal's program, seeing in it not only an opportunity for personal political involvement, as in the case of Foreman, but more importantly, a powerful ally in the effort to liberalize southern life. In 1938, Foreman coauthored a *Report on the Economic Conditions of the South*, which referred to the South as the

76. Chicago *Defender*, Nov. 25, 1933. Foreman's speech was printed in the *Defender*, Nov. 18.
77. See "Introduction" in Ickes, *New Democracy*, ix.
78. *South Today* (Spring 1942), 52.

nation's "number 1 economic problem." The *Report* gained considerable publicity because of its public endorsement by President Roosevelt; and it reflected clearly Foreman's belief that federal economic intervention was crucial both to alleviating the region's major economic difficulties and to establishing a new basis for interracial unity. From the perspective of a southern race liberal, economic reconstruction and racial reconstruction were always considered interdependent.[79]

To a black audience in Chicago, Foreman interpreted the New Deal as a government experiment designed to steer a course "between the Communistic dictatorship of Russia and the Fascist dictatorship of Italy"; through "democratic control," the government would operate in the "best interests of the country." The goal of the administration was to direct the "country into a more humane economic organization, where the chief aim . . . will be the well-being of our citizenry rather than gold in our banks." Such "well-being," Foreman believed, could be achieved only by a strong government which would exercise controls over the entire economic system and force a redistribution of economic power throughout the country.[80]

State control was particularly relevant to the special problems of black workers. Under the old "system of laissez-faire," Foreman noted, "the Negro was used largely as a reserve group from which employers would call additional laborers either to fill gaps or break strikes or undercut the existing labor group when it strove for higher conditions." Under such a system, buttressed by a labor movement which "jealously protected" its "vested interests," blacks had been economically isolated and relegated to a "subsidiary and marginal" position in American industrial life "with fluctuating fortune and no security."[81] Under the National Recovery Administration, the situation would be different. "The whole question of the future of the Negro," Foreman stated in early 1934, was "intimately involved in the administration's attempt to regulate and plan industry."[82] Not only was the NRA providing guarantees for labor organizing and collective bargaining, which would benefit black workers; it was also assuming central control over the entire labor market. In the long

79. Sosna, *In Search of the Silent South, passim*, esp. 60-89.
80. Chicago *Defender*, Nov. 18, 1933; New York *Times*, Apr. 15, 1934. For a general discussion of New Deal economic philosophy in respect to the NRA and blacks, which Foreman's ideas closely followed, see Wolters, *Negroes and the Great Depression*, esp. 83-97.
81. Chicago *Defender*, Nov. 18, 1933.
82. New York *Times*, Apr. 15, 1934.

run, this would be of most significance to Negroes. The NRA's purpose was to coordinate industrial development to "achieve the greater distribution of buying power in the country"; this meant that the "pool of reserve labor, which was used by industry for its reservoir to its own advantage . . . will be drained." No longer would "individuals be kept in semi-starvation so that big profits" might accrue to only a few; now, "those unemployed through no fault of their own will be kept in a decent standard of living." If the New Deal was successful, he was convinced that the "Negro race will benefit proportionately more than the white race because more [blacks] have heretofore been consigned to that miserable pool. A government guarantee of a decent livelihood to all would have a revolutionary effect on our Negro population."[83]

Privately, Foreman sometimes showed concern over certain aspects of the NRA's relationship with black Americans. Within the Interdepartmental Group and in correspondence with Ickes, he pressed the cause for black representation on the NRA's Labor Advisory Board; no one in NRA, he argued, with the exception of R.W. Lea, assistant administrator for industry, was concerned with Negro needs or understood their problems.[84] Like many black spokesmen, he was apprehensive also about organized labor's power provided under the NRA and in Senator Wagner's proposed labor relations bill. Although a strong supporter of trade unions, he felt that black people would not profit as they should from union activities unless antidiscriminatory guarantees were established.[85] For these and other reasons, he favored Robert Moton's proposal for a separate "advisory committee." "I believe," he wrote Ickes in December 1933, that "with the development of difficulties . . . throughout the recovery program in the NRA, CCC, CWA and AAA, a small and important advisory group dealing with the economic future of the Negro would be very helpful."[86]

Black objections to NRA policies, however, were more fundamental. In respect to the industrial codes which Foreman praised, they pointed out that in the case of Negroes the codes were frequently

83. Chicago *Defender*, Nov. 18, 1933; New York *Times*, Apr. 15, 1934.
84. See "Minutes of the Interdepartmental Group . . .," Mar. 2, 30, 1934, NARG 48; Foreman to Ickes, Dec. 13, 1933, *ibid.*
85. "Minutes of the Interdepartmental Group . . .," Mar. 2, 1934, *ibid.* For the objections of blacks to the Wagner Act, see Wolters, *Negroes and the Great Depression*, 169-87, and Irving Bernstein, *Turbulent Years: A History of the American Workers, 1933–1941* (Boston, 1970), 189-90.
86. Foreman to Ickes, Dec. 22, 1933, NARG 48.

evaded through devices such as occupational and geographic job classifications, wage loopholes, or simply lack of NRA enforcement. Yet when the minimum wage and hour standards were adequately enforced, they often had equally harmful effects on black laborers. Particularly in the South, blacks were frequently displaced by whites when industries were forced to conform to a uniform higher wage, or else they lost their jobs when, unable to compete in compliance with NRA wage levels, a number of enterprises closed their doors.[87] Foreman conceded that in certain instances Negroes did suffer from NRA policies, but he believed that this had to be seen as a natural result of the transition from a laissez-faire to a planned economy. It was inevitable, he maintained, that in the "effort to regulate industry," some blacks "employed by unsound or marginal industries" would lose their positions. He remained convinced, however, that in the long run, with the "development of a planned economic life and the prosperity of industry" constructed on a fair wage standard for all, there was "every reason to believe that Negroes will gain directly and indirectly from the more wholesome situation."[88] Responding in 1934 to criticisms by John P. Davis, labor leader A. Philip Randolph, and Roy Wilkins that the root problem was the administration's failure to deal with the special racial factors confronting blacks, Foreman stated that nothing could be better as far as Negroes were concerned than "to have the government ignore [them] as a racial group and . . . leave [them] to act as workers and consumers."[89]

Foreman's thesis, then, was that despite the acknowledged shortcomings of the NRA, despite the immediate labor setbacks, black integration into the national industrial system through a uniform federal labor policy would be of ultimate "revolutionary" import to the "Negro population." The implication was that, as a result of strong federal policies, black labor and consumer standards would inevitably prosper along with those of the rest of the country. Yet when Foreman turned from strictly industrial matters to the plight of

87. Wolters, *Negroes and the Great Depression*, 83-215, esp. 113-35, has a full discussion of these and other difficulties confronted by Negroes under the NRA. Wolters states that with displacement and loss of jobs resulting from NRA codes, blacks probably "benefited from the NRA's inability and unwillingness to enforce its wage and hour provisions," 147. Thus, black workers "benefited" only when the NRA did not work according to Foreman's rationalization of its supposed purpose and goals.

88. New York *Times*, Apr. 15, 1934; Pittsburgh *Courier*, Apr. 14, 1934.

89. Pittsburgh *Courier*, July 28, 1934. See also *Courier*, Apr. 14, 1934; Wolters, *Negroes and the Great Depression*, 136-37. The conference Foreman participated in with Davis, Randolph, and Wilkins was sponsored by the Pullman Porters' Union.

southern rural blacks, he took a different approach. Here, uniformity gave way to an emphasis on Negroes as "a racial group," an emphasis he saw as detrimental to black interests when applied to industrial labor considerations.

Writing for *Opportunity* in April 1934, Foreman noted that the condition of the southern Negro was the "worst on the North American continent." "Downtrodden and terrorized into peonage by those who claim[ed] that 'white supremacy' " had to be insured, the majority of rural blacks were "confined to abject servitude and hopeless poverty." The only way to attack such conditions was for the government to evolve a strategy that was "realistic" and "motivated by sentiment possibly, but based on observable facts." It was true, he believed, that the "greater the area of government, the less it will be influenced by local prejudices"; and there was every reason to hope that once the New Deal extended its control, "federal authority will succeed in finding some way of rescuing the rural Negro." Whatever steps the federal government took "in the direction of greater federal control over agriculture should be welcomed by Negroes."[90]

Foreman, of course, was acutely aware of the depth of local southern white hostility to blacks. The crop reduction and farm subsidy policies of the AAA indicated the limitations for Negroes of federal agricultural programs when complicated by traditional southern racial customs. Though he supported the AAA idea in general as a step toward extending federal influence in the South and praised the FERA's attempts to provide relief assistance to poor Negroes and whites, the scheme he seized upon as being of most value to black farmers was subsistence homesteads. Characteristically, he saw the strength of the subsistence plan emanating from the "fact that the federal government would be behind the people . . . and would therefore inevitably assume the responsibility for a fair plan." Like NRA, he considered subsistence homesteads as "revolutionary" in their "potential effect on the rural Negro population."[91]

But in contrast to his ideas on industrialization, his agricultural proposals did not contemplate the immediate or even long-term integration of blacks into the southern farm economy. He advocated instead federal financing of separate Negro and white homesteads; specifically, he wanted federal assistance to those communities where blacks were in a numerical majority. In an interview in the

90. Foreman, "What Hope for the Rural Negro," *Opportunity* 12 (Apr. 1934), 105.
91. *Ibid.*, 106, 126.

Chicago *Daily News* (and reprinted in the *Defender* under the caption, "U.S. Government to Indorse Race Segregation: Scheme for Jim Crow Communities Told by Ickes Aide"), he elaborated on the theme. He was, he stated, in basic agreement with W.E.B. Du Bois that the "only way the Negro can develop is through group effort"; he proposed therefore that the Public Works Administration help blacks build their "own self-sufficient communities." These communities would be only a start, providing black people with "little plots of ground to sustain themselves, with a beginning on housing." But from there, the possibilities became much greater; "financed by their own people . . . and by the Public Works Administration, they would construct their own public utilities. With power and fuel and water developed by their own activities they could next turn to industry." He was certain Negroes could move from the homestead base to the establishment of black-operated industrial centers. He saw little difficulty in their competing under these circumstances with white-dominated business enterprises. "I do not recognize any limitation upon" the black man's ability; "reared with an inferiority complex because of the great handicap under which he has always labored in a mixed community, he makes his own limitations."[92]

Nor did he believe his scheme would inevitably strengthen the separation of blacks and whites. He was not advocating "segregation" but that "communities should be Negro built, Negro controlled, so that the colored people would have freedom for exercise of their own abilities, an outlet for the leadership which has been developed." The satisfactory completion of that, he affirmed, could "solve the economic problem of 13,000,000 people."[93]

Considering that a similar idea put forward by Du Bois was then under strong attack from the NAACP leadership, it is no wonder that Foreman's farm proposals, in contrast to his labor ideas, did not find universal acceptance within the Negro community.[94] Yet there was support for such schemes in the Interior Department. Bruce L. Melvin, head of minority affairs for the Division of Subsistence Homesteads, wrote to Du Bois in early 1934 congratulating him on his January *Crisis* issue, which had inaugurated the "segregation" debate within the NAACP. Opponents of Du Bois, Melvin believed,

92. Chicago *Defender*, Oct. 14, 1933.
93. *Ibid*.
94. See, for instance, Chicago *Defender*, Oct. 21, 1933; Pittsburgh *Courier*, Nov. 11, 1933. For a lengthy essay by a black "economist" supporting Foreman's subsistence homestead idea, see article by G. Victor Cools, reprinted in *Defender* and *Courier*, Nov. 11, 1933.

had confused the "question of segregation . . . with discrimination." Negroes had been coming to him and "asking for the establishment of subsistence homesteads to be led by colored people." If the administration followed the "logical conclusion" that "no project should be established in which colored people, alone, would be placed or in which white people, alone, would be placed, we would have to turn down colored people and their requests merely because they are colored people."[95]

Whatever the soundness of the Melvin and Foreman idea, the philosophical justification for it was not consistent with Foreman's defense of NRA policies. His NRA argument was based on the assumption that it was important to ignore blacks as "a racial group" if they were to benefit in the administration's attempt to "regulate and plan industry." In contrast, support of separate Negro homesteads was seen as a means, perhaps the only means, of assuring blacks some federally financed agricultural aid. One approach was particularly sensitive to prevailing racial attitudes and patterns and their effect on black economic and social welfare; the other assumed that such attitudes and patterns were inconsequential.

Yet despite the apparent incongruity, there was a certain consistency. Within both industrial and agricultural areas the key element for Foreman in dealing with the "Negro problem" was the federal government's provision of basic economic assistance to black Americans. A student of his later career has observed that he was a "deeply traditional—if not stereotypical—American progressive. The Southern question, for him, was at bottom an economic question; the South's poverty and the South's colonial economy were at the root of her major problems. The Southern question had an economic answer: Northern-style industrialism humanized by New Deal social reforms."[96] The "Negro question" had essentially the same answer. Economic "readjustment," the Georgian believed, was being made "quite peacefully and . . . without any serious class or race bitterness." As a result of New Deal planning, America would no longer sanction the idea that "any race is sub-normal nor that any section of our population should be deprived of decent standards. . . . Prejudice, unfair discrimination and exploitation" would be made "unprofitable under the New Deal."[97]

---

95. Bruce J. Melvin to W.E.B. Du Bois, *Crisis* 40 (May 1934), 145. On Melvin, see Paul K. Conkin, *Tomorrow a New World: The New Deal Community Program* (New York, 1959), 101, 200, and Kifer, "The Negro Under the New Deal," 161.

96. Krueger, *And Promises to Keep*, 104.

97. Pittsburgh *Courier*, Apr. 14, 1934.

Believing that all else would follow—the end to "prejudice, unfair discrimination and exploitation"—if the New Deal was able to carry out its economic reforms, Foreman might, therefore, accept a little inconsistency in the racial application of those reforms. What was important, however, was faith in the long-term result. In this regard, though he came to affirm economic reform as the surest way to securing for blacks a better life in the future from a somewhat different perspective, his ideas and those of Harold Ickes were identical. As a southerner and a race liberal, Foreman perceived the progress of the South and that of the Negro as inextricably linked. He had no difficulty applying that same principle to the nation and to black people everywhere, thus concluding that the hope of all rested with the continuation of the New Deal.

Writing for the New York *Times* toward the end of his service as adviser, he acknowledged that discrimination had "occurred in local communities in the administration of several of the government's programs" and that in "too many cases local prejudice" had thwarted the "best plans of the central authority." Yet he was steadfast in the belief that the federal government was aware of its "obligations to the Negro population and has undertaken them with an energy comparable to its activities in other fields of reconstruction." Ultimately, he concluded, "everyone interested in achieving a fair opportunity for advancement on the part of the colored population must welcome the social theories of the New Deal and the clear intention of the administration to apply these theories without reference to race."[98]

Liberal reformism was seen as *the* means through which racial progress in the thirties and later might be accomplished. Foreman and Ickes became architects of an emerging racial liberalism which held that white hostility toward blacks could be overcome by making white and Negro partners in a national social, political, and economic reformation. Convinced of the basic soundness of New Deal reform and its capacity to address the major problems confronting black people, without engendering more intense black-white antipathies, Ickes and Foreman gave support to a new hope and sense of confidence among liberal interracialists. This was especially true in the case of southern race liberals who, given their unique position within the South and the nation, made an important contribution to the New Deal's response to racial concerns. Indeed, as was reflected

98. New York *Times*, Apr. 15, 1934.

in the appointment of Clark Foreman, race liberals from the South played a major role in encouraging and justifying the particular manner in which the Roosevelt administration sought to include black Americans within its reform agenda.

The Southern Perspective
on Race

I.

With the exception of Harold Ickes and Eleanor Roosevelt, the most influential New Deal interracialists were southerners. Clark Foreman was only one of many who found a home during the 1930s and 1940s in the Roosevelt administration; and of whites outside the administration who had an impact on the government's racial stance, the southern-bred Edwin Embree was clearly the most energetic.

The reasons for the predominance of southern race liberals in the New Deal are not totally clear; no doubt Franklin Roosevelt's personal attachment to the South resulting from his long-time association with Warm Springs, Georgia, had something to do with it. More important, probably, was that the "Negro problem" during the 1930s was still largely identified with the South, and it was assumed that southern whites were the most knowledgeable about racial matters in their region. Moreover, while the liberalism of the South was frequently linked to the race issue, that was not true of liberalism elsewhere, as most northern progressives had no articulated position on the question in the early 1930s.[1]

Whatever the reason, there was an impressive group of southern activists who made their way into the Roosevelt administration and helped mold reform programs to fit what they considered were the primary needs of black Americans: Clark Foreman; George S. Mitchell of the Resettlement and Farm Security Administrations; Aubrey Williams of the Federal Emergency Relief Administration, later director of the National Youth Administration; Will Alexander, head of the Farm Security Administration; Mark Ethridge, first chairman of the Fair Employment Practices Committee; and Jonathan Daniels, appointed as an assistant to Franklin Roosevelt in 1943 to look after race concerns during the war. They were only the most prominent of a southern contingent that combined support for

1. Sosna, *In Search of the Silent South*, chs. 4-5; George B. Tindall, *Emergence of the New South*, chs. 6, 8. Also see Friedel, *F.D.R. and the South*.

the New Deal with a wish to see the American interracial climate improved; many others served in lesser positions in federal departments and agencies.

Not every southerner who supported the Roosevelt administration, of course, was a race liberal; nor was every southerner who was liberal on race an advocate of the New Deal. Robert Fechner, director of the Civilian Conservation Corps, was known widely for his unsympathetic attitude toward the Negro. In contrast, the prominent University of North Carolina sociologist Howard W. Odum, who was close to Alexander, Foreman, and Mark Ethridge and identified with their racial efforts, was a critic of many New Deal measures.[2]

Southern race liberals did not always agree either on strategy for improving the Negro's situation. Some, like Ethridge and Jonathan Daniels, generally shied away from any approach they thought might seriously endanger the delicate relationship of blacks and whites in the South. Others, especially Foreman and Aubrey Williams, became more militant in their civil rights activities as the years progressed, particularly after they left the government.[3] And then there were those like novelist Lillian Smith, discussed later in this chapter, who neither served the New Deal in any official capacity nor wrote much about it, but whose ideas increasingly raised questions about the relevance of the southern liberal response to black conditions in American life.

II.

The "pivotal figure" among southern liberals during the Roosevelt years, as noted historian of the South George B. Tindall has called him, was Will W. Alexander. Not only did Alexander keep "in touch with all the current movements" in his native region, his involvement with the Commission on Interracial Cooperation and his friendships with Edwin Embree, Charles Johnson, Walter White, and others kept him close to most interracial activity in the 1930s

2. For a discussion of the CCC's racial policies and Fechner's leadership, see John A. Salmond, "The Civilian Conservation Corps and the Negro," *Journal of American History* 52 (June 1965), 75-88, and Arthur F. Raper, *Preface to Peasantry* (Chapel Hill, 1936), 263. On Howard Odum, see R. Alan Lawson, *The Failure of Independent Liberalism, 1930-1941* (New York, 1971), 140-43, 170-73; Sosna, *In Search of the Silent South*, 90-91.

3. Sosna, *In Search of the Silent South, passim*, but esp. ch. 8 for the later career of Foreman and Williams.

and 1940s.[4] Rexford G. Tugwell, who brought the former Methodist minister to Washington in 1935 as his assistant in the Resettlement Administration, considered him the "most knowledgeable man in the country on interracial matters" and also "the best."[5]

Whether that was true or not, Alexander was clearly one of the most active. Even before joining the administration, he was busy with his friends Embree and Johnson submitting the names of Negroes for possible governmental positions and lobbying for safeguards to assure blacks adequate coverage under New Deal reforms. Alexander may well have had a hand in Harold Ickes' PWA quota scheme, and he was certainly a powerful voice behind the passage of the Bankhead-Jones Farm Tenant Act and the creation in 1937 of the Farm Security Administration.[6] In 1935 Alexander, Embree, and Johnson published their widely noted *Collapse of Cotton Tenancy*, which graphically depicted the economic and social plight of tenant farmers and sharecroppers and their traditional neglect by federal and state governments. The same year Alexander was made a member of President Roosevelt's Commission on Farm Tenancy, which played a major role in securing passage of the Bankhead-Jones Act.[7]

4. Tindall, *Emergence of the New South*, 632.
5. Quoted in Dykeman and Stokely, *Seeds of Southern Change*, 24.
6. Writing to Edwin Embree in early 1934, Alexander noted that "one of the things we agreed should be done was to get Negroes scattered all over the departments in Washington. That is literally happening." Alexander to Embree, Jan. 31, 1934, Rosenwald Fund Archives, Box 94. On Alexander's involvement in the PWA quota plan, see Dykeman and Stokely, *Seeds of Southern Change*, 244. Whether Alexander actually had an influence on the quota idea is not clear, since many people apparently claimed responsibility for it. In this connection, see Jane R. Motz, "The Black Cabinet: Negroes in the Administration of Franklin D. Roosevelt," (M.A. thesis, Univ. of Delaware, 1953), 44-45; Kruman, "Quotas for Blacks," 39-47; Wolters, *Negroes and the Great Depression*, 200-3. Sidney Baldwin, *Poverty and Politics: The Rise and Decline of the Farm Security Administration* (Chapel Hill, 1968), 114-15, 157-92, discusses Alexander's efforts on behalf of the Bankhead bill. Baldwin notes (p. 150) that Alexander was distressed at the lack of strong black support for the proposed farm legislation. Also see "Reminiscences of Will Alexander," Columbia Oral History, 596-97. For discussion of black objections to Bankhead see Wolters, *Negroes and the Great Depression*, 60-69.
7. *Collapse of Cotton Tenancy* (Chapel Hill, 1935), 48-61, contains the authors' attack on the failure of the AAA to assist marginal farmers. With financial aid from the Rosenwald Fund, the three organized a conference in Washington in 1934 on "Negroes and Economic Reconstruction" in which they made public some of their findings later published in *Collapse of Cotton Tenancy*. For reference to this, see Will Alexander to Stacy May, Dec. 26, 1934; Memorandum of Conference on Negroes and Economic Reconstruction, Jan. 28, 1935, Charles S. Johnson Papers, Box 78. Stacy May was connected with the Rockefeller Foundation, which also helped finance the research of Alexander, Embree, and Johnson.

Nor did his taking over from Tugwell as head of the Farm Security Administration mean that he severed ties with those outside the government. With New Dealers Gardner Jackson and Aubrey Williams, Alexander was considered by the Southern Tenant Farmers' Union to be among its "most sympathetic and understanding" friends in Washington. H.L. Mitchell, chief organizer of the SFTU, praised him for his willingness to level with farmers and to inform them of what they were "up against in trying to get the machinery of government moving in a crisis."[8]

Alexander's tenure with the FSA and, in the war years, with the Minorities Branch of the Office of Production Management gave him considerable experience in the difficult task of persuading government to respond to social concerns. Under Alexander, the FSA moved away from Tugwell's stress on green belt cities and emphasized financial aid and relief to poor white and black farmers.[9] "The principal function of the Farm Security Administration," he wrote W.E.B. Du Bois in 1939, "is to make small loans, coupled with guidance in sound farming practices, to needy and low-income farm families, who cannot obtain adequate credit from any other source." Alexander was particularly pleased that FSA loans had "been made to approximately 50,000 Negro families since the program was initiated three years ago."[10]

To facilitate Negro participation in FSA programs, Alexander encouraged their appointment to advisory posts both in Washington and on state and regional boards and committees. By 1941, each of the three southern regional directors had a black adviser; and Joseph H.B. Evans was selected to assist Alexander in the national FSA office, in much the same way that Robert Weaver aided Ickes at Interior. Compared with that of most other administration departments and agencies, Farm Security's record in this regard was quite good.[11]

8. Quoted in Dykeman and Stokely, *Seeds of Southern Change*, 24. According to Donald H. Grubbs in *Cry from the Cotton: The Southern Tenant Farmers' Union and the New Deal* (Chapel Hill, 1971), while Gardner Jackson was in the AAA he was the outstanding administration supporter of the STFU. See Grubbs, *ibid.*, 88-107, and "Gardner Jackson, That 'Socialist' Tenant Farmers' Union, and the New Deal," *Agricultural History* 42 (Apr. 1968), 125-37. For reference to Alexander's sympathy for the STFU, Grubbs, *Cry from the Cotton*, 94-95.

9. Baldwin, *Poverty and Politics*, 218-29; Kifer, "The Negro Under the New Deal," 170, 207.

10. Alexander to Du Bois, Apr. 14, 1939, Aptheker, ed., *The Correspondence of W.E.B. Du Bois*, II (Boston, 1976), 192.

11. Baldwin, *Poverty and Politics*, 279, 306-7, 332; Wolters, *Negroes and the Great Depression*, 72-73; Kifer, "The Negro Under the New Deal," 207-9.

Yet there remained serious shortcomings in the FSA's contribution to enhancing the condition of the southern black farmer. As Alexander acknowledged to Du Bois, the FSA had limited impact on Negro sharecroppers who lived on large plantations and were dependent on white landlords both financially and in other ways.[12] And despite his urgings, blacks were never able to penetrate the crucially important FSA state committees, where discrimination was most likely to occur. Alexander blamed in part his superior, Agriculture Secretary Henry A. Wallace, for this failure, charging Wallace with an unwillingness to buck southern politicians when they protested black representation on local Farm Security boards. Wallace was "terribly afraid of this race issue," Alexander recalled, "and just couldn't stand up under it. . . . He was always afraid of me—distrusted me—and I think it was on that issue."[13]

But the "race issue" was a source of considerable apprehension for Alexander as well. Though far more willing than Wallace to guarantee Negro participation in governmental programs—throughout the 1930s, Wallace fought against what he felt was the "special treatment" accorded black Americans—he was no more prepared than the Agriculture Secretary to make a direct attack on the fundamental southern principle of race segregation. During most of the Roosevelt years, the former Interracial Cooperation leader conformed to the traditional southern liberal stance on segregation; although personally and morally opposed to it, he refrained from any open denunciation. The primary "political means" of southern liberals for overcoming the evils of racial prejudice and poverty in the South, Gunnar Myrdal noted, had been "conciliation, moral persuasion and education."[14] During Alexander's directorship, the FSA followed, at least in regard to the Jim Crow issue, a similar approach. One student of the Farm Security Administration states that Alexander and his associates, many of whom, like George Mitchell, were recruits from the southern interracial struggle, pursued agrarian reforms that "avoided open violation of the rules of southern life." Particularly "in matters of race, the leaders of the FSA were careful. In their allocation of loans and grant funds, in their personal appointments, in their cooperative and group enterprises, in their resettlement projects, and in their public information activities, they

12. Alexander to Du Bois, Apr. 14, 1939, Aptheker, ed., *Correspondence of W.E.B. Du Bois*, 192.
13. "Reminiscences of Will Alexander," Columbia Oral History, 607-8.
14. Myrdal, *American Dilemma*, II, 847. For a good discussion of the traditional southern liberal race philosophy, see Sosna, *In Search of the Silent South*, ch. 2.

adhered fairly consistently to southern attitudes and practices regarding race."[15]

In 1940, Alexander resigned from the Security Administration and accepted a full-time position with the Rosenwald Fund. But World War II produced new challenges in race relations, and he returned to government to serve as director of the Minority Groups Service in the OPM with Robert Weaver. As they had in the thirties, Alexander and Weaver endeavored to secure for Negroes a place in an economic system which was then being geared for war; and, as earlier, they ran into considerable opposition. Even before Pearl Harbor, Alexander wrote Edwin Embree that the "lack of any sense of responsibility on the part of most great employers in the field in which we are working seems to me to be terribly discouraging." Following a meeting with a vice president of the Du Pont Corporation, he noted that management was "greatly interested in the problem of the adjustment of the Negro to the economic life of the nation and I think all were impressed, but so far as I could see, they felt that when the Du Pont Company had turned out explosives for the defense of the nation, they had no further responsibility. The social illiteracy of these tycoons is a most depressing aspect of the national scene."[16]

Yet what was even more distressing during the war to Alexander and to other liberals from the South was the interjection of race into the mainstream of American political and social life. Though sympathetic to the goals of Negro militants like A. Philip Randolph, whose proposed March on Washington in 1940 and 1941 was designed to force open both the armed forces and the nation's defense industry to black soldiers and workers, Alexander feared the repercussions from such tactics, especially in the South. After the Japanese attacked Pearl Harbor, he told Embree, he had "listened with great care to the broadcasts on Sunday night. It seemed to me that there were too frequent references to the color of our enemy. In my opinion the real enemy is Hitler, and to make this specific sector a race war will leave us with very serious problems on our hands when it is over." Given the circumstances, he believed it was extremely important for "responsible Negro leaders" and especially the black press, which was helping lead the fight for armed forces desegregation, to publicly express their loyalty to the Allied cause. "I have no doubt whatever that the overwhelming majority of our

15. Baldwin, *Poverty and Politics*, 279. Sosna (p. 64) quotes Alexander to this effect.
16. Alexander to Embree, May 27, 1941, Rosenwald Fund Acchives, Box 94.

colored citizens are loyal, and it would make trouble in the future, as well as create difficulties now, if any other impression should get abroad throughout the country. This is a delicate matter. . . . The mood of the country is that we are in for a life and death struggle, and that anything else is extraneous. I think it would make a bad impression if Negro leaders, in what they say, should try to use this occasion to bring to the front even their just grievances."[17]

Displeasure with both white insensitivity to Negro needs and the potential harm created by black militant rhetoric was a long-time southern liberal preoccupation. Like so many white interracialists, Alexander saw himself as straddling a line between racial extremists: black revolutionaries and die-hard white segregationists. Since World War I, his life had been committed to isolating these two elements in the hope of improving relations between the two races. Within the hostile environment of the South, he had sought to better the Negro's condition, expand the black man's white allies—"in search of the silent South"—and build a future where class and racial unity might become a reality rather than simply a dream, as well as possibly an example to the rest of the nation. It was out of this experience and vision that Alexander derived so much initial hope with the coming of the New Deal and the presidency of Franklin D. Roosevelt. The tendency to subordinate race to class and economic considerations, to interpret the Depression as the beginning of a new day of social interdependency and cooperation, conformed closely to the southern liberal's racial philosophy.

Long believing that the special problems of Negroes would be "eased" by economic and other reforms coming to the entire South, Alexander thus stressed the need for a black and white common cause, for a cooperative effort of black and white farmers and laborers, and for a mutual understanding of their problems. There was "no way under the sun by which Negroes could be saved except as part of the whole South," he wrote in 1933, and it went "without saying that there is no way by which the South can save itself economically or culturally which does not also save the Negro."[18] Commenting in 1940 on the Clark Foreman–inspired "Report on the Economic Conditions of the South," he observed that the central

17. Alexander to Embree, Dec. 13, 1941, *ibid*. Also Sosna, *In Search of the Silent South*, 105-7.

18. Alexander, "The Slater and Jeanes Funds: An Educator's Approach to a Difficult Social Problem," *Occasional Papers No. 28* (John F. Slater Fund, June, 1934), 14. Alexander's paper was part of a speech delivered at Hampton Institute, Apr. 27, 1933.

dilemma confronting the South was finding the means "by which the southern rural poor can be given an opportunity to live decently where they are." The South could solve that dilemma, he felt, only with the cooperative assistance of federal, state, and local governments and with the "cheerful cooperation . . . of the Southern people," including both whites and Negroes. It was necessary, he added, to see that this was a "long-time problem, requiring long-time, large-scale planning such as we have never done before."[19]

Planning, cooperation, common interests—these constituted the underlying themes of Alexander's commitment to racial betterment and Roosevelt reformism; and during the 1930s, before World War II seemed to put both goals into jeopardy, Will Alexander carried his message to representatives of both races.

In an article written for *Opportunity* in 1934, Alexander urged Negro workers to take more advantage of the growing influence of the federal government's support of labor unions.[20] The black worker, he insisted, must become a part of the total labor force. Blacks as well as whites had to learn to transcend the "fixed traditions and deep-rooted attitudes" of the past, which were primarily responsible for isolating black people from the ranks of organized labor. Although noting trade union discrimination, he emphasized the need for blacks to acknowledge their common working-class ties with whites. "Because of their past experience," he argued, "Negro workers as a class have been led to think of themselves as a special group. Frequently, they have found it necessary to accept a lower wage in order to secure a foothold in a particular enterprise." But the future of black laborers demanded that "this assumption of separateness be overcome"; they must come to think of themselves simply as workers, not "Negro workers." Skilled and unskilled black laborers, he suggested, should be provided "opportunities for supplementary training which will help them to overcome handicaps growing out of lack of experience in industry." Likewise, it was necessary for Negroes to gain greater awareness of the "history, principles and methods of the labor movement." Only when this was achieved would the "inferiority complexes which are the result of generations of segregation and discrimination . . . be rooted out."[21] Speaking at the Howard University Charter Day celebration in March 1934, he concluded that there was no "future for Negro

19. Alexander, "The South's Problem Number One, "*Southern Frontier* I (Mar. 1940), 6.
20. Alexander, "A Strategy for Negro Labor," *Opportunity* 12 (Apr. 1934), 102.
21. *Ibid.*, 102-3.

workers in this country as a group of workers; they must become a part of the working group. The Negro . . . must be encouraged to become more class conscious and less race conscious."[22]

Alexander was aware of the difficulty of building a class consciousness and cohesion among blacks and whites. Therefore, he believed it was necessary to educate both races concerning the folly involved in their obsession with "race-conscious" thinking. Addressing himself directly to whites in an essay entitled "The Negro As a Human Person," he attacked the prevalent white tendency to view all blacks as "special kinds of people." To single out Afro-Americans as somehow being different from other American citizens led to the fallacious but widespread racist conclusion that "Negroes as a group" were inherently inferior. As a result, he said, it has "been supposed that Negroes are incapable of acquiring the tools of culture necessary for full participation in American life." As a progressive thinker, Alexander naturally discounted the idea that hereditary racial characteristics determined human motivation or progress. Recent studies, he noted, had shown that traditional religious, anthropological, and historical arguments supposedly supporting belief in innate race inferiority were "entirely unscientific." Such irrational and groundless notions, he was convinced, had been the basis for perpetuating racial discrimination and segregation in American life, past and present. Believing that blacks were inferior to whites had become the primary—if not, in Alexander's mind, the only—justification for continued separation of black and white in schools, industry, and all social levels of society. But this desire to "give a racial explanation to everything distinctive in the Negro community in America" was, "like so many other folkways," devoid of any rational defense.[23]

Thus, one of the first significant steps in developing a new consciousness among the races was for whites to rid themselves of their "unscientific" concepts and to "establish in the thinking of people generally the idea that the Negro is a normal human being."[24] Black people, Alexander assured readers at a later time, desired simply to "live in America," to enjoy the opportunities and rights guaranteed to the population as a whole. If Negroes were granted that freedom,

22. Pittsburgh *Courier*, Mar. 17, 1934.

23. Alexander, "The Negro As a Human Person," *The Missionary Review of the World* 59 (June 1936), 292. See also Alexander, "A Strategy for Negro Labor," 103.

24. Alexander, "The Negro As a Human Person," 292.

they would be entirely able to assume the responsibilities expected of other groups; Alexander's defense of FSA programs, of the integration of black workers in war industries, and of FEPC legislation was based on that assumption. Testifying before a congressional committee in 1945 on behalf of a permanent FEPC, he maintained that the experience of blacks in the defense industries had shown the inaccuracy of the oft-repeated idea that Negro laborers were inherently incapable of performing the same employment tasks as white workers.[25] Before the Civil War, he noted on a number of occasions, blacks had comprised a majority of the skilled workers in the South; it was not because of their "inherent biological qualities" that they had been later deprived of good jobs and wages but because of "their inheritance" of racial discrimination and segregation.[26]

Yet it was not enough for an emancipated white like himself to convince other whites that their racial stereotypes were erroneous. "Negroes themselves were refuting the popular belief as to their inferiority," he noted in 1936, and in this they were being strongly supported by the New Deal. Federal assistance to education, in the South and elsewhere, the entrance of more Negroes into professional and graduate schools, economic and social reforms which exposed blacks to new skills and trades, all helped undermine the myth of Negro inferiority. And Alexander was certain that "improvement in race relations" would be possible to the extent that the "opportunity for acquiring the tools of knowledge is extended to the masses of Negroes."[27]

Like many white liberals and black leaders, he looked to the educated Negro as critically important in the process of building black confidence and easing white hostility. Those who had acquired the "tools of knowledge" assumed a special role in the long-term process of educating members of both races. With Alexander's encouragement, Edwin Embree and the Rosenwald Fund established fellowships and financial aid programs to promote the development of black leaders, particularly in the South. In 1943, Alexander appealed to Harvard University's James B. Conant in urging the American Council of Education to supplement the

25. U.S. Congress, Senate, Committee on Education and Labor, *Fair Employment Practice Act, Hearings, before a subcommittee of the Committee on Education and Labor*, Senate, on S. 101 and S. 459, 79th Cong., 1st sess., 1945, 28.

26. Alexander, "The Negro As a Human Person," 292; Pittsburg *Courier*, Mar. 17, 1934; U.S. Cong., Senate, *Hearings*, 1945, 28.

27. Alexander, "The Negro As a Human Person," 293-94.

Rosenwald program in order to provide training for the "best brains among the talented tenth of our Negro population."[28]

Whether they liked it or not, prominent Negroes, those in the public eye, were seen as representatives of their race. They were therefore in a crucial position to persuade other blacks of their common bonds with whites and to argue the wisdom of identifying their cause with the larger cause of social and economic reform represented by Roosevelt's New Deal. Likewise, by their examples as knowledgeable experts, they could seriously weaken the false perceptions whites held concerning the abilities of black people.

For Alexander, therefore, the type of black chosen by the federal government to represent the views of Negro Americans was extremely important. When Aubrey Williams contacted him in early 1934 to discuss possible choices for a racial advisory position in the FERA, Alexander gave him the names of three individuals, all of whom had been or were then affiliated with the National Urban League: Forrester Washington, Ira deA. Reid, and James Hubert. The final selection, however, was between Washington, dean of the Atlanta School of Social Work, and another NUL official, Jesse Thomas, who was the League's southern field representative.[29] Noting the background of both men, Alexander indicated to Williams why he preferred Washington. "First, so far as I have been able to see, he belongs to no particular clique or section of Negro opinion. Second, the whole situation in America makes it impossible for a Negro, however well educated, not to 'think black.' To a surprising degree, Washington seems to me to be able to view the problems of Negroes with the minimum of racial feeling."[30]

Even more so than Forrester Washington, Alexander considered Robert Weaver, with whom he worked closely in the late thirties and

28. Alexander to Embree, Nov. 10, 1943, Rosenwald Fund Archives, Box 94. Quote is included in Alexander's letter to Embree in which he discussed his meeting with Conant and other members of the American Council on Education. For discussion of Rosenwald Fund fellowships, see Embree and Waxman, *Investment in People*, and Embree to Alexander, Nov. 28, 1939, Rosenwald Fund Archives, Box 94.

29. Williams first called Alexander, who was still with the CIC, about problems facing blacks under the FERA and the best method of meeting them. The idea of a race relations adviser was discussed, but it is not clear whether it was Williams' or Alexander's idea. Jesse Thomas' name was suggested by Eugene Kinckle Jones, director of the National Urban League and then a race adviser in the Commerce Department. See Alexander to Williams, Jan. 16, 1934, CWA, NA, Box 83.

30. Alexander to Williams, Jan. 16, 1934, CWA, NA, Box 83. In his second letter to Williams (Jan. 25, *ibid.*) Alexander also stressed the fact that Washington was well known in the North and had contacts with organizations such as the Russell Sage Foundation and the Phelps-Stokes and Rockefeller Foundations.

early forties, to be an ideal Negro spokesman who could serve black needs and challenge white social attitudes. "He wasn't interested much in the race problem. . . . He was an economist—a kind of social engineer. He could write as good a book about some other aspect of economics as he could about Negro economics." Weaver was, Alexander concluded, "a thoroughly emancipated Negro."[31] And agreeing with his friend's assessment, Edwin Embree in 1946 praised Weaver as a "first class administrator with ability to cooperate with associates. . . . Keen scholar, suave manners, tough mind, excellent personality."[32]

It was because of his own extreme sensitivity to white attitudes toward the Negro and the certainty that those feelings must be addressed in any struggle to improve the condition of Afro-Americans that Alexander disliked the "think black" Negro. The strong racial emphasis produced by the war, the increase in black militancy, the upsurge of racial hostility in the South, and the riots in New York and Detroit were all sources of discouragement to him in the 1940s. Writing at the end of the war, he expressed considerable pessimism about the effects of the black economic cooperative movement which, during the 1930s, enjoyed some popularity within a number of northern urban ghetto communities. "To adopt economic segregation as a means of solving the economic problems of Negroes," he insisted, "bears on its very face the stamp of futility." There could be "no adequate provision for the economic life" of thirteen million black Americans "except as they share in the general economic life of the country."[33]

Alexander's career as an interracialist had been devoted to seeing that Negroes received their proper "share." The New Deal's importance in this regard was critical; for the first time and on a large scale, the federal government was providing economic and other assistance to blacks and whites previously excluded from the American system. The participation of the Negro in Roosevelt administration reforms thus symbolized the long-awaited break in the vicious cycle of black oppression and exploitation. The success of that adventure was always dependent, however, on the ability of black and white to surmount their "race-conscious" mentality. For blacks, it meant being an "emancipated Negro" and minimizing the tendency to

31. "Reminiscences of Will Alexander," Columbia Oral History, 692.

32. Embree to E. X. Mohr, Feb. 4, 1946, Rosenwald Fund Archives, Box 132.

33. Alexander, "Our Conflicting Racial Policies," *Harper's Magazine* 210 (Jan. 1945), 177. For the difficulties southern race liberals like Alexander and others faced as a result of the war and black militancy, see Sosna, *In Search of the Silent South*, ch. 6.

"think black" when addressing those problems that confronted the Negro community. For whites, it meant perceiving the black man as a "human person" and not as a racial stereotype. For both, it indicated the need to acknowledge common economic bonds and to approach the dominant issues of the 1930s and 1940s from the vantage point of class and not race. Blacks and whites shared the same ideals of individual freedom and equal opportunity, according to Alexander. There was only one future for black Americans, and that lay in their inclusion within a reformed American socio-economic and political system. By "subjecting Negroes to American education we have made them Americans"; black people desired nothing more than the "freedom and opportunity to live as Americans."[34]

Anything that aggravated tensions between blacks and whites, inflamed feelings of race antagonism, distracted blacks from stressing class rather than race priorities, or supported the natural white tendency to see Negroes as "different" made Alexander's contribution, and that of the New Deal's, much more difficult. "Economic segregation" had such an effect. So also might government policies which failed to "adhere" to prevailing white "attitudes and practices regarding race." There was a built-in limit, then, to what the government could do. The New Deal's primary role was to give blacks an equal opportunity to raise their economic and social position; as a social by-product, racial tensions would be lessened when class "differences" between the races gradually diminished. Given the "maximum amount of freedom," he concluded in his most comprehensive statement on the race issue, written in 1945, "white and colored Americans could probably adjust amicably most of the difficulties that arose between them."[35]

In order to ease white apprehensions over possible implications of New Deal support for blacks, however, Alexander believed it necessary to point out distinctions between social and economic equal opportunities. In 1936 he observed that although Negroes were

34. Alexander, "Our Conflicting Racial Policies," 179, 177.
35. Ibid., 177. Dykeman and Stokely, Seeds of Southern Change, 272, refer to the Harper essay as Alexander's most extensive analysis of race segregation and a "minor landmark, both in national understanding of the race problem and in Dr. Will's personal involvement in the question of segregation." For a slightly different interpretation, see Sosna, In Search of the Silent South, 154-55. Clark Foreman, who had gone beyond Alexander's cautious approach to the race segregation issue, praised his former mentor and noted that the essay had "caused a great deal of favorable comment." Foreman to Alexander, Jan. 11, 1945, Rosenwald Fund Archives, Box 121.

indeed Americans like everyone else, there were perhaps in their "African background certain influences that persist" among them even to the present.[36] Exactly what those "influences" were or what they represented, he never made very clear. But in 1945 he assured whites that the end of legal segregation would not automatically bring with it the feared bugaboo of racial intermarriage. "Left free, human beings group themselves according to their tastes, interests and cultural backgrounds." Afro-Americans did not want the "opportunity to mingle with whites"; even without "arbitrary segregation, common interests and common backgrounds would probably lead most American Negroes to develop their own way of living and find much of their association among themselves as other groups do."[37]

Alexander's ideas and activities indicated the complexity of racial attitudes which underlay much of the New Deal's effort on behalf of Negroes during the Roosevelt years. Believing, as did all white New Deal liberals, that there was inherent within the Roosevelt reforms a potential for effecting a major transformation in the economic and social existence of American people, and committed to seeing that blacks were included in that transformation, the problem for Alexander and other liberals remained one of overcoming prevailing racial theories which complicated their successful execution of government policies. Emphasizing class rather than racial or ethnic loyalties was crucial, not only because it fit conveniently with the tone of New Deal reformism and his southern perspective, but because Alexander saw it as affording the surest way to transcend racial barriers between black and white and bring into existence a harmonious interracial community. Like Harold Ickes, he assumed that once Negroes were able to achieve "maximum freedom" through educational and economic opportunities, the historic rationale for white racism would disappear.

Toward the end of his life, Alexander stated that "the thing that I'm willing to stand by, more than anything else, is the friendly feelings and the effort I've made to make life more livable for Negroes."[38] As much as anyone in the Roosevelt administration, he was committed to assuring blacks a "life more livable" by their

36. Alexander, "The Negro as a Human Person," 292.
37. Alexander, "Our Conflicting Racial Policies," 177.
38. "Reminiscences of Will Alexander," Columbia Oral History, 701. Sosna, *In Search of the Silent South*, 170, discusses the last years of Alexander's life when he became "despondent" over the rise of the Ku Klux Klan in North Carolina and felt he was being "shunned" by former friends at the Univ. of North Carolina.

inclusion in the new federal welfare programs. The increased concern liberals gave to civil rights and the "Negro problem" after 1945 was partly a result of Alexander's presence in the 1930s and 1940s and his desire to see that black progress was linked to progressive reform.

Yet his long-time fear of the race issue as a disrupting influence in ameliorating black and white relations, and his sense of the New Deal as a means of salvation for both the South and the black man, created a certain ambivalence in Alexander's racial philosophy. Concerned that even the minimum advantages won in improving race relations would be jeopardized by tactics that exacerbated tensions between the races, he cautioned blacks to refrain from "race-conscious" thinking and race-dominated programs; in effect, he asked them to challenge the racial assumptions of whites by emulating white America's social and economic values and status symbols. But to offset white anxiety over increased black and white social relations possibly emanating from New Deal reforms, he drew an artificial barrier between black and white by arguing that the "common interests" and "common background" of black people would assure that they would continue "their association among themselves" and not "mingle with whites." In the end, despite his intentions, Alexander's attempt to clarify the entangled racial conceptions held by black and white was no more satisfying than the attitude of the segregationists, whose ideas he characterized in 1945 as "so inconsistent as to be completely bewildering to Negroes." Often, he concluded, blacks simply "cannot tell just what is expected of them."[39]

III.

In the late 1950s and early 1960s, when black America's campaign for equal justice included a more systematic attack against racism and segregation, it had a powerful ally in novelist Lillian Smith. During the thirties and forties, Smith represented a dimension of southern race thinking not characteristic of Will Alexander or of most liberals of the period. In contrast to Alexander, Aubrey Williams, and Clark Foreman, whom she knew well, Lillian Smith did not engage in New Deal policy-making, nor did she, as did her friend Edwin Embree, attempt to influence governmental programs from

39. Alexander, "Our Conflicting Racial Policies," 173.

outside the Roosevelt administration.[40] She was also far less concerned than New Deal advocates with the importance of federal aid as a weapon in the restructuring of southern life and customs.

Yet Smith had much to say about black and white relations, the nature of the "Negro problem," and the manner in which America addressed racial questions in the Roosevelt era. Her ideas provide a means of understanding some of the tensions in southern liberalism—and liberalism in general—in regard to the race question, and they offer an example of what one articulate reformer from the South thought were serious flaws in the liberal response to the struggle for equal rights.

In 1937, with her close friend and associate Paula Snelling, Smith founded the literary and social journal *North Georgia Review*, which became better known in the forties as *South Today*. Through the journal and other writings she became recognized as one of the South's most militant white critics of race discrimination and segregation. When she published her controversial novel *Strange Fruit* in 1944, a story centering on a complex and tragic interracial love affair in the South, she became a figure of national prominence.[41]

Strange Fruit symbolized her philosophical preoccupation with race and Negro-white relations. She was foremost a writer and a student of psychology, involved in comprehending the complexities of the total human experience, the tug and pull of emotional and rational needs, loves, and hates, and the contradictions which invariably evolved from such dichotomies. Almost all her writings were exercises in individual and group self-analysis, searchings for a sense of what she considered to be the most overwhelming predicament confronting the South, the nation, and the world at large—race conflict.[42]

Smith frequently drew on personal experiences to analyze racial issues. She described herself as a "southern woman born in that

40. There were a few exceptions to Smith's general ignoring of New Deal politics; see "Dope with Line," *North Georgia Review* 5 (Spring 1940), 4. In reference to FDR and a third term, Smith commented that "Roosevelt has done some good things for this country but he is not doing them now . . ."; she opposed his reelection. Also, references to war and domestic policies are noted in *North Georgia Review* 5 (Summer 1940), 12; criticism of the CCC and praise for the work of the NYA in the South are contained in *North Georgia Review* 6 (Winter 1940-1941), 94.

41. Discussion of the Smith and Snelling friendship and support they received from Edwin Embree and the Rosenwald Fund in the beginning of their journalistic and literary careers is found in Sosna, *In Search of the Silent South*, 178-84.

42. The best biographical material on Smith comes from her own writings; see particularly in this regard, *South Today* 7 (Spring 1943), 41-42; Smith, "Growing Into

region of all the earth where race prejudice is sharpest, where it has its bitterest flavor, its deepest roots, where the relationship of the two races has become so intertwined with hate and love and fear and guilt and poverty and greed, with churches and with lynchings, with attraction and repulsion that it has taken on the ambivalent qualities, the subtle conflicts, of a terrible and terrifying illness." *White suprem-acy, segregation,* and *the Negro's place* were not simply words to her but a "way of life, a tragic way" which she and others, "white and Negro, have lived since birth." From the day she was born, she had learned that it was possible, as a white person, to "be a Christian and a Southerner simultaneously; to be a gentlewoman and an arrogant callous creature in the same moment; to believe in freedom, to glow when the word is used, and to practice slavery from morning to night."[43]

Thus she considered it entirely feasible for one to hold to certain traditional American virtues like "freedom" and "equality of oppor-tunity" while at the same time denying those virtues to people whose skin was black. Racial superiority was so deeply ingrained in the entire fabric of the nation's life that white Americans had developed a schizophrenic response to the racial issue. White emotions were "blunted" when it came to perceiving "Negroes as human beings." It was as "if we had segregated an area in our minds, marked it Colored, and refused feelings to it." White people in the South had excelled through the years in developing rationalizations to ease their guilt and to preserve their "superiority" over blacks. They had never concerned themselves with their "own problem of white superior-ity" or their "own sick obsession with skin color" but had always concentrated on blacks, hoping that they could be "changed to fit the pattern more harmoniously." When the white South talked about *race relations*, it meant a "more harmonious adjustment of the Negro to the white man's pattern"; and it had "sold the idea to the North" as well.[44]

Because the majority of whites failed to acknowledge their re-sponsibility in creating conditions daily confronted by black Ameri-

---

Freedom," *Common Ground* 4 (Autumn 1943), 47-52. Many of her essays as well as biographical data are included in her book, *Killers of the Dream* (New York, 1949). Also useful are Sosna, *In Search of the Silent South*, ch. 9, and Louise Blackwell and Frances Clay, *Lillian Smith* (New York, 1971).

43. "Growing Into Freedom," 47-48.

44. "Putting Away Childish Things," *South Today* 8 (Summer 1944), 63. This essay was also published in different form as "Humans in Bondage," *Social Action* 10 (Feb. 15, 1944), 6-34, and "Plain Talk for U.S. Whites," *Negro Digest* 2 (May 1944), 21-25.

cans, Smith said, they were seldom able to deal honestly with racial considerations in any form. Most whites, she wrote in 1944, continued to think and feel as white people; most still wanted the "priorities" which they enjoyed "under the White Supremacy system," and they feared that "when segregation goes," their priorities would "go with it." As a result of "having calloused our imaginations with daily rubbing of one stereotype against another," whites seemed incapable of truly realizing what they were saying when they calmly exclaimed that racial questions "must be changed very slowly, that the Negro must 'prove' himself and then he will be 'accepted' by the white man." What white America had done, in effect, was to drop the "heavy millstone of Jim Crow about the Negro's neck" and then turn "away from seeing what it does to the man beneath it."[45]

It was now time, Lillian Smith wrote in 1942, for white America to "assess the damage that we are responsible for," telling the "total deficit over and over to ourselves, rubbing it in like salt until it stings us into action."[46] Two years later, in an important essay in the *New Republic*, she addressed herself specifically to the white liberal community and to shortcomings she considered inherent in the liberal's approach to racial matters. Instead of talking about the "Negro problem," she maintained, the time had come "for us to right-about-face and study the problem of the white man" and the "deep-rooted needs that have caused him to seek those strange regressive satisfactions that are derived from worshipping his own skin-color." It was the "white man himself," she concluded, who was "one of the world's most urgent problems today, not the Negro, not other colored races. We whites must learn to confess this."[47] She was convinced that unless liberal Americans looked more deeply into their own attitudes and values, they would never get to the root of their country's racial crisis. One could not consider racial segregation "apart from man's whole personality, apart from his own culture." It was impossible to "separate men's specific needs from the destructive effects of a *way of life* . . ."; nor could one "meet these specific ends, one by one, first, and then hope that somehow in the shuffle this schizophrenic philosophy of death will change into a philosophy of creative living."[48]

---

45. "Putting Away Childish Things," 62.
46. "Addressed to Intelligent White Southerners: 'These Are Things to Do,'" *South Today* 7 (Autumn-Winter 1942), 35.
47. "Addressed to White Liberals," *New Republic* 111 (Sept. 18, 1944), 331.
48. *Ibid.*, 332.

The basic weakness of those who professed to want change for the black population was their refusal to deal with the totality of the racial dilemma, a totality which affected black and white equally. Somehow they found it necessary or expedient, Smith asserted, to support policies and propose solutions which dealt only with the peripheral aspects of the black condition. "Hard as it is to acknowledge, the simple truth is that the South's and nation's racial problems cannot be solved by putting a loaf of bread, a book and a ballot in everyone's hand." Although these were obviously important to Negro welfare, they could only partially solve the problem, and she seriously questioned the motives of those who believed they were anything more than half solutions. She concluded that it was the "fear in the white man's heart that makes him more willing to work for specific, short-range goals such as the vote, better schools, better jobs for Negroes, than to change his own attitude about himself and his white race."[49]

More than any other white exponent of black equality in the period, Smith challenged her own race to perceive its failure to transcend a color-oriented mentality. Until they did, she believed, whites—particularly liberals—would continue to cling to the "belief that the problem of race relations is the 'Negro problem,' " that the solution to that problem was "a matter of economics," and that it would "take a long time to 'educate the Negro' " and even longer for the "Negro to get to the place where he is worthy of democracy." Such theories derived from white inability to "face the fact that race prejudice and the cultural and psychological patterns of segregation" were rooted in white people's own "complex feelings about skin color"; that those feelings had profoundly affected their actions and those of their children "on every level of our life and culture."[50]

Like other liberal thinkers, Smith believed it was essential to see blacks not as a "problem" but as fellow "human beings"; but she was certain that this would remain an impossibility until whites freed themselves of their "white supremacy" notions. It was imperative in this regard that the white man use his imagination and intelligence to "put himself in the Negro's place and learn *how it feels* to be there."[51]

49. *Ibid.*
50. *Ibid.*
51. Editorial, "Are We Not All Confused," *South Today* 7 (Spring 1942), 30. For references to "Negroes As Human Beings," see "Dope with Line," *North Georgia Review* 2 (Summer 1937), 24, and Smith's review of E. Franklin Frazier, *The Negro Family in the United States* (New York, 1939), in *North Georgia Review* 5 (Summer 1940), 38.

One way in which this might be accomplished, she felt, was for Americans to become better acquainted with the literature by and about black people. From the very beginning, Smith and Paula Snelling included in their journal reviews and analyses of current and past works dealing with the Afro-American experience and the history of race relations. Writing to "intelligent white Southerners" about the "simple, undramatic things we can do," she put at the top of her list books by noted black authors W.E.B. Du Bois, Richard Wright, Franklin Frazier, Claude McKay, Benjamin Brawley, and Hortense Powdermaker.[52] *South Today* also frequently published accounts of studies such as Wilbur J. Cash's *Mind of the South*, John Dollard's *Caste and Class*, and Karl Menninger's *Man Against Himself*. All these books, Smith maintained, would give white Americans an opportunity not only to learn about black life but also to determine where the "racial pressure-points" were in American society.[53] Referring to Franklin Frazier's *The Negro Family in the United States*, for example, she stated that through Frazier one was able to view the black man "in his human context, as a member of a family, as an individual in a web of personal relationships; and one sees the family as it has been shaped by social, racial, psychological pressures, into what it is today."[54]

Smith thus interpreted segregation as a "way of life" affecting whites as well as blacks, a point she was far more willing to bring home to her fellow whites than were other race liberals like Will Alexander. The duality of the black American experience had produced, she believed, its counterpart in a white American schizophrenia. For every Negro child "shut off from schooling," there was "a white who deliberately shuts himself away from knowledge and honest thinking"; for every black man kept in his place, there was a white man who was "lynching the spirit" of his own children. America's racial crisis would not be overcome through piecemeal measures, through appeals to economic change, through granting to a few blacks political patronage, or through any other means white racial liberals generally proposed. In short, there would be no solution to the oppression of black people as long as whites continued to isolate their own involvement from that oppression and considered the crisis simply a "Negro problem."[55]

52. "Addressed to Intelligent White Southerners," 36.
53. *Ibid.* See also *North Georgia Review* 2 (Spring 1937), 21; *ibid.*, 3 (Spring 1938), 16-17; and Sosna, *In Search of the Silent South*, 179-181.
54. Smith, review of *Negro Family* in *North Georgia Review*, 38-39.
55. "Growing Into Freedom," 51-52; editorial, "Are We Not All Confused," 32.

The failure of white America to grasp that reality became very clear to Smith as a result of two events in the early 1940s. One was the response of a number of liberals to the activities of black leaders and organizations involving racial discrimination in war industries and the armed forces and the evasiveness which many whites showed in their reaction to the race riots of 1943. A second issue that disturbed her concerned the public stance on segregation taken by the newly formed interracial Southern Regional Council.

Many liberal whites, of course, gave support to Negro efforts to gain admission on a nonsegregated basis into the armed forces, and initially they backed President Roosevelt's FEPC order. Southern New Dealer Aubrey Williams had encouraged FDR to create an FEPC, and Mark Ethridge of the Louisville *Courier-Journal* became the FEPC's first chairman. Yet many of these same liberals showed considerable annoyance and displeasure over A. Philip Randolph and the black press's unwillingness to be satisfied with government efforts and their push for stronger guarantees. Like Alexander, what they feared above all was the effect of an increased black militancy on white attitudes.[56]

But Lillian Smith did not. In an editorial in *South Today* entitled "Are We Not All Confused?" she responded to some of those who challenged the March on Washington and the support given it by the black news media. It was first of all essential to recognize, she affirmed, that there were 11 million Negroes in this country, not one of whom "has his full constitutional rights as a citizen." In some areas of the country, a black man was "permitted many of these rights"; but in other regions he had few of them and in some none at all. "In the South, the Negro loses out on all counts; education, health, recreation, housing, the vote, jobs both as to pay and kind, civil liberties, right of free movement, right to the courtesies of address which civilized countries accord citizens regardless of race and economic

56. Virginius Dabney, editor of the Richmond *Times-Dispatch*, and an influential figure among liberal southerners, attacked northern blacks, accusing them of stirring up race trouble and undermining the white liberal's position in the South. This view is found in Dabney's essay reprinted in *Southern Frontier* 3 (July 1942), 1, 4. *Southern Frontier* was the official journal of the Commission on Interracial Cooperation and later of the Southern Regional Council. It is significant that very little coverage was given Randolph's MOWM by *Southern Frontier* during the movement's entire existence in the early 1940s. For an analysis of Dabney's ideas, see Sosna, *In Search of the Silent South*, ch. 7, and his ch. 6 for discussion of other southern liberals and the trauma the war created for them.

status." Under such conditions, she could not comprehend how well-known southern liberals like Virginius Dabney and John Temple Graves, "both of whom in peacetime made honorable efforts in defense of the Negro," could now be hostile to black demands. After eighty years "in legal freedom," in which they had endured the pattern of race discrimination and segregation, the black man had the right "not as a slave but as an American citizen" to ask *"When will the patterns be changed?"* The Negro American rightly believes, she argued, "that the government which requires him to pay taxes and conscripts his sons to go fight its war owes him democracy's privileges as well as its duties. He believes quite simply that as a citizen he has an inalienable right to protest the nation-wide denial of his Constitutional freedoms."[57]

Liberals were telling A. Philip Randolph and others that "the time is not 'right' " to pursue their just demands. But, Smith asked, "when will the time be 'right' and 'right' for whom?" That was what Randolph and black people wanted to know, and that was exactly what white America refused to tell them. These were "questions which bore deep into the core of American democracy. They are questions to be answered; not questions to be dismissed by hush-hush campaigns, or avoided by talks of morale, or settled by white men calling in Negro leaders, closing doors, and laying upon Negro shoulders the heavy responsibility for averting 'race trouble.' " The "common complaint" that "this was not the right time" betrayed the "liberals mistaking for 'Christmas' the Negro's basic claim to democracy." If liberals in the South and elsewhere continued to " 'solve' deep fundamental conflicts by silence and evasion, pep talks, quiet pressures, or by criticism of Negroes who are attempting to pull their race toward freedom, much of the responsibility for the violence which may result will be theirs—as it has been theirs in the past." "We white liberals," she concluded, "cannot in honesty blame the demagogues for stirring up 'race trouble'; nor can we in decency accuse Negro leaders of exploiting the war emergency. We do our full share of both by our faint-heartedness, our covering up of actual conditions, our personal snobbery, our selfish habit of putting private affairs, state, politics, business interests and desire to be 'gentlemen' ahead of deep fundamental human needs."[58]

57. Editorial, "Are We Not All Confused," 30-31. Also Sosna, *In Search of the Silent South*, 185.
58. Editorial, "Are We Not All Confused," 30-34.

The racial violence which broke out in Detroit and then in Harlem and Los Angeles in 1943 seemed to only confirm Smith's fears. "In 1943," she noted, "men dreamed of brotherhood and filled the American calendar with days of rioting and bloodshed, with obscene talk of White Supremacy, with bus fights and death, with smear stories and rumors, with all the fury that destroys good feelings for each other and makes understanding so difficult."[59] The reaction of many whites to the "rioting and bloodshed" convinced her that Americans did not want to be bothered by the deeper issues of race relations. "All most of us want," she lamented, "is to be assured that there will be no more race riots; no more lynchings; no more killings on buses; no more flares of violence calling attention to a way of life in which we all willingly participate and are willing to continue to participate, if only the Negroes will be more contented; if only the psychotic, the delinquent, the criminal, the sick will not use 'race' as a way of expressing their frustrations, although we give them a green light to do so." The so-called "good people—the intelligent, even the wise" continued to "accept without protest" the spiritual lynching which goes on around them in "every town, every city, every part of our nation." Riots would continue and race conflicts would intensify as long as southern and northern white people maintained that "segregation cannot be abolished" and that "whatever is done 'for' the Negro must be done under the very system which lynches his spirit and mind every day he is under it."[60]

The equivocation over segregation expressed by many "good people," some of whom Smith considered close friends, led her to denounce the efforts of southern liberals who in 1943 formed the Southern Regional Council. In October 1942 a group of moderate blacks, predominantly from the South, met in Durham, North Carolina, to discuss the war and its effect on race relations. Representing for the most part the professional classes, college presidents and school principals, publishers, businessmen, doctors, and social workers, the blacks affirmed as their "first loyalty" the American and Allied war policies. Such loyalty, they maintained, should not distract Negroes from considering the present "problems and situations that handicap the working out of internal improvements in race relations essential to our full contribution to the war effort." Yet, although they were "fundamentally opposed to the principle and

59. Smith, "Putting Away Childish Things," 61.
60. *Ibid.*, 62.

practice of compulsory segregation," they believed it was neverthe-less more "sensible and timely to address ourselves now to the current problems of racial discrimination and neglect." Following the lead of the Durham blacks, a hundred or so prominent white southerners met in Atlanta and affirmed the black leaders' inten-tions; and in June 1943, meeting out of joint committees, the Durham and Atlanta delegations agreed to form the Southern Reg-ional Council.[61]

Including among its officers and active supporters noted southern white liberals Howard W. Odum, Guy Johnson, and Ralph McGill and moderate blacks like Charles S. Johnson, C.C. Spaulding, Ira de A. Reid, and P.B. Young, the SRC was designed as an interracial organization along the lines of the Commission on Interracial Coop-eration. Shortly after the SRC's founding, the CIC officially disbanded and merged its operation with the Council.[62] Committed to improv-ing race relations and the condition of black Americans in the South through education and through the urging of greater governmental consideration of black social and economic needs, the SRC's stand on the segregation question was, like that of the CIC before it and the Durham group, vague and equivocal. In effect, the priorities set by the Council did not include any direct attack on segregation at all, a point made clear by the SRC's white director, University of North Carolina sociologist Guy Johnson. The Southern Regional Council believed, Johnson remarked in 1944, that it was "more realistic to base a movement on the support of thousands who are willing to do something than on the support of a few lonely souls who denounce segregation and are powerless to do anything about it."[63]

Whatever the tactical wisdom of that position, it was not a view which satisfied Lillian Smith. Writing in *Common Ground* in the spring of 1944, she sharply rebuked the SRC for its failure to confront

61. Quotes from J. Saunders Redding, "Southern Defensive—I," *Common Ground* 4 (Spring 1944), 37. For a discussion of the Durham meeting and the creation of the Southern Regional Council, see Krueger, *And Promises to Keep*, 119-21, and Sosna, *In Search of the Silent South*, 114-20, 152-67.

62. *Southern Frontier*, Jan. 1943 through Dec. 1944, contains a good description of the development of the SRC and of the CIC's merger with it. The last issue of *Southern Frontier* as the CIC's official organ was in Feb. 1944; see editorial, "The Curtains Drop on the Old Order," 2. For the philosophy of SRC, see Guy B. Johnson, "Southern Offensive," *Common Ground* 4 (Summer 1944), 87-93, and *ibid.*, 93 for a list of officers and board members of the SRC. Also Sosna, *In Search of the Silent South*, 119-20, 152-61.

63. Johnson, "Southern Offensive," 91.

the segregation question.[64] Racial problems in America, she argued, were much like a "knotted skein of yarn," and it was necessary for people to untangle it "by pulling here . . . working on one thread, then another, until the skein is at last unraveled." The crucial issue was whether "we want the tangled race skein completely unraveled" or "are we merely trying to avoid more race riots, and lynchings, more 'tensions' which embarrass white folks? Do we want human equality for the Negro or only a better reputation for the white man?" Again she asserted that one could not believe in "human equality" and "segregation" simultaneously and still claim to be in favor of racial progress. Segregation was not simply a "Southern tradition" or a regional problem; it was the "basic problem of every human being on the face of the earth." She sadly concluded that it was very difficult for her to believe that any group, particularly the SRC, was " 'doing good' when the fundamental ideology of the group is a regressive belief in segregation." Howard Odum, she noted, frequently spoke of "good men in the South doing bad things," but was it not the case now that Odum and others in the SRC were "men who wish to be thought good" and were "doing bad things"?[65]

Smith believed it was a "pity" that the Southern Regional Council was being given so much publicity in the race relations field since the Council was not, in effect, committed to "racial democracy." What the SRC should do, she argued, was clearly state that its purpose was to "improve the economic life of our region, to help raise, whenever possible, the levels of our people's life (black and white) whenever it can be done without upsetting the basically undemocratic and inhumane patterns of our demagogues, our economic exploiters, our own fears and guilts which have been imposed upon us."[66] The great tragedy of the liberal position as reflected in the SRC's philosophy was that it would tend to raise people's hopes momentarily while it would ultimately increase the bitterness of blacks and other Americans "when it fails," as it was "bound to." The individuals who made up the SRC and supported its weak thesis of racial improvement were not inherently "bad people" or "conscious hypocrites"; nor had they "sold out to any vested interests." But they were "confused. And

64. Smith, "Southern Defensive—II," *Common Ground* 4 (Spring 1944), 43-45. Many of Smith's criticisms of the SRC were similar to those expressed by J. Saunders Redding writing in the same issue, "Southern Defensive—I," 36-42. Johnson's essay in the summer 1944 issue of *Common Ground* was a response to both Smith and Redding, although most of Johnson's comments were addressed to Redding's attack on the SRC.
65. Smith, "Southern Defensive—II," 43-44.
66. *Ibid.*, 45.

confused people can do harm that they do not intend." The only real hope for black freedom would come when white liberals "cherished with their minds and their spirits the concept of human equality"; when they "prized it so highly that they are not willing to give up big ends for little ends." She was "left with the feeling that not much is going to be done to bring racial democracy" by way of the Southern Regional Council "until its leaders accept and acknowledge publicly the basic truth that segregation is injuring us on every level of our life and is so intolerable to the human spirit that we, all of us, white and black, must bend every effort to rid our minds and hearts and culture of it."[67]

Shortly after her attack on the SRC, Smith was asked to become a member of the Council's Board of Directors. But in a letter to Guy Johnson she politely refused the offer, reasserting her criticisms of the organization's stand on segregation and maintaining that what was required was a "more profound philosophy" combined with new techniques to confront directly the fundamental racial questions in American life.[68] Many of her comments to Johnson were later incorporated in her *New Republic* essay in which she expanded her criticism to include not only southern liberals but white liberalism in general.[69] She determined finally that the liberals' hesitancy to challenge openly the segregationist and racist values of America had rendered meaningless their contribution to the black American's struggle for freedom. As long as whites refused to "break the conspiracy of silence which has held us in a grip so strong that it has become a taboo," they would remain a part of the very "problem" which they honestly seemed to feel they were striving to overcome.[70]

IV.

The contribution of southern race liberals like Will Alexander to the New Deal's incorporation of Negro Americans into the welfare state system of the 1930s was considerable. With a few exceptions, such as Harold L. Ickes and Eleanor Roosevelt, it was the liberal

67. *Ibid.*, 45, 44.

68. Smith to Guy B. Johnson, June 12, 1944, copy in Rosenwald Fund Archives, Box 345.

69. Smith, "Addressed to White Liberals," 331-33. This essay and her "Humans in Bondage," *Social Action*, 6-34, and "Southern Defensive—II" provide a good summary of her ideas and her criticisms of white liberal race thought and activity in the 1940s.

70. "Addressed to White Liberals," 333.

southerner who most consciously brought black concerns to the attention of the Roosevelt administration and endeavored to see that those concerns were acted upon. In this regard, the New Deal's stress on economic reform and the ideas of individuals like Ickes fit in with their own special need to reduce the South's isolation from the rest of the nation and the liberal's isolation from his fellow white southerner. The solution liberals envisaged was massive federal aid to the entire South, which they hoped would bring major benefits to blacks along with the rest of the populace. In the process, the southern liberals assumed, the historic obsession with race—which they believed to be the source of the South's economic and social backwardness—would decline as the system was made more open for the advancement of all classes and minority groups, especially for black Americans.

For Lillian Smith, however, such a perspective symbolized white liberalism's failure to confront the root cause of black oppression, a cause often manifested through economic exploitation but emanating in her opinion primarily from widespread adherence to "white supremacy." One could never overcome the racism which had been built into the institutions of American life for centuries by simply changing the structural nature of those institutions; one had ultimately to challenge directly and transcend the value system, the white racial ideology, which lay behind the institutions themselves. Her liberal New Deal friends were not entirely wrong in their proposals, but they were basically "confused." They were confused because they naïvely assumed that a program of economic reform combined with a moderate attempt at racial education would overcome the irrationality of white supremacy ideology. But this approach would always be insufficient, she maintained, because for "those economic powers who have a stake in race tensions, who have used their power so unscrupulously and so furtively, more than green curtains will have to be used; and far more than education."[71] Along with any economic and political reforms proposed, it would be necessary to apply additional measures directly related to racial segregation in order to assure black people their full participation in American life. This would mean, she believed, among other things, strong government pressure on labor unions, constitutional amendments, new laws, and "presidential war decrees." In short, "as much power must be used to control" white racists "as they now use

71. "Addressed to Intelligent White Southerners," 43.

to control the race situation—and that is a very great deal of power indeed."[72]

Perhaps it was because Smith came to her understanding of America's racial dilemma with a different perspective from that of most liberals in the Roosevelt era that she remained skeptical of their response. Unlike Alexander and Foreman, who emphasized economic and political considerations, Smith viewed black-white tensions through the eyes of a writer and a student of psychology. She remained outside the mainstream of most movements for racial change during the period because she believed that few of them truly faced the essential cause of racial animosity. As a consequence, her impact on the forces shaping policies and programs for blacks was far less immediate than that of Will W. Alexander.

For Alexander and most southern race liberals, the importance of the Roosevelt New Deal extended beyond its ability to improve the condition of blacks. Certainly the problem of race relations was central to their thought, but what they saw in the administration was a powerful force for building a new South. Thus, a southern liberal like Alexander brought to government the conviction that change in the South—and in the status of Negroes—was strongly dependent upon the successful continuation of a national reform movement, which the New Deal represented. Preservation of that movement was the southerner's foremost concern, even when he was forced to acknowledge, like Alexander, that the government's response to black needs was less than adequate.

Lillian Smith's lack of political or personal ties to the New Deal may have allowed her to view the southern and liberal racial approach more critically. At any rate, she was convinced that most liberals failed to understand the manner in which race dominated black and white thought and activity; and she remained one of the few white reformers who challenged the evolving liberal racial attitudes of the Roosevelt years. Those attitudes were often tested by the events and shifting circumstances of the 1930s and 1940s. No one symbolized better the strengths and weaknesses of the liberal racial vision than another articulate woman of the time, Eleanor Roosevelt.

72. *Ibid.*

FOUR

Eleanor Roosevelt
and the Evolution of
Race Liberalism

I.

Liberal reform was never a fully formed political philosophy, either before or during the Roosevelt era. What we have come to identify as the liberal vision—concern for social welfare, equal opportunity (especially economic), planning, and reliance on government regulation and control—evolved over the years as a mix of an earlier progressivism and New Deal pragmatism. Developments such as the rise of organized labor, the conservative renaissance in the late thirties, the coming of World War II, and war and mobilization considerably affected liberal thinking. Many of these developments and the changes they forced in government policies also produced a redefining of liberal attitudes on race-related matters; and so did the activities of black Americans who responded to many of the same issues.

Through most of the 1930s and 1940s, the general public, and Afro-Americans in particular, identified New Deal concern for minorities with one particular individual, Eleanor Roosevelt. The NAACP's Roy Wilkins observed that Franklin D. Roosevelt was considered a friend of the black "only insofar as he refused to exclude the Negro from his general policies," but it was his wife's "personal touches" and her "personal fight against discrimination" which truly won the affections and support of most blacks.[1] Walter White, the National Association's executive secretary during the Roosevelt years and a close friend of the First Lady, noted in his autobiography that in moments of deep despair, his awareness of Mrs. Roosevelt's presence often renewed his faith and kept him from hating all white people.[2]

1. Roy Wilkins, Columbia Univ. Oral History Collection, 1960, 100.
2. White, *A Man Called White* (New York, 1948), 199.

Yet Eleanor Roosevelt's awareness of the Negro American was fairly limited when she and her husband came to the White House in 1933. Unlike Harold Ickes, Will Alexander, or Aubrey Williams, who influenced her racial perspective, she had little prior experience in interracial work and few direct contacts with black people. In 1927 she met Mary McLeod Bethune, the dynamic black president of Bethune-Cookman College; and during the Roosevelt presidency that friendship grew, as did her dependence on Bethune for understanding the black condition. During the thirties and the war years Mrs. Roosevelt and Walter White were extremely close, and he too encouraged her commitment to race justice. But in the early days of the New Deal, it was concern for the "underdog" and the "unfortunate" of America which essentially drew her to the cause of black people.[3]

Mrs. Roosevelt's willingness to respond to difficult racial issues, her openness to the opinions of others on matters relating to the Negro, and her struggle through the long years of depression and war to link civil rights with New Deal reform make her a person of major significance in understanding the evolution of racial liberalism.

In many ways she was in a unique, albeit delicate, position as the wife of the President. Whatever her actual influence on Franklin Roosevelt's views on race, blacks as well as racist whites saw her as a powerful voice in the administration. She claimed that she spoke only for herself when addressing racial issues, which prompted Socialist Norman Thomas to remark that she allowed the President to have it "both ways"—to garner support from Negroes as well as southern conservatives.[4] But she was willing to defend both her individual prerogative to speak her own mind and her husband's

3. For discussion of Mrs. Roosevelt's limited background to racial matters prior to the 1930s and her close association and popularity with Negroes during the thirties and forties, see especially Joseph P. Lash, *Eleanor and Franklin* (New York, 1971), chs. 44 and 53, and *Eleanor Roosevelt: A Friend's Memoir* (Garden City, N.Y., 1964), 133, 168-69, 199, 216-17; Tamara K. Hareven, *Eleanor Roosevelt: An American Conscience* (Chicago, 1968), 112-29; Allen Morrison, "The Secret Papers of FDR," *Negro Digest* 9 (Jan. 1951), 4-12. In the NAACP Papers, Ms. Div., LC, "Eleanor Roosevelt Correspondence," File C-73, are numerous letters from Walter White to Mrs. Roosevelt asking her advice on how the NAACP might pursue certain strategies in respect to government policies affecting blacks. Mrs. Roosevelt's voluminous correspondence with White, other black leaders, and hundreds of individual Negroes who wrote to her for aid and comfort can be found in the Eleanor Roosevelt (ER) Papers, Franklin D. Roosevelt Library (FDRL), Personal Correspondence.

4. Norman Thomas, Columbia Univ. Oral History Collection, Part II, 1966, 96.

stance on civil rights. When, in 1942, a young black woman denounced FDR's lack of concern for the Negro, Mrs. Roosevelt responded that "of course I can say just how I feel, but I cannot say it with much sense of security unless the President were willing for me to do so." It was "easy for us as individuals," she added, "to think of what we would do if we were in office, but we forget that with the election to the office of President go at the same time infinite restrictions and the kind of responsibility which is never ours as private citizens."[5]

Nevertheless, as the President's wife, as the close confidante of many New Deal administrators, and as the friend of numerous important blacks, Eleanor Roosevelt was perceived, at least within the black community, as the official interpreter of the New Deal and its commitment to minority rights. Indeed, her own commitment to black equality has been described as the "best expression of her social thought and activities" and the "cardinal point upon which the various aspects of her thought converged; her faith in democracy, her struggle for social justice and equality, and her support of a pluralist society."[6]

Eleanor Roosevelt often urged whites to join in the effort to make democracy a meaningful reality for all groups and to translate the American traditions of fair play and equal opportunity into relevant programs of social change. "Democracy is never safe," she stated in 1940, "when it isn't safe for all citizens."[7] Democratic government depended upon the unity of every class and race. The "day of selfishness" was now over, she predicted as early as 1934; "the day of really working together has come, and we must learn to work together, all of us, regardless of race or creed or color; we must wipe out, wherever we find it, any feeling that grows up of intolerance, of belief that any group can go ahead alone. We go ahead together or we go down together."[8] Speaking to A. Philip Randolph's Sleeping Car Porters' convention, she assured delegates that people were "beginning to realize that we can't let any group suffer because it then becomes a menace to the whole group."[9]

5. ER to Pauli Murray, Aug. 3, 1942, ER Papers, Box 1654.
6. Hareven, *Eleanor Roosevelt*, 112.
7. Eleanor Roosevelt, "Defense and the Minority Groups," *Opportunity* 18 (Dec. 1940), 356.
8. Eleanor Roosevelt, "Address," *The National Conference on Fundamental Problems in the Education of Negroes, Washington, D.C., May 9-12, 1934* (U.S. Dept. of Interior, Office of Education, 1935), 10.
9. New York *Times*, Sept. 17, 1940.

Her early optimism on race relations was predicated on a belief that Americans were becoming increasingly aware that democracy's future was dependent upon greater mutual respect among all groups and classes. White Americans, if for no other reason than their own survival, could not indefinitely deprive blacks of their rights to "equal justice, equal opportunity and equal participation in the government."[10] During the early war years, she included such rights as part of her "Four Freedoms"—equality of law, education, economic opportunity, and expression—domestic freedoms designed to rally American citizens in the same manner as the four international freedoms proclaimed by FDR in the Atlantic Charter.[11] Poverty, discrimination, and illiteracy were not, in her mind, the sole concern of those who suffered most directly; in a democracy, they mattered to everyone. Speaking at the first conference on the "Negro and Negro Youth," organized by her friend Mary McLeod Bethune, then an assistant in the National Youth Administration, she declared that low standards of black health, housing, and education were problems not only for Negroes but for the entire nation. "We are all equally responsible for all of us, and for that reason wherever our communities may be, we have an equal responsibility for everyone in our community."[12]

Increased social responsibility, which implied a more tolerant attitude toward black people, was for a number of reasons, she believed, a greater possibility in the 1930s. Like Ickes and Foreman, she felt that the Depression had increased the American people's awareness of their common needs and wants. "Rugged individualism" could no longer be considered the dominant American value in an increasingly urbanized and industrialized society. The "era of the pioneer and rugged individualist" had to give way to the "era of careful planning." She acknowledged to those critical of her views on individualism that America had "gone very far in a material way"; but the ultimate test for a country was the "general happiness of the great mass of our people." The United States, she maintained, had come "to a point where the material way is good only for a limited number of people, and now we must turn and develop the

10. Eleanor Roosevelt, "Social Gains and Defense," *Common Sense* 10 (Mar. 1941), 72.

11. New York *Times*, July 15, 1943.

12. Eleanor Roosevelt, speech to the first "National Conference on the Problems of the Negro and Negro Youth," Jan. 6, 1937, Social Science Research Council, NARG 316, Box 22.

other side of life so that these material benefits may be more widely spread."[13]

Less inclined than some New Dealers to sanction the expansion of federal authority, she nevertheless agreed that the economic collapse had created circumstances that necessitated greater governmental activity in order to assure social justice and minimum economic security. Judicious programs of reform could produce a more democratic environment. A strong democracy required healthy citizens, she told the NAACP convention in 1939; but one could not enjoy "physical health, mental development, spiritual happiness" unless one lived "in an environment that makes it possible."[14]

Eleanor Roosevelt's advocacy of New Deal reform thus fused with her democratic and religious principles. Together they represented what she considered the strongest hope for the future of black people—the creation of a more democratic and virtuous society in which each individual would be granted the freedom to progress according to his own capabilities. She acknowledged at times that this was often more of a hope than a reality, that people unfortunately were still handicapped simply because of their race. She noted further that there were areas where black people had not been fairly considered by New Deal legislation, and she strongly urged that the government remedy those omissions.[15]

In this connection, speaking personally and not for the New Deal, Mrs. Roosevelt supported an expanded social security law that would include in its provisions black and white farm workers and household domestics. In addition, she urged guaranteed minimum wages and maximum hours for domestic workers; a quota system, established under civil service guidelines, to increase the number of Negroes in governmental employment; and federal and state aid to equalize educational opportunities for all citizens.[16] In the area of public housing, she maintained that the federal government not only had an obligation to furnish citizens with decent dwellings but also

13. *Woman's Home Companion* 61 (Nov. 1934), 14; undated speech, 1935, "Need for Change," ER Papers, Box 3032.

14. For her views on government expansion see Hareven, *Eleanor Roosevelt*, 130-32. On the NAACP speech, delivered on July 2, 1939, see Eleanor Roosevelt, "Presentation of Spingarn Medal to Marian Anderson," *Crisis* 46 (Sept. 1939), 285.

15. See, for instance, Eleanor Roosevelt, "The Negro and Social Change," *Opportunity* 14 (Jan. 1936), 22; "Remarks," *Proceedings of Second Conference*, 1939, 82-89, *passim*; "Freedom: Promise or Fact," *Negro Digest* 1 (Oct. 19, 1943), 8-9; and New York *Times*, Aug. 5, 1942.

16. "Remarks," *Proceedings of Second Conference*, 83-87.

must work more closely with state and local authorities to ensure that "opportunities for good living" existed in every American community.[17] Although hesitant about having her name associated with any organized movement which pressed for a federal anti-lynching law, she spoke on numerous occasions in favor of its passage. She doubted that such a law would actually eliminate the evil of lynching, but she advocated legislation since it would put the nation "on record against something which we should certainly all . . . anywhere in this country be against."[18] For much the same reason, she backed efforts during the war to gain equal treatment of blacks and other minorities in defense industries and the armed forces.[19]

For Mrs. Roosevelt, the New Deal symbolized more than the granting of jobs and financial aid to minorities like black Americans. It also stood as the guarantor of equal opportunity, as an example of individual and group responsibility, and as a beacon for a more just, equitable, and moral democratic environment. In a society committed to economic and social security, to tolerance and respect for the individual, Negroes would be able to enter more fully into the mainstream of American life. Like other New Deal liberals, she felt that there were also obligations which blacks must assume if freedom and justice were to become realities. Blacks needed to take advantage of reforms which afforded them the possibilities for advancement. To do this, they must become aware of every facet of a fast-changing society. Speaking at the Urban League convention in 1935, she argued that the Negro "must be able to understand the economic conditions and changes which are coming not only in our country, but throughout the world."[20] To Hampton Institute students, she declared that ignorance was the "greatest danger to democratic forms of government." Democracy required "from every

17. Eleanor Roosevelt, "Social Gains and Defense," 71.
18. For her thoughts on lynching, her activities on behalf of an anti-lynching law, and her reluctance to support certain anti-lynching activities, see correspondence between Mrs. Roosevelt and Walter White, ER to White, Mar. 23, 1935, NAACP Papers, LC File C-73; ER to White, Mar. 19, 1936, White to ER Mar. 9, Mar. 16, 1936, ER Papers, Box 1411. For a good discussion of Mrs. Roosevelt's anti-lynching concerns, see Lash, *Eleanor and Franklin*, 671-77. Also Hareven, *Eleanor Roosevelt*, 119-22; Eleanor Roosevelt, "Defense and Minority Groups," 357. Quote is from Eleanor Roosevelt, "Remarks," *Proceedings of Second Conference, 1939*, 77.
19. Eleanor Roosevelt, "Defense and Minority Groups," 357; "Social Gains and Defense," 71-72; "The Democratic Faith," *Common Ground* 2 (Spring 1942), 9-10; and Hareven, *Eleanor Roosevelt*, 168-70.
20. Eleanor Roosevelt, "Negro and Social Change," 22.

citizen far more intelligent citizenship than does any other form of government."[21]

For a minority, long oppressed and separated from the dominant values and institutions of society, it was critically important then to become educated to the new conditions, to develop skills required to advance in a changing social and economic order. Blacks who had overcome the adversities of prejudice and poverty should become examples to their race. "Anyone in a minority group has got to strive to do a better job," she noted, "not just for himself as an individual but because it is going to help the whole group that he belongs to and because it is going to have an effect on what all the others are going to be able to do."[22] Addressing the Harlem Hospital School of Nursing graduating class, she admonished them to be just a little better and a little more committed than others in their professions. As black nurses they had "an obligation as well as an opportunity to help" their own people "in many ways that are not strictly nursing."[23] Like Will Alexander, she believed that successful blacks offered a dramatic refutation to the white stereotype of Negro inferiority; when she praised individuals like Marian Anderson or her friend Mary McLeod Bethune, she praised them as symbols of the best of black America. "There is now a great group of educated Negroes," she wrote for the *New Republic* in May 1942, "who can become leaders among their people, who can teach them the value of things of the mind, and who qualify as the best in any field of endeavor."[24]

In urging Negro Americans to work hard, develop their skills and abilities, and set examples of which both the white and black races might be proud, there was much in Eleanor Roosevelt's race philosophy that was similar to that of Booker T. Washington and even W.E.B. Du Bois. Like Washington and Du Bois, she considered it important for blacks to establish a sense of pride in their own cultural attributes. The "Negro race," she noted, has "tremendous gifts to bring to this country in the way of artistic development"; blacks had an "appreciation of art and of music and of rhythm" that came to them naturally and that whites acquired only "through education." Black people should thus be proud of their talents, which could be

21. New York *Times*, Apr. 22, 1938.

22. Eleanor Roosevelt, "Address," *Education of Negroes*, 9-10; "Negro and Social Change, 22-23; "A Guest Editorial," *Opportunity* 18 (March 1940), 66; "Presentation of Spingarn Medal," 265, 285; New York *Times*, Apr. 22, 1938.

23. New York *Times*, Feb. 8, 1941.

24. Eleanor Roosevelt, "Race, Religion and Prejudice," *The New Republic* 106(May 11, 1942), 630.

"utilized for the good of the whole nation." In a pluralistic society like that which Mrs. Roosevelt desired, the society which she believed the New Deal was committed to promoting, blacks would be able to make their contributions along the lines that gave them their greatest "joy."[25]

Tamara Hareven, who has studied Eleanor Roosevelt's social philosophy, argues that Mrs. Roosevelt did not perceive the true racial dimensions of the "Negro problem" until sometime after 1945; "earlier she had considered it mainly in the framework of social justice."[26] There is support for this view when attention is focused primarily on the First Lady's public comments; but analysis of her private correspondence, especially during the war years, complicates such an interpretation.

In discussing the Negroes' future, Mrs. Roosevelt, like other race liberals, emphasized the importance of expanded economic, educational, and political opportunity. Like Ickes and Alexander, she believed such opportunity was being made available through the administration's general reform program. During the war, she outlined four "fundamental rights that democracy had to grant to all of its citizens": equal justice before the law, equal educational opportunity, equal employment opportunity according to one's ability and training, and equal participation in the political process. These were, she noted often, "citizenship rights" which a just government could and should provide its citizens through the promotion of jobs and essential public conveniences such as improved health and housing facilities.[27]

Mrs. Roosevelt was certainly aware that race prejudice and discrimination often made it difficult, if not impossible, for most Negroes to enjoy fully the "fundamental rights" of democracy. But she had considerable doubt as to the ability of government to eliminate racial obstacles. Though instrumental in helping blacks secure a presidential order banning discrimination in defense employment, she questioned its ultimate effectiveness. To a black man who wrote asking why she did not advocate an executive decree to prohibit

25. Eleanor Roosevelt, "Address," *Education of Negroes*, 9-10. See also Hareven, *Eleanor Roosevelt*, 113-14, for discussion of her ideas here; and for an excellent analysis of the philosophies of blacks, in particular Washington and Du Bois, see August Meier, *Negro Thought in America, 1880-1915* (Ann Arbor, Mich., 1963).

26. Hareven, *Eleanor Roosevelt*, 204.

27. For expression of these ideas, see ER to J.T. Netterville, June 28, 1943, ER Papers, Box 1693; ER to Catherine D. Stallworth, Aug. 26, 1944, *ibid.*, Box 1746; ER to Pauli Murray, Oct. 3, 1944, *ibid.*, Box 1735.

discrimination in the armed forces, she replied that "you cannot police everybody, and no Executive Order issued to the Army would stop discrimination." That approach had not eliminated prejudice against Negroes in defense jobs because there "should always be 'good reasons' for doing things when individuals want to do them" regardless of laws. "This change has to come slowly from the human heart and it takes a long while to bring about great changes."[28]

It was not so much, as Hareven suggests, that Eleanor Roosevelt failed to see race as part of the "Negro problem"; rather, she confined it to the realm of the "personal," thereby eliminating racial considerations from any meaningful governmental action. And because it was "personal," it was inevitable that change would come slowly. "Citizenship rights" and what she termed "social equality" were, in her mind, very different. By "social equality" she meant the "relationships which you choose to have with friends." What she wanted "for all people of all races is economic and civic equality"; she would leave "people's contacts, which are their individual interests, to them to settle as they see fit." To a charge made by a white woman from Alabama in 1944 that she promoted racial mixing, Mrs. Roosevelt replied that she had "never advocated any social equality whatsoever and I do not know of any Negro leaders who advocate it. In this country we are completely free to choose our companions and no one has any right to interfere."[29]

But the system of race segregation in the South and discrimination elsewhere in the country against blacks in reality denied that freedom to the majority of Negro Americans. It was hard therefore to see how "civic equality" could be realized without challenging the racial laws, customs, and values which rendered "citizenship rights" impossible for so many. "Social equality" might mean to Eleanor Roosevelt simply "personal relationships," but in a society where race touched every aspect of black people's existence, distinctions between personal and public relationships were not very meaningful, and clearly not the kind segregationists made in the racist system they constructed.

Like many white interracialists, Mrs. Roosevelt found in World War II a heightened sense of what Joseph Lash has referred to as "consciousness of color." More than some of her friends, she was willing, at least privately with the President and others, to press the

28. ER to Rev. Clarence Nelson, Oct. 30, 1943, *ibid.*, Box 1693.
29. ER to Catherine Stallworth, Aug. 26, 1944, *ibid.*, Box 1746; see Stallworth letter to ER, Aug. 18, 1944, *ibid.*, which prompted her comments. Also, ER to Irene Stephens, Sept. 25, 1944., *ibid.*

cause of race justice as a necessary part of America's wartime involvement.[30] Nevertheless she remained, as did the majority of liberals, deeply distressed over the increased militancy among blacks and the racial violence which erupted throughout the war years, particularly in the Detroit and New York riots of 1943.

The emphasis given to race consciousness strained her belief in improving race relations through the vehicle of liberal reform. Yet it did not destroy her faith in the ultimate wisdom of that approach. As her comments on "social equality" suggest, she struggled to assume a posture which she hoped would further sympathy for equal rights and temper extremists on both sides of the race question.

As a result, Mrs. Roosevelt and other New Deal race liberals found themselves often in uncomfortable positions in the 1940s. "A number of people have been asking me to make a statement on segregation," she wrote in 1944 to a militant young black woman, Pauli Murray, whom she had befriended in the late thirties, but "I do not want to make it until we have achieved the four basic citizenship rights because I do not think it wise to add any antagonism that we do not have to have." "Of course," she told Murray, who later became well known as a civil rights attorney, poet, and feminist, "public places should be open to all citizens." However, the time was not right to make that a central cause; perhaps when the war was over and "we get our four basic rights accepted," a statement opposing segregation might be effective.[31]

Earlier, in 1942, she expressed agreement with Virginius Dabney's criticism of the Negro press for its interjection of race into the American war effort; and the following year, in spite of her friend Walter White's strong dissent, she found much to praise in a similar attack on black journalists by Warren H. Brown in an essay that was

---

30. Lash, *Eleanor and Franklin*, ch. 53, esp. 863-78. As Lash and others have noted, it was also during the war that racial attacks against Mrs. Roosevelt by southern segregationists became particularly vitriolic—see Lash, 867-68.

31. ER to Pauli Murray, Oct. 3, 1944, ER Papers, Box 1735. As Joseph Lash notes (*Eleanor and Franklin*, 683, 866-67, 870), Murray provided Mrs. Roosevelt with the views of a young and militant black which she did not often get through her relationships with Walter White and Mary McLeod Bethune. The Eleanor Roosevelt–Pauli Murray correspondence began in Dec. 1938 and continued throughout the war years; it was a frank yet always respectful communication, and Mrs. Roosevelt employed her influence on a number of occasions to assist Murray in her career. Murray, at one time, had been turned down by the Univ. of North Carolina Law School and eventually went on to graduate from Howard Univ. Law School; in this connection, see Sosna, *In Search of the Silent South*, 85-86.

reprinted in the *Reader's Digest*.[32] Though she did not read the Negro press regularly, she wrote White, she was "often sent clippings, and the headlines and articles seem pretty extreme at times."[33]

Nevertheless, she tried to maintain a perspective on the question. She noted to Dabney that liberals "must remember that if morale was built for most of the people in this nation in the homes and in the schools, it is not very astounding to find it a little dulled in the Negro race."[34] When the riots broke out in Detroit and New York City, she acknowledged in *Negro Digest* that "if I were a Negro today, I think I would have moments of bitterness. It would be hard for me to sustain my faith in democracy and to build up a sense of goodwill toward other men."[35] And her response to Pauli Murray's angry poem attacking Franklin Roosevelt's insensitivity to the Detroit racial encounter was a simple "I understand."[36]

In the end she returned to her original theme, noting in the same *Negro Digest* essay that "too much demanding" by black Americans might produce conditions which would permanently impair the opportunities they had already achieved. Black people needed to be "realistic" and to keep in mind their primary objectives. With the racial situation as bleak as it was in 1943–44, it was especially important for American Negroes to decide exactly what their "real rights as a citizen" were and to begin working for "those rights first, feeling that other things such as social relationships might well wait until certain people were given time to think it through and decide as individuals what they wished to do."[37]

32. Eleanor Roosevelt, "What Is Morale?" *Saturday Review of Literature* 25 (July 4, 1942), 12. Mrs. Roosevelt's comments directed to Dabney were related to an article he wrote for the same issue: Dabney, "Press and Morale, "*Saturday Review*, 5-6, 24-25. Warren Brown's essay was also originally published in the *Saturday Review*. See Brown, "A Negro Warns the Negro Press, "*Saturday Review of Literature* 25 (Dec. 19, 1942), 5-6, reprinted under the same title in *Reader's Digest* 42 (Jan. 1943), 32-34. Brown was the director of Race Relations for the Council of Democracy. See also Lash, *Eleanor and Franklin*, 869.

33. Eleanor ER to White, Jan. 4, 1943, ER Papers, Box 1642.

34. Eleanor Roosevelt, "What Is Morale?" 12.

35. Eleanor Roosevelt, "Freedom: Promise or Fact," 8.

36. ER to Pauli Murray, July 26, 1943, ER Papers, Box 1692. Murray's poem, included in the above, was dated July 21, 1943. See also Lash, *Eleanor and Franklin*, 870.

37. Eleanor Roosevelt, "Freedom: Promise or Fact," 9, 8. In a letter to Rev. Clarence Nelson, cited in note 28, Nov. 11, 1943, Mrs. Roosevelt attempted to explain that what she meant by "too much demanding" was that Negroes would "probably get further if the white people who believe as they do, were urged to do most of the fighting and demanding. . . . Dr. Will Alexander, for instance, can do

II.

Worried as she sometimes was about black and white relations and the effect of the war, Mrs. Roosevelt remained generally optimistic about the future of black Americans. That optimism was sustained in large part by the faith she shared with other New Deal interracialists in the viability of liberal reform and its continued importance for America in the decades ahead.

Throughout the Roosevelt years there were, of course, many critics of New Deal liberalism and its relevance to racial concerns. But what must certainly have given confidence to many a New Dealer was the inability of most critics to launch any meaningful alternative to the government's approach. Much has been written about the "failure of independent liberalism" and radicalism to proceed very far against the Franklin Roosevelt style of reform; that lack of success applied as well to the administration's philosophy on race.[38]

In many respects, the failure of an independent racial liberalism was even greater. The anti–New Deal left's frequent attacks against administration programs and reform ideology seldom involved a sustained criticism of the government's handling of racial matters. Before the advent of the Popular Front, the Communist party did concentrate on winning black support and gave considerable attention to civil rights issues. But the Communists were never a serious threat to the New Deal, though they helped generate protests against government policies, including those affecting the black population.[39]

Under the leadership of Norman Thomas, American Socialists endeavored to move beyond their historic perspective, which viewed the lot of blacks as identical to that of all oppressed workers

---

twice as much with a Southern audience" as she believed she could. Yet Alexander, and Mrs. Roosevelt herself, felt restrained in their own protests involving the war and its impact on race relations.

38. See, for instance, the excellent studies of Richard Pells, *Radical Visions and American Dreams*, and R. Alan Lawson, *The Failure of Independent Liberalism, 1930-1941*, both previously cited.

39. The relationship of Communists and black Americans is discussed briefly in ch. 7. For an earlier and generally negative view on Communist civil rights activities, see William A. Nolan, *Communism Versus the Negro* (Chicago, 1951); Wilson Record, *The Negro and the Communist Party* (Chapel Hill, 1951), and *Race and Radicalism: The NAACP and the Communist Party* (Ithaca, N.Y., 1964). For a recent analysis of that party's more positive accomplishments in shaping the cause of racial justice, see Harvard Ira Sitkoff, "The Emergence of Civil Rights As a National Issue: The New Deal Era" (Ph.D. diss., Columbia Univ., 1975, chs. 4, 7, 8, 11, *passim*.

and the Negro's salvation as linked to the successful achievement of a classless society.[40] Thomas did affirm that vision, but he also attempted to address the "special needs" of blacks. Writing for Negro publications like *Opportunity* and the *Crisis*, organizing the interracial Southern Tenant Farmers' Union, and devoting an entire chapter to the "Negro problem" in his most extensive analysis of the Depression, *Human Exploitation*, he made many trenchant criticisms of the New Deal's inability to protect the rights of Negro Americans.[41]

Yet much of what Thomas had to say in *Human Exploitation* and elsewhere about race was aimed at attacking "black nationalist" thought and the racial separatist tendencies he associated with a number of black struggles of the 1930s. The politics of race, he argued (logically, from his perspective), jeopardized the formation of working class solidarity, which was indispensable in the battle to defeat capitalism.[42] Writing in *Opportunity* during the 1932 election, he maintained that the "root of race prejudice" was "planted deep in the soil of economic inequality." "White arrogance," he concluded, was simply the "product of accidental economic advantage"; only by the "establishment of economic justice and the end of a class division of society" would Americans acquire any "sanity concerning race relations. Indeed, the union of workers across race and language

40. For background on the Socialist party's attitude toward black Americans, see David A. Shannon, *The Socialist Party of America* (New York, 1967), 50-53; Ernest Doerfler, "Socialism and the Negro Problem," *American Socialist Quarterly* 3 (Summer 1933), 23-36; Margaret I. Lamont, "The Negro's Share in Socialism," *American Socialist Quarterly* 4 (Mar. 1935), 41-51; R. Luwrence Moore, "Flawed Fraternity— American Socialist Response to the Negro, 1901-1912," *The Historian* 32 (Nov. 1969), 1-18.

41. Thomas, "Can America Go Fascist?" *Crisis* 41 (Jan. 1934), 10; "For the Socialists," in "Symposium for 1932 Presidential Candidates," *Opportunity* 10 (Nov. 1932), 340; "Greetings" to the 1935 NAACP convention, in Thomas to Walter White, June 13, 1935, NAACP Papers, LC, Box C-76; *Human Exploitation in the United States* (New York, 1934), 258-83. For Thomas' involvement with the STFU and other efforts on behalf of blacks, see Grubbs, *Cry from the Cotton*, 5-145, *passim*; Jerold S. Auerbach, "Southern Tenant Farmers: Socialist Critics of the New Deal," *Labor History* 7 (Winter 1966), 3-18; M.S. Venkataramani, "Norman Thomas, Arkansas Sharecroppers, and the Roosevelt Agricultural Policies, 1933-1937," *Mississippi Valley Historical Review* 47 (Sept. 1960), 225-46; Harry Fleischman, *Norman Thomas: A Biography* (New York, 1964), 144-51; W.A. Swanberg, *Norman Thomas: The Last Idealist* (New York, 1976), 158-60. Analysis of Thomas' racial ideas can be found in John B. Kirby, "The New Deal Era and Blacks: A Study of Black and White Race Thought, 1933-1945" (Ph.D. diss., Univ. of Illinois, 1971), 243-56.

42. Thomas, *Human Exploitation*, 268-70, 280-82.

barriers for the cooperative commonwealth" would of itself be "the greatest solvent of our racial jealousies and hates."[43]

Thomas distinguished himself in the early part of the thirties by his strong commitment to social justice and racial equality. Yet toward the end of the decade, as war in Europe seemed imminent, his attention focused increasingly on what he feared was the spread of fascism at home and abroad. He tied that fear to some degree to his continued support of Negro rights, arguing, as he did at the 1937 convention of the National Negro Congress, that the "war against fascism" should begin in "our country" against the evils of Jim Crowism, labor discrimination, and the Ku Klux Klan.[44] Gradually, however, his sympathy for the black struggle and the creation of a solid black and white labor front became secondary to his opposition to internal fascism and to America's entrance into World War II. As early as 1936, it was evident that whatever his personal commitment to black justice, he did not see Negro people as constituting a major force in the fight against New Dealism or in the building of a socialist society. In his 1936 campaign pamphlet, *After the New Deal*, little mention was made of the plight of black Americans, and they were conspicuous by their absence from his section devoted to the "dynamic forces of change."[45]

In the mid-1960s, Norman Thomas reflected on his experiences in the thirties and his efforts on behalf of the Negro and lamented that he had not "emphasized more strongly than I did my real feelings on this race issue. I regret that I didn't work in the party harder for a separate program. . . . I do think that it would have been good to work then in the Socialist party at a very detailed program such as everybody has been working at in the last few years." Yet he felt that it had been difficult to do that in the New Deal era, as the "whole liberal American-left position had definitely become sapped and excessively dependent upon a personality—upon the personality of Roosevelt, so that it lost intellectual content." And Thomas believed that in spite of his and the party's failure to develop a specific program for blacks, he received "no response from Negroes

43. Thomas, "For the Socialists," 340.
44. New York *Times*, Oct. 17, 1937.
45. Thomas, *After the New Deal, What?* (New York, 1936). See also Thomas, *Socialism on the Defensive* (New York, 1938), and *We Have a Future* (Princeton, N.J., 1941), for increasingly limited reference to race issues.

to what I did do"; "Negroes themselves . . . were curiously quiet for a long time."[46]

Though he may have been right that blacks did not fully appreciate his contributions to racial justice, Thomas exaggerated their silence during the Depression years. The failure of Socialists and others on the liberal left to win blacks away from the New Deal was not the fault of black Americans. The problem lay in the essential similarity of the pro– and anti–New Deal interracial perspectives. The basic racial assumptions of Thomas' "Socialist commonwealth" and New Dealer Harold Ickes' "New Democracy" bore, in effect, a close resemblance. Both philosophies were grounded on a belief that race differences were contrary to reason and derived from emotional and irrational attitudes which racists employed to separate blacks and whites and prevent them from recognizing a common economic and political destiny. Both Thomas and Ickes asserted that through education and economic reform, racial divisions would cease to be important. Where they disagreed, of course, was in respect to the economic changes required; liberal New Dealers, unlike Thomas and others of the left, were unwilling to eliminate private ownership.

No doubt that was an important distinction, but given the problems confronting the black masses in the 1930s and 1940s, it was essentially an academic distinction. Since it was the New Deal liberal who held power during the period, it was thus understandable that most Negro Americans, faced with two philosophies of so little difference, would not flock to what the black intellectual Ralph J. Bunche characterized in 1939 as "virtually a paper party."[47] Without political influence or a racial ideology to distinguish them from the Roosevelt administration, Socialists and many of their colleagues on the independent left won little support from the black community.

That gave some assurance to the policies and racial assumptions pursued by New Deal and pro-administration interracialists. Though there were differences among them, white liberals like Eleanor Roosevelt, Harold Ickes, Clark Foreman, and Will Alexander shared a number of key ideas which helped determine the federal government's approach to racial concerns.

Of central importance was their belief in the government's power to effect major economic, political, and social change in the existing American system. The New Deal was a personal experience for

46. Norman Thomas, Columbia Oral History, II, 93-96, 143-44.

47. Ralph J. Bunche, "Extended Memorandum on the Programs, Ideologies, Tactics and Achievements of Negro Betterment and Interracial Organizations" (unpubl. memorandum for the Carnegie-Myrdal Study, New York, 1940), NYPL, 787.

them; it represented an opportunity to become part of a comprehensive reform movement, to realize programs and dreams which they had considered for years. This was particularly true, as has been noted, for southern race liberals, who had long operated at the margin of southern life. Aubrey Williams, as associate and close friend of other New Deal liberals and, like them, committed to improving the black condition, expressed this sentiment in his unfinished autobiography, *Southern Rebel*. Listening to President Roosevelt's inaugural address in 1933, he felt FDR had "put something together" inside him that day: the "government suddenly became real. He brought me into a circle which in many ways was totally new. It was a mutual community . . . with the government. . . . becoming my government . . . a joined and connected amorphous mass, a continuum. In short, he made me a member of the nation. I belong."[48] And, in spite of an occasional clash with the President over what Williams considered to be a lack of sensitivity on racial issues, he acknowledged that "I really rather worship this man. He was just about what I wished I was."[49]

That feeling of "mutual community" and of belonging to "government" and "nation" which the New Deal inspired in Williams and other liberals carried over in their interpretation of the Roosevelt administration's importance to black Americans. New Dealers believed, in short, that a combination of factors, emanating essentially from the Depression, had generated a host of new conditions which made the future of Negroes and black-white relations appear extremely hopeful. The economic collapse in 1929 signified the end of a distinctive phase in American life, a phase characterized predominantly by an obsession with individualism. Eleanor Roosevelt referred to it as the "era of the pioneer and rugged individualist"; Harold Ickes called it the era of the exploiter. But whatever its name or whatever its previous strengths or attributes, it was an era that no longer existed.[50] And with its passing went the American faith in unending economic and physical expansion, boundless affluence, and unlimited technological development, as well as the ideology that sustained that faith. The "frontier" was gone; America had emerged, whether by choice or by necessity, as a more constrained

48. Aubrey Williams, "A Southern Rebel" (unpubl. ms.), Aubrey Williams Papers, FDRL.
49. Quoted in John Salmond, "'Aubrey Williams Remembers': A Note on Franklin D. Roosevelt's Attitude Toward Negro Rights," *The Alabama Review* 25 (Jan. 1972), 67.
50. *Woman's Home Companion* 61 (Nov. 1934), 14; Ickes, *New Democracy*, 32, 43.

and closed society, economically and socially as well as physically. The 1930s were the "beginning of a new era," one which no longer assumed that laissez-faire and individual liberty were the guiding American principles but which now stressed faith in planning and in the need to enhance human equality and the quality of American life. As Steven Kesselman has noted in a study of New Deal ideology, what inevitably followed from the "kind of thinking about the closing of the frontier" and the "end of economic expansion" was belief in the "need for, and the possibilities of, coordinated planning from above."[51]

The conviction that the combined effects of the Depression and the New Deal were fundamentally restructuring American institutions and values dramatically influenced the manner in which white New Dealers interpreted the "Negro problem" in the 1930s and 1940s. Seen in light of the historic conditions plaguing the black population, as the New Dealers defined those conditions, the Depression indeed became a turning point, a significant departure in the black American experience. The "Negro problem" had always been at its root an economic problem, they argued. Certainly the black man's situation had been complicated and made worse by political opportunism in the past and by the existence of unscientific theories regarding race inferiority. But these factors were simply manifestations of the deeper dilemma; they were rationalizations for the economic oppression and exploitation of black people. It was, as Eleanor Roosevelt expressed it, essentially because "colored people, not only in the South, but in the North as well have been economically at a low level . . . that they have been physically and intellectually at a low level."[52] What the Depression had done was to underline that fact by showing clearly the basic economic instability of the black position in American life.

New Deal liberals maintained further that the Depression's devastation had the effect of transcending racial classifications and considerations. In the 1930s, whites as well as blacks were in need of economic security. That common adversity would thus create a bond among diverse racial and ethnic groups, as they became aware that they all suffered from similar deprivations. Creation of a sense of shared values and goals was of prime importance in building the interdependency and unity necessary for centralized government planning and for construction of the "new democracy."

51. Steven Kesselman, "The Frontier Thesis and the Great Depression," *Journal of the History of Ideas* 29 (April-June 1968), 264.
52. Eleanor Roosevelt, "The Negro and Social Change," 22.

Following these assumptions, New Dealers regularly emphasized Negro class conditions and the mutual economic interests of black and white. This perspective owed less to Marxist theory than to a number of philosophical and political needs of liberals, especially the justification of the New Deal's relevance to both black and white and the search for a common denominator by which the races might unify and discard "race-conscious" notions that had separated them in the past. Class analysis was, of course, a dominant feature of the times, shared not only by New Dealers and Socialists like Norman Thomas but by a significant segment of the liberal-left community. A student of northern liberal race thought argues that in the thirties liberals "considered class problems the important ones and looked at race primarily as a distraction, a lesser problem that would most likely be cleared up when a few court decisions secured equal justice for blacks and some economic or political reforms made possible the passage of an anti-lynching law."[53] Defining the "Negro problem" as essentially economic, liberal interracialists within the New Deal allowed themselves considerable freedom to push for reforms they believed would benefit every American, regardless of color.

The success of this approach was dependent primarily on faith in the New Deal's power to achieve certain long-range changes in black standards and white attitudes. Clark Foreman's assertion that under the New Deal "prejudice, unfair discrimination and exploitation" would be made "unprofitable" indicated the depth of that faith. Believing in the ultimate correctness of their approach, Foreman and others could accept certain immediate disappointments that resulted from an unsympathetic Congress, from colleagues who did not share their commitment, from periodic outbreaks of racial hostility, from local white resistance to their programs, and from the discriminatory treatment of blacks in the defense industries and the armed forces during the 1940s. Convinced, however, that people's attitudes would change as the material condition of blacks improved, they believed it important to caution Negroes to be patient, to take advantage of the opportunities which were being created, and not to push too hard for rights which were more social than economic and which aggravated racial passions and complicated government efforts on their behalf. Within the New Deal reforms, they asserted, there would be the practical educational experience of blacks working with whites in a truly interracial endeavor. But like all educa-

53. Peter J. Kellogg, "Northern Liberals and Black America: A History of White Attitudes, 1936-1952" (Ph.D. diss., Northwestern Univ., 1971), 20.

tional experiences, it would take time for the full benefits to be realized. People must be allowed to "think through and decide as individuals what they wished to do." As Ickes noted, you could not "force people on each other who do not like each other," and Mrs. Roosevelt affirmed that even the government could not force industry to accept blacks in its employment until there was "created opinion sufficiently strong to make people want to do the fair thing."[54] "I believe that your cheerful disposition, your faith, your loyalty and your lack of resentment," Ickes told the NAACP in 1936, "are some of the qualities that have brought you the success that already is yours."[55] To expand that success, he called upon blacks to maintain those same qualities.

The white liberal approach to the "Negro problem" in the 1930s and 1940s was elitist. The black leaders whom New Dealers relied on for racial advice were elites from the black community, and the nature of "planning from above" was predicated on elitist principles.[56] In championing the cause of Negroes within the administration, white New Dealers tied the black future to the successful fulfillment of the Roosevelt reform program. In the process, they identified their own faith in the New Deal's potential, their tolerance of white prejudice, their belief in economic priorities, and their acceptance of existing institutions and values with black needs, black endurance, black priorities, and continued black loyalty to the American way of life. The solution to the "Negro problem" ultimately hinged upon the interplay of a number of factors—expanded economic opportunities and security, the power of education to modify traditional beliefs, the steady rise in black standards, and the eventual decrease in white bigotry. Within this complex interrelationship there were established limits on the government's activities in dealing with racial questions. Those limits involved basically the degree to which the white population would accept the inclusion of blacks in New Deal housing, labor, education, and health programs, limits within which white New Dealers felt they must operate if any assistance to black Americans was to be ever realized.

54. Ickes, *Secret Diary,* II, 115; Eleanor Roosevelt, "Remarks," *Proceedings of Second Conference, 1939,* 85-86.

55. Ickes, "The Negro As Citizen," 231.

56. An excellent analysis of New Deal elitism, including discussion of black New Dealers, is Thomas A. Krueger and William Glidden, "The New Deal Intellectual Elite: A Collective Portrait," in Frederic Cople Jaher, ed., *The Rich, the Well Born, and the Powerful: Elites and Upper Classes in History* (Urbana, Ill., 1973), 338-374. For comments on certain black figures who later formed within the Roosevelt administration the "Black Cabinet," see Motz, "Black Cabinet," 21-32, 72-76.

Not until World War II were they forced to acknowledge certain difficulties inherent in their approach, though by then the welfare system they had helped create was rapidly becoming institutionalized. Peter Kellogg, an historian of the racial attitudes of liberals associated with the *New Republic* and the *Nation* from the mid-1930s through the early 1950s, maintains that the racial implications of the war confronted the liberal community for the first time with the centrality of race in American life. "During the New Deal years," Kellogg notes, northern liberals "had stressed the importance of class unity and denied the significance of racial divisions until they had almost no sense of race as a public issue when World War II began. The war raised racial issues in a very stark, moral form."[57]

For liberal southerners, the war was even more catastrophic in its impact on their race relations ideas. Morton Sosna's recent study indicates that the impetus given to black militancy and to racial hostilities by the war "deflated the white Southern liberal's prewar hope of subordinating the race issue to other problems," and the difficulties southern reformers faced "resulted from the fact that the entire Jim Crow system had finally come under attack."[58] For a number of the South's liberals, like Virginius Dabney, the inability to keep the racial genie in the bottle led to an increasingly conservative stance on race reform; others, Clark Foreman and Aubrey Williams for example, who left the Roosevelt administration in the early 1940s, became more outspoken in their denunciations of racism and, in particular, segregation.[59]

For Will Alexander and Eleanor Roosevelt, who remained in the government, the war abroad and racial strife at home were particularly trying. Neither gave up the commitment to black people; both continued to work and speak out for greater racial understanding and equal opportunity. Yet the ascendancy of race in discussions involving the Negro often disheartened and confused them. Mrs. Roosevelt's struggle to hold in balance her concepts of "social equality" and "citizenship rights" without inciting "passions" typified the difficulties she and others faced. Few liberal interracialists, in fact,

57. Kellogg, "Northern Liberals and Black America," 427-28.

58. Sosna, *In Search of the Silent South*, 107, 110.

59. On Dabney and other liberal southerners who became more conservative on the race question, see Sosna, *In Search of the Silent South*, ch. 7, and for his brief comments on Foreman and Williams, 140-50, 169-70. Also Krueger, *And Promises to Keep, passim*, esp. ch. 8, for post–World War II activities and Foreman's support of Henry A. Wallace's presidential candidacy in 1948.

were able to discard the basic assumptions they had developed before and during the years of New Deal domestic reform. Their hope for a more cooperative social order and for interracial unity, coupled with their fear that racial conflict and violence were indeed probable without that order or unity, deterred them from embracing the full implications of racism in American society. Thus, despite the threats the war posed to their beliefs, their faith in the soundness of the New Deal response remained essentially unchanged.

The ideas of Roosevelt liberals affected not only their own strategies but those of the black community as well. Since they considered the manner in which Negroes carried on their activities to be of major importance in the ultimate success of the New Deal's program, they spent considerable time and effort advising blacks of their primary responsibilities. And since they occupied important positions within the government or had direct access to those who did, it was inevitable that liberal race thinking would significantly influence the tactics, goals, and general framework used by New Deal and non–New Deal blacks in pursuing their objectives. The liberals' influence was further enhanced by the weak economic and political position in which most black Americans found themselves during the administration of Herbert Hoover.

FIVE

Black America and the Coming of the New Deal

If white interracialists had been in a quandary as to how they might better America's racial climate in the years immediately preceding the New Deal's arrival, a majority of black Americans experienced an even more intense feeling of disorientation. For most Negroes, the collapse of the American economy after 1929 simply aggravated an already desperate situation. Passed by during the boom times of the twenties, they found their precarious hold on social and economic opportunity further eroded by the Great Depression. A National Urban League report in 1933 indicated that over 17 percent of the entire black population was on relief. In northern urban centers, where black southerners continued to migrate, there was unrelenting despair: Gary, Indiana, showed over one-half of its Negro citizens unemployed and on relief; in Pittsburgh, blacks accounted for 43 percent of those on local relief rolls. The jobless rate for black males by the early 1930s ran between 40 and 60 percent in major industrial cities like New York, Chicago, Detroit, and Philadelphia. In the cities of the South conditions were worse, because there state and private charity organizations often refused aid to Negroes. And in southern farm belts, black tenant farmers and sharecroppers sank deeper into debt while the few landowning Negro farmers struggled at barely subsistence levels.[1]

What intensified the situation for the Afro-American was his lack of meaningful options, an historic condition made worse by the Negro's forced isolation from any political and economic influence in the twenties. It was not simply that black Americans lacked

---

1. Myrdal, *American Dilemma*, I, Part 4, contains useful information on black economic conditions prior to and after the Great Depression. Chs. 11 to 13 are especially relevant to the early 1930s. See also Weiss, *National Urban League*, 237-40; Buni, *Robert L. Vann*, 188, for reference to Pittsburgh; Sterner, *The Negro's Share, passim*. Useful also are Charles S. Johnson, *Shadow of the Plantations* (Chicago, 1934), for discussion of rural conditions in the South, and the National Urban League's *The Forgotten Tenth: An Analysis of Unemployment Among Negroes and its Social Costs, 1932-1933* (New York, 1933).

financial resources to draw on when the hard times came, but that they lacked other resources as well.

Still, for many blacks, despite "normalcy" and the Ku Klux Klan, the decade of the twenties had been a time of some positive accomplishment. The growth of a distinctive Afro-American identity, sparked by the race philosophy of Marcus Garvey and the cultural achievements of those talented writers and artists associated with the "Harlem Renaissance," was of major importance to black people both during and after the New Era years. Garvey and the Renaissance contributed greatly to Negro Americans' sense of personal worth and collective pride and offered some compensation to a people who suffered pain and hurt simply because they were black.[2]

Yet racial self-awareness offered little compensation for those after 1929 who were confronted with a threat to individual and collective survival. "At no time in the history of the Negro since slavery," the Urban League's T. Arnold Hill exclaimed in 1931, had the Negro's "economic and social outlook seemed so discouraging."[3] The dream of Garvey and black cultural thinkers in the 1920s—that the black man might free himself from his dependence on white America—was dashed finally by the economic fallout which came in the 1930s. As Garvey well understood, cultural and economic independence were interwoven; and when the stock market crashed in 1929, both hopes crashed with it. It was difficult to hold on to racial pride or pride in anything when over a quarter of the population, white and black, was out of work.

Organizations traditionally concerned with black welfare, like the National Association for the Advancement of Colored People and the National Urban League, opposed to Garvey in the twenties, were little better prepared to deal with the conditions produced by the Depression. The NAACP and Urban League had not been inactive, however, in the years between World War I and 1929. Founded in 1909, the NAACP continued to emphasize in the postwar years legal, educational, and propagandistic means to win equal rights for the Afro-American. Particularly in the courts, the Association counted a number of significant victories, the most important being

2. On Garvey, See Cronon, *Black Moses*, and Amy Jacques-Garvey, ed., *Philosophy and Opinions of Marcus Garvey*, 2 vols. (New York, 1923-1925). An excellent discussion of the Renaissance is Huggins, *Harlem Renaissance*, previously cited. See too, S.P. Fullinwider, *The Mind and Mood of Black America* (Homewood, Ill., 1969), ch. 6; Stephen H. Bronz, *The Roots of Negro Racial Consciousness: The 1920s: Three Harlem Renaissance Authors* (New York, 1964).

3. New York *Times*, Apr. 5, 1931.

the 1927 *Nixon v. Herndon* ruling by the United States Supreme Court which weakened the Democratic "white primary."[4]

The NAACP also expanded its educational activities, lobbying for equal federal and state support to black schools, a pursuit that led ultimately to the Association's successful challenge of the "separate but equal" doctrine itself. Perhaps more significant for the Roosevelt era was the NAACP's involvement in certain economic issues in the 1920s. Though its efforts never satisfied the ambitions of *Crisis* editor W.E.B. Du Bois, the NAACP did commit legal and propaganda resources to challenging labor union discrimination and trying to force the American Federation of Labor and its affiliates to open their ranks to Negro workers.[5]

For the most part, however, the NAACP continued to defer to the National Urban League on economic matters. Created shortly after the NAACP in 1910 with the strong backing of Booker T. Washington, the League's original mandate was to assist southern black migrants in their difficult adjustment to the conditions of northern city life and industrial employment. Historian Nancy Weiss states that in the twenties the NUL "generally eschewed active reform" and sought to "strengthen and broaden the social service efforts it had begun during the 1910s."[6] With Charles S. Johnson serving as the first director, the Urban League established a Department of Research in 1921 and intensified its campaign to persuade employers to hire Negroes. But efforts to "integrate white capitalism" met with only limited success, as did the League's struggle to convince the AFL to employ its organizing talents on behalf of the black laboring class. Beginning in 1918, the NUL went on record in favor of collective bargaining, and throughout the 1920s, with little encouragement from the labor leadership, it endeavored to overcome the historic anti-union feelings of many Negro workers. Still, by the end of the decade, little more than 80,000 blacks were affiliated with the union movement, and those were concentrated in a handful of internationals such as the Longshoremen and United Mine Workers, the Sleeping Car Porters, and a number of independent black unions.[7]

Perhaps the most important changes in the twenties involving the National Urban League and the NAACP were internal ones. Interra-

4. Ross, *J.E. Spingarn*, 108-9.
5. *Ibid.*, 106-7.
6. Weiss, *National Urban League*, 163.
7. Irving Bernstein, *The Lean Years: A History of the American Worker, 1920-1933* (Boston, 1960), 107-8; Weiss, *National Urban League*, 212-13. In Weiss, chs. 11-14, there is a fine discussion of the League's activities during the 1920s.

cial both in philosophy and membership, the NUL and the NAACP had from the start been extremely dependent upon their white friends for financial support and expertise. During the twenties, neither the goal of integration nor the fact of economic dependency changed, but a shift did take place in organizational leadership. This was especially true in the case of the NAACP, which had claimed only one black, W.E.B. Du Bois, among its original board of directors.

In 1921, the poet and novelist James Weldon Johnson became the first black NAACP national secretary; and ten years later, when he retired, he was replaced by his Negro assistant, Walter White. While the national secretary's position was being assumed by blacks, the focus of authority within the Association shifted from the board of directors to the secretary's office; when Joel E. Spingarn resigned as chairman of the board in 1935 and the noted black surgeon Louis Wright took his place, that shift became complete.[8] Given the priorities of the NAACP, even more significant was the gradual dominance of black lawyers on its legal staff, culminating in the mid-thirties with Charles F. Houston and William Hastie taking over the major responsibility for the National Association's litigations.[9]

Change was less pronounced in the National Urban League. Nevertheless, during the twenties the League expanded its activities in the deep South, created a new research office, and added to its staff individuals like Jesse Thomas, T. Arnold Hill, and Charles S. Johnson, who considerably strengthened its operations and leadership.[10]

As important as these events were, especially for the later years, the two major civil rights and black welfare organizations were faced with possible extinction shortly after 1929. Unlike the NAACP, the NUL had never drawn much financial support from the Negro rank and file; in the best of times operating on a shoestring budget, the League found its foundation support and other philanthropic assistance dramatically weakened by the Depression. Only through astute management and the elimination or reduction of valuable services

8. Elliott Rudwick and August Meier, "The Rise of the Black Secretariat in the NAACP, 1909-35," in Meier and Rudwick, eds., *Along the Color Line: Explorations in the Black Experience* (Urbana, Ill., 1976), 94-127. On Spingarn's resignation, Ross, *J.E. Spingarn*, 242-43.

9. August Meier and Elliott Rudwick, "Attorneys Black and White: A Case Study of Race Relations Within the NAACP," in Meier and Rudwick, *Along the Color Line*, 128-73. A shorter version of this essay appeared under the same title in *Journal of American History* 62 (Mar. 1976), 913-46.

10. Parris and Brooks, *Blacks in the City*, 156-204; Weiss, *National Urban League*, ch. 10.

did it manage to avoid bankruptcy during the 1930s.[11] Despite its broader support, the NAACP was not much better off. After 1929, it was primarily the financial expertise of its president, Joel E. Spingarn, a small surplus inherited from the 1920s, and continued foundation aid that saved the Association from a "complete financial collapse."[12]

The threat of their own demise certainly did not enhance the capabilities of the NAACP and the NUL in aiding Depression-shocked black Americans. With little direction from the Hoover administration, Negro leaders, like other Americans, floundered as the times worsened. The Urban League found itself petitioning Hoover simply to give more attention to the condition of the black unemployed, while it struggled to assure the Afro-American citizen an equitable share of government and private relief funds.[13] Continuing its assault on lynching and educational discrimination, the NAACP joined the League and the black National Bar Association to protest the exclusion of Negro workers from the construction of the Hoover Dam and Hoover's appointment of a white racist judge to the United States Supreme Court.[14] Successful largely because of the aid received from organized labor, the NAACP victory over Hoover's nomination of John J. Parker to the Court seemed small when it was compared with the unimpeded erosion of the Negro's economic status in America by the early 1930s.

A more direct response to the Depression occurred outside the NAACP and NUL in the form of the "Don't-Buy-Where-You-Can't-Work" campaigns. Originating in Chicago in 1929, the "Don't Buy" movement spread to other black communities, primarily in the North. The objective was, through picketing and boycotting, to force business establishments located in Negro neighborhoods to hire black personnel or, at the very least, not to replace Negro employees with whites. "Don't Buy" struggles were usually led by individuals indigenous to their communities, though at times during the thirties both the Communist party and the NAACP offered support. Perhaps the "Don't-Buy-Where-You-Can't-Work" movement

11. Weiss, *National Urban League*, 155-62, 242-48.

12. Ross, *J.E. Spingarn*, 131; see also 130-38, 115-24.

13. Weiss, *National Urban League*, 238-49; Parris and Brooks, *Blacks in the City*, 214-27.

14. Charles Radford Lawrence, "Negro Organizations in Crisis: Depression, New Deal, World War II" (Ph.D. diss., Columbia Univ., 1953), 133-53; Bunche, "Programs, Ideologies, Tactics," Carnegie-Myrdal, 23-300, discusses activities of the NAACP and the Urban League in early Depression and New Deal years.

was a significant legacy for civil rights and other activists of the 1950s and 1960s, but it had only limited impact on the economic dislocation and race discrimination experienced in the 1930s by most black people.[15]

It was difficult for Negro Americans to fix on any meaningful strategy to relieve the Depression's misery. In 1931, Oscar De Priest, who had been elected as a Republican congressman from Chicago's South Side in 1928 (the first black to achieve that distinction since early 1900), called for a "non-Partisan Negro Conference" to assess the mounting problems confronting his race.

Meeting in Washington, D.C., in early December, representatives from various black political, religious, and civil organizations listened for three days to stories depicting the dismal conditions that existed in black American communities. Writing later to the NAACP's Walter White, who had attended the conference, De Priest noted that his own travels and the reports from other delegates had shown him that there was "a serious and deep-seated dissatisfaction among all classes of Negroes in every section of the country." It was time, he felt, "for concerted action."[16]

But there was little "concerted action" proposed at the De Priest gathering. Instead, delegates appealed to President Hoover and Congress to end discrimination in federal employment, enact a federal anti-lynching law, and provide federal aid to black schools. They urged labor unions and management "in this dark day of industrial uncertainty" to set aside "their customary intolerance" and share with Negroes the "limited opportunities." In what was perhaps its most "radical" expression, the conference indicated the growing black disillusionment with Hoover and the Republicans by urging Negroes to seek support in both major political parties. "We have been chiefly the beneficiaries of one party against the overt or covert unfriendliness of the other. . . . But today, party creeds are crumbling and party differences dwindling to the point of indistinction. The last two party platforms adopted in 1928 differ only in phraseology." Thus, the Negro was admonished to "dispose his mind to

---

15. August Meier and Elliott Rudwick, "The Origins of Nonviolent Direct Action in Afro-American Protest: A Note on Historical Discontinuities," in Meier and Rudwick, *Along the Color Line*, 314-32. Also see Ralph J. Bunche, "A Critical Analysis of the Tactics and Programs of Minority Groups," *Journal of Negro Education* 4 (July 1935), 313-14.

16. De Priest to White, Dec. 17, 1931, NAACP Papers, File C-64.

independent political action" and to "build up a basis of effectiveness and influence inside of both parties, so that when the wheels of political fortune bring the one or the other into national control, the race may not be without friends at the seat of power."[17]

Conferees eschewed involvement of blacks in third-party politics, especially the brand espoused by Communists, who by 1931 were taking an active interest in civil rights issues. "We warn members of the race," one resolution read, "against the specious pleas of Communism, whose basic principles are vitally at variance with our received ideals of free institutions." Assuring all who might have some doubts of their "undeviating devotion to the principles of American institutions," the Non-Partisan Conference concluded by calling upon black people to be "thrifty, frugal, and industrious, reliable and dutiful in the performance of any tasks which their hands may find to do."[18]

Oscar De Priest considered the 1931 Negro Conference a "success"; in reality, it revealed the impoverished thought of a black leadership forced to respond to the manifest failures of the Hoover administration's Depression policies. The 1920s had not prepared blacks any more than it had whites for the kinds of problems the Depression created; neither Garvey's black capitalism nor the Urban League's integrated capitalism made sense when capitalism itself had failed. What the "Negro needs is a definite economic program," stated the NAACP at its annual convention in 1932.[19] But not until the following year did the Association or other rights organizations begin to suggest the outlines of such a program.

In March 1933 the executive secretary of the National Urban League, Eugene Kinckle Jones, called upon the federal government to expand its efforts in public works, initiate a low-income housing program (to be funded through the Reconstruction Finance Corporation), and declare a moratorium on farm mortgages. Two months later, the Rosenwald-backed "Conference on the Economic Status of the Negro," noting that the "economic future of the Negro worker is linked with the economic future of American labor generally," urged not only the inclusion of blacks in the collective bargaining process and a just distribution of federal relief assistance, but

17. "Findings of the Negro Non-Partisan Conference," included in *ibid*.
18. *Ibid*. Prominent black leaders who attended the Conference were W.E.B. Du Bois, William Monroe Trotter, Robert L. Vann, and Howard University President Mordecai Johnson.
19. "The 23rd Conference, N.A.A.C.P.," *Crisis* 39 (July 1932), 219.

increased "social and economic planning" at every level of government.[20]

A similar wish for more planning by government was expressed in an NAACP memorandum issued to members of the organization's resolutions committee who met prior to the Association's convention scheduled for Chicago in July 1933. "The paramount concern of the Negro today is his economic status," read the statement; and with his fellow white workers, the Afro-American sought a "redistribution of wealth through systematic taxation of large incomes and the conduct of industry and government for the benefit of the many and not of the few." Further, black people required unemployment insurance and federal aid for their sick and elderly, "access without discrimination to all forms of education," and the "right to equal employment in private industry and in federal public works."[21]

What obviously encouraged black spokesmen and rights organizations to sharpen their demands for Negro people in 1933 was the election of Franklin D. Roosevelt and the reform legislation passed by the United States Congress. Like most Americans, blacks took a close look to see how they might fare with the new government in Washington. For some, the signs were clearly hopeful. In the November 1933 issue of the *Crisis*, one writer predicted that "in this New Deal the Negro has an unusual opportunity of getting in on the ground floor" and of "profiting by his past experiences of missing the country's bounties." The Depression, she concluded, might indeed be a blessing to the black man; by "correct vigilance and action," it was possible "for him to lift himself out of the category of the Forgotten Man by means of the New Deal."[22]

Some months earlier, a less optimistic, though still hopeful, interpretation of the New Deal was expressed by those who gathered at the estate of NAACP president Joel Spingarn. Convened as the Second Amenia Conference (an earlier one had taken place in 1916), black leaders sought not only to evaluate critically the "Negro's existing situation in American society" but also to chart possible new directions for the NAACP and black people. Like other racial conferences during the spring and summer of 1933, the Amenia

20. Pittsburgh *Courier*, Mar. 4, 1933, for reference to Jones; and "Findings Committee" report from Conference on Economic Status of the Negro, in letter of Charles S. Johnson to Walter White, June 19, 1933, NAACP Papers, File C-230.

21. "Memorandum in the Resolutions Committee," June 20, 1933, *ibid.*, File C-73.

22. Hazel W. Harrison, "The Status of the American Negro in the New Deal," *Crisis* 40 (Nov. 1933), 256, 262.

representatives affirmed the "unseparable" tie between white and black workers, arguing that what was required was a "new labor movement" devoted to organizing the "great mass of workers, skilled and unskilled, white and black." Though such a movement was never clearly outlined, one of its assumed goals was pressuring the federal government to expand its social and economic programs and to guarantee black involvement in those programs.[23]

In assessing what they believed constituted the three alternatives to the present political system—fascism, communism, and reform democracy—Negro spokesmen endorsed the last, therefore giving their support, if only indirectly, to New Deal reform. Yet they were clear in maintaining that no meaningful reform for either black or white could be forthcoming until "white paternalism in government" was eliminated. Thus, they held it to be "absolutely indispensable" that any "attempt of the government to control agriculture and industry" involve "adequate Negro representation on all boards and field staffs."[24]

By mid-1933, then, many black leaders were in agreement with white interracialists like Edwin Embree and Will Alexander that the "center" of action was the Roosevelt administration, and that whatever hope existed for Negro Americans rested in large part on their understanding what was happening in Washington and within the ever-increasing complex of departments and agencies to which the New Deal was giving birth. "Obviously the Negro had to be included," the NAACP's Roy Wilkins noted, but the question was "how was he going to be included and how was he going to be treated." [25] Two courses of action immediately presented themselves to Wilkins and blacks attending Amenia and other strategy sessions in 1933: to secure direct representation within the administration and to organize political pressure outside the government. In effect, the purpose of both strategies was the same—to influence New Deal policies and assure their relevance to black America's needs.

It was clear also that neither activity was exclusive of the other, since the success of one approach would often depend on the success of the other. But regardless of the approach, a new chapter in the black struggle for justice and equality in American life had emerged, and the overwhelming force behind it was the New Deal of Franklin D. Roosevelt.

23. "Youth and Age at Amenia," *Crisis* 40(Oct. 1933), 226-27.
24. *Ibid*. For general discussion of the Amenia Conference, see Ross, *J.E. Spingarn*, 178-85; Wolters, *Negroes and the Great Depression*, 219-29; and Bunche, "Programs, Ideologies, Tactics," Carnegie-Myrdal, 208-10.
25. Roy Wilkins, Columbia Oral History, 164.

SIX

Blacks in the New Deal

CONFRONTING THE PRIORITIES

I.

The black press and the NAACP strongly opposed, at least initially, the Roosevelt administration's selection of Clark Foreman to be black America's "adviser"; but they did not oppose the sentiment behind the nomination. In fact, most Negro leaders believed that their first priority was to gain a direct voice for the black perspective within the New Deal. Certainly, those attending the race gatherings in 1933 were in accord with the Amenia Conference's statement calling for "adequate Negro representation on all boards and field staffs" involving administration agencies and departments. And that representation was considered even more immediately critical given the rapidity with which the Congress passed, and Franklin D. Roosevelt signed, reform and recovery measures in early 1933. When Foreman assumed office in August, the National Recovery Administration, the Tennessee Valley Authority, the Civilian Conservation Corps, and the Federal Emergency Relief Administration were already established, and it was clear that keeping up with the proliferation of new federal "alphabet agencies" would be of crucial importance to blacks throughout the Roosevelt years.

By 1940, over 100 Negroes had served the New Deal in some appointive capacity. The idea of placing blacks in federal positions was not new (Republicans had selected Negro Americans for government jobs in the Treasury, the Post Office, and the diplomatic and consular services since Reconstruction days); but in the opinion of some, those chosen in the 1930s and 1940s were unique.[1] One writer has observed that "in the quality of their training and performance and in their numbers, the members of this group represented something new in the Administration of our national affairs."[2] Ralph J. Bunche, often critical of New Deal policies, wrote

1. Bunche, "Political Status of the Negro," Carnegie-Myrdal Study, 1359-78; Motz, "Black Cabinet," 8-10; Roi Ottley, *New World A-Coming": Inside Black America* (Cleveland, 1943), 256.
2. Lawrence, "Negro Organizations in Crisis," 216.

in 1939 that the "positions held under the New Deal represented a radical break with the past because of their novelty and the entirely different character of the appointee, as well as the method of appointment."[3]

What Bunche and others considered different was the background of many black New Dealers and their essentially nonpolitical appointment. The majority of blacks who came into the federal government in the 1930s and 1940s were middle-class; most were college graduates and highly trained professionals. Few had been involved in partisan politics or worked for the Democratic party prior to the thirties.[4] Of course political consideration was involved, since the presence of Negroes in the government provided the Roosevelt administration with a favorable image in the black community at a time when black votes were considered increasingly important. The nomination of Pittsburgh *Courier* editor and publisher Robert L. Vann as Assistant Attorney General clearly fit that interest. And Vann, who had made a dramatic shift in his political allegiances and worked for Roosevelt's election in 1932, assumed that part of his role in the administration would be to promote black political patronage.[5]

But most Negroes selected for New Deal service were chosen more for their ability to define issues relevant to the black community than to pay off political debts. Richard Bardolph has seen Robert Weaver as an "example of the highly trained expert" who was "drafted by a liberal administrator, in part as a concession to the Negro electorate, in part for his own qualifications, and retained by his proven worth." That characterized the majority of black officials who by the late 1930s were often referred to as the New Deal's "Black Brain Trust."[6]

3. Bunche, "Political Status of the Negro," 1361. For a similar interpretation, see Ottley, *"New World A-Coming,"* 254-58; Krislov, *The Negro in Federal Employment,* 23-25; Henry Lee Moon, *Balance of Power: The Negro Vote* (Garden City, N.Y., 1948), 28-30; Motz, "Black Cabinet," *passim,* esp. 25, 28-30, 60-61, 80-83. For a favorable view by a contemporary black, see Kelly Miller's comments in Pittsburgh *Courier,* July 17, 1934.

4. As was true for most blacks, many advisers considered themselves Republicans prior to 1932, including Mary McLeod Bethune and Forrester Washington; see Bunche, "Political Status of the Negro," 1440-50.

5. Buni, *Robert L. Vann,* 198-207, discusses this and Vann's general frustrations in realizing his patronage ambitions.

6. Bardolph, *The Negro Vanguard* (New York, 1959), 362. Support for that interpretation and its application to other black advisers is noted in Motz, "Black Cabinet," 23-30, and William A.H. Birnie, "Black Brain Trust," *The American Magazine* 135 (Jan. 1943), 26-37, 94-95.

Yet the New Deal's willingness to include the problems of Negroes within the spectrum of its social and economic reforms defined the circumstances that distinguished black appointees of the 1930s from those of an earlier time. Unlike the Reconstruction era or the 1960s, under Franklin Roosevelt's leadership the federal government did not champion civil rights legislation; nor did it publicly endorse racial desegregation. Instead, New Deal economic and class-oriented reform affirmed the ideal of an equal opportunity society. It was that ideal which pro-administration race liberals most often espoused and which many assumed included racial integration as its ultimate end, albeit not absolutely.

As has been noted, the unwillingness of liberal whites to commit themselves openly to integration and to oppose desegregation stemmed not from personal preference as much as from their fear of the possible political recriminations directed against blacks and their belief that race harmony might be realized by an active avoidance of racial confrontation. As attacks against them testified, the white interracialist approach did not always pacify unreconciled Negrophobes like Senator Theodore G. Bilbo or Governor Eugene Talmadge. Yet the unwillingness of the President to back publicly a federal anti-lynching bill, Eleanor Roosevelt's restrictive interpretation of "social equality," and the economic rationale given New Deal reforms did deflect possibly stronger criticisms aimed at the administration's racial assumptions.

In any event, the black New Dealer had to work within the existing political and ideological framework. For some Negroes, that posed little difficulty because they could accept the priorities such circumstances seemed to demand, or they were fortunate enough to be assigned to administrators who provided, as Ralph Bunche noted, the "latitude" to pursue their objectives.[7] Others, however, did not acquiesce so easily to their conditions of employment, and many did not enjoy support from their superiors. Nevertheless, all blacks had to operate within the limits of their officially defined positions as "race relations advisers."

From the perspective of the Roosevelt administration, the race adviser's primary function was providing information concerning the needs of the black community to federal agency or department heads and performing as public relations spokespersons for New Deal programs. The majority of blacks held strictly advisory responsibilities; few were actually accountable for carrying out government

7. Bunche, "Political Status of the Negro," 1455.

policy. Their ability to influence policy depended largely on the "liberality" of those they worked for and the authority and whatever abilities their superiors might possess in circumventing bureaucratic restrictions.[8]

Thus, even though it became standard New Deal practice by the early 1940s to include in each department or agency at least one black as a special "race adviser," the scope and purpose of the office was never uniformly agreed upon. In some cases, most notably in the Interior Department and the National Youth Administration, autonomous departments were created for blacks which even included small staffs. At the other extreme, the existence of a race adviser was looked upon by many agencies and departments as more a nuisance than a help. Edgar Brown, who served with the CCC, was given an office that consisted of a "panel placed across a space at the end of a corridor." Robert Vann claimed he was in the Justice Department a month "before they knew I was there," and it is possible that Vann never met his boss, Attorney General Homer Cummings, during his entire two years in Washington. Even the most resourceful and powerful black New Dealer found taxing the government's complex bureaucratic structure with its numerous chains of command and petty jurisdictional rivalries.[9]

Negro officials encountered other problems in their relationships with the black community. Since many Negroes saw them as their "race representatives," they often demanded that black New Dealers produce immediate and tangible results. Kelly Miller, for example, a well-known voice of moderation among the black intelligentsia, lauded those blacks appointed by 1934 as the "most intelligent and thoughtful group of colored men" that had ever been recruited to government service. But Miller cautioned that these "well trained and highly equipped Negro experts must shortly give an account of their stewardship or stand belittled, if not discredited, in the public estimation."[10]

One student has observed that the "ideal Negro leader is one who

8. Motz, "Black Cabinet," 19-20, 52-83; Bunche, "Political Status of the Negro," 1452-60; Moon, "Racial Aspects of Federal Public Relations Programs," 66-72; and especially for a discussion of bureaucratic structures, Ross, "Mary McLeod Bethune and the National Youth Administration," 1-28, *passim.*

9. Motz, "Black Cabinet," 62-73; Kifer, "The Negro Under the New Deal," 65; Bunche, "Political Status of the Negro,"1414-24. The Vann quote is from Buni, *Robert L. Vann,* 205. See also Ross, "Mary McLeod Bethune and the National Youth Administration,"13-28.

10. Pittsburgh *Courier*, July 7, 1934.

can appear to Negroes as absolutely uncompromising, and to whites as reasonable."[11] That has always been a difficult task, and in the Roosevelt years, given black New Dealers' limited authority and the enormous problems confronting their people, it was virtually impossible to achieve. Black advisers were caught frequently between the need to "give an account of their stewardship" and the "latitude" granted them by the government. Of course it was possible to use black community pressure to enhance their own influence in the administration, and many Negro New Dealers attempted to do just that. But the effectiveness of that tactic often depended on circumstances beyond their control, such as the organized nature of black community involvement and the understanding that community leaders possessed of government programs. Finally, what determined the value of the Negro adviser– administration relationship depended in part on how black officials interpreted their governmental objectives and the vision they held of the New Deal as a meaningful vehicle for black progress.

II.

An additional problem for those in government was the impermanence of their appointments, since most blacks were assigned jobs in emergency agencies such as the FERA, CCC, PWA, and WPA. By 1939 one fourth of the black appointees had left the New Deal and returned to private positions.[12] Interestingly enough, however, the two most prominent and influential Negro advisers, Mary McLeod Bethune and Robert Weaver, were chosen for posts in temporary agencies, and both remained in the administration until almost 1944. Obviously one reason for their lengthy tenure lay in the strong working relationships they had with their white supervisors. Bethune spent her entire time in the National Youth Administration, from 1935 until 1943, under the supervision of Aubrey Williams. Weaver, brought into the New Deal in 1933 by Clark Foreman, served respectively under Harold Ickes, Nathan Straus in the USHA, and Will Alexander in the Office of Production Management until he left the government in 1944.

In spite of differences in age, background, and involvement in the New Deal, Bethune and Weaver shared a number of basic assump-

11. Motz, "Black Cabinet," 74. See also Bardolph, *Negro Vanguard*, 140.
12. Bunche, "Political Status of the Negro," 1454.

tions. Both saw integration as the ultimate goal of black Americans and looked upon their own positions in government as designed, in part, to attain that goal. They also agreed on the need to provide immediate assistance to the black masses during the Depression and to ensure broader Negro participation in the planning and administration of the government's operations on national, state, and local levels. With Bethune as chairman and Weaver as vice chairman of an informal gathering of black advisers known as the Federal Council or the "Black Cabinet," they worked closely to coordinate Afro-American opinion both in and outside the New Deal.[13] They also kept close ties with certain black and interracial organizations through active memberships, attending meetings and conferences, and writing in publications such as *Crisis, Opportunity, the Journal of Negro Education*, and the *Journal of Negro History*. Such contacts served two functions: they allowed Weaver and Bethune to obtain knowledge of Negro opinion and needs (at least as determined by the organizations they consulted) and helped them articulate New Deal programs to the black population. In both connections, these two individuals performed an important service to white administrators like Ickes and Alexander, providing them with an indirect link to a segment of black America.

Mary Bethune also shared a number of attitudes with her white friends, Eleanor Roosevelt and Aubrey Williams; she believed, as did they, in the fundamental commitment of the New Deal to assist the black American's struggle and in the need for blacks to assume a number of responsibilities to help win that struggle. Unlike those of her white liberal associates, however, Bethune's ideas had evolved out of a long experience as a "race leader." Founder of a small black college in Florida patterned after the educational philosophy of Booker T. Washington, she had become widely known by 1935 as an organizer of black women's groups and as a civil and political rights activist. Deeply religious, certain of her own capabilities, she held a relatively uncluttered view of what she felt were the New Deal's and her own people's obligations to the cause of racial justice. Unafraid to speak her mind to powerful whites, including the President, or to differing black factions, she combined faith in the ultimate willing-

---

13. For reference to the Federal Council or "Black Cabinet," see Motz, "Black Cabinet," 22-23, 26-28; Bunche, "Political Status of the Negro," 1450; Rackham Holt, *Mary McLeod Bethune: A Biography* (New York, 1964), 197-99.

ness of whites to discard their prejudice and bigotry with a strong sense of racial pride and commitment to Negro self-help.[14]

No doubt much of her faith in the New Deal came from her friendship with Eleanor Roosevelt and other white officials. She referred to Aubrey Williams as one of her "favorite people" and "one of America's foremost fighting liberals who has made a very real contribution to the Negro's cause."[15] Mrs. Roosevelt, she believed, had "done more to better race relations and to give the 'human touch' to the affairs of state and the democratic struggle than any other woman."[16] With help from Williams and the First Lady, for whom she was a major source of understanding in the period, Bethune was one of the few Negroes to have any direct communication with the President. She later noted that between 1933 and 1945, she had met with FDR on the average of six or seven times a year.[17]

Because of Bethune's accessibility to the President and to other New Dealers, she was sought out as a spokesperson by administration blacks and by different Negro leaders, such as the NAACP's Walter White and John P. Davis of the National Negro Congress.[18] As a dominant figure in the "Black Cabinet," she was expected by other black advisers to transmit their ideas and suggestions to the President. In 1937 and 1939, she organized two major conferences on the "Problems of the Negro and Negro Youth" which were sponsored by the NYA; not only did she send copies of the conference report to FDR but she also included specific recommendations on how he might implement their proposals.[19] As head of the

---

14. On Bethune, see Sadie Iola Daniel, *Women Builders* (Washington, D.C., 1931), 79-106; Edwin Embree, *13 Against the Odds* (New York, 1944), 9-24; Holt, *Mary McLeod Bethune*; Emma Gelders Sterne, *Mary McLeod Bethune* (New York, 1947); Ross, "Mary McLeod Bethune and the National Youth Administration," 1-28 *passim*.

15. Bethune, "My Secret Talks with FDR," *Ebony* 4 (Apr. 1949), 42-51, reprinted in Bernard Sternsher, ed., *The Negro in Depression and War: Prelude to Revolution, 1930-1945* (Chicago, 1969), 59.

16. Bethune, "My Secret Talks," 61. For additional references to Bethune's relationship with Mrs. Roosevelt, see Eleanor Roosevelt, *The Autobiography of Eleanor Roosevelt* (New York, 1961); Lash, *Eleanor and Franklin*, 670, 681-83; Motz, "Black Cabinet," 67-68.

17. Bethune, "My Secret Talks," 63.

18. Indication of Mrs. Bethune's correspondence with numerous black leaders can be found in FDRL, "National Association for the Advancement of Colored People, 1933-1945," OF 2538 and PPF 4266; NAACP Papers, File C-63.

19. Bethune to FDR, Jan. 1937, Report of the *National Conference on the Problems of*

"Negro Affairs" section of the NYA, she traveled extensively around the country talking to black leaders and groups in numerous communities. Through these excursions and in articles she wrote for the Chicago *Defender* and the Pittsburgh *Courier*, she tried to bring the New Deal's accomplishments directly to the Negro population. Thus, in both her personal and professional relationship to the administration, she served as an important bond between blacks and the government.[20]

Bethune's faith in the New Deal was rooted in more than her personal relations with the President and his wife or her official position in the federal bureaucracy. She felt strongly that since black people constituted the lowest social and economic strata in society, they could begin to achieve upward mobility only through the help of a sympathetic national government. In one of her first meetings with FDR, she asserted that the black man could not "find his way to the opportunities that are opening unless he has someone to guide him."[21] Considering black people's oppression, she argued that even if New Deal social and economic reforms were not aimed primarily at their particular condition, they still warranted Negro support. In every respect, she wrote in 1938, the Negro was "the real 'sick man' of America" and thus in "need of every liberal program" designed to benefit the masses. Government was "of, for and by the people," and the "problems of the people are the problems of the Government." Any government which could "conscript in times of war" could provide for people "in times of economic stress and uncertainty."[22] The federal state might be limited, she acknowledged in 1933, in its ability to alter people's fundamental attitudes, but government policies did "influence thinking trends which develop attitudes."[23] A strong government was thus imperative in providing for the basic

---

the Negro and Negro Youth (Washington, D.C., 1937), and Bethune to FDR, Jan. 1939, *Proceedings of Second Conference*, 1939. Also see Bethune to FDR, "n.d.," included with memorandum, Bethune to Aubrey Williams, Oct. 17, 1939, NYA, Office of Negro Affairs, NARG 119.

20. Bethune wrote long reports of her visits to various black communities which were included in her newspaper columns for the *Defender* and *Courier*. Examples can be found in NYA, NARG 119, Box 637. See also George Philip Rawick, "The New Deal and Youth: The Civilian Conservation Corps, the National Youth Administration and the American Youth Congress" (Ph.D. diss., Univ. of Wisconsin, 1957), 242-43.

21. Quoted in Holt, *Mary McLeod Bethune*, 193.

22. Bethune, " 'I'll Never Turn Back No More!' " *Opportunity* 16 (Nov. 1938), 325.

23. Pittsburgh *Courier*, Mar. 4, 1933.

material requirements of black and white and in initiating programs that might shape new attitudes of tolerance and respect in the future.

In this and in other respects, Bethune's ideas paralleled the thought of white liberals. Particularly in her more optimistic moments, she believed that the New Deal could provide most of the tools blacks required to achieve their essential rights. In 1937 the *Literary Digest* quoted her as saying that "never in American history has the Negroes' future seemed so secure." Everywhere, she exclaimed, were signs of "great inter-racial understanding . . . a growing feeling on the part of ever-increasing numbers of white people that Negroes should have a larger participation in the civic program of the communities in which they live." The following year she wrote that "these are times of a great awakening and new opportunities for all; the spirit of democracy is being galvanized into realistic action." All the goals which Negroes sought had not been achieved, but "we are on our way"; it was truly a time of "our golden harvest." Even while criticizing the President and the administration for going too slow, she acknowledged black debts to New Deal reforms. In 1937 and 1939, in letters to Roosevelt accompanying reports detailing the federal government's shortcomings in providing aid to her people, she was careful to note "the many, many benefits" that had come to black Americans which they did not have before. They were, she assured Roosevelt, "grateful."[24]

With so many changes emanating from a sympathetic federal government, black people could not remain passive; in fact, the very success of the administration's programs depended on their active response. It was necessary for race leaders to "encourage our people to see the need for becoming more and more an integral part" of the progressive movement. "We must continually educate our people to the great benefits of our national progress so that we may cooperate with orderly social reform and social legislation rather than to the quicksands of revolution or the false promises of communism or fascism." Low-income housing, social security, aid to education, increased health facilities, and apprenticeship training were of tremendous value to blacks, who as a "definitely underprivileged people" had "everything to gain in a program of social reform."[25] To ensure their participation in the movement for social change, she

24. *Literary Digest* 123 (Mar. 6, 1937), 9; Bethune, " 'I'll Never Turn Back!' " 324; Bethune to FDR, with memorandum, Bethune to Williams, Oct. 17, 1939, NARG 119, and "Final Report, Division of Negro Affairs," 1943, *ibid*.

25. Bethune, " 'I'll Never Turn Back!' " 324-26. Also see Bethune, "Education

urged Negroes to assume a greater role in the political life of their own communities; they had to learn about political techniques and organization and prepare for leadership positions in the state and national governments. "In large measure," she noted, "the whole of our national life is directed by the legislation and other activities of our governmental units." Those who had achieved "through discipline and training a measure of culture" must become examples to others less fortunate than themselves; those who understood the movement for social change must fully identify with it and "interpret it to others."[26]

More than her liberal white friends, Bethune argued for a strong and direct black voice in initiating and shaping government policy. She pursued this in her conversations with FDR, in numerous memoranda to Aubrey Williams, and in her administrative work as head of NYA's Office of Negro Affairs.[27] With the assistance of Williams, she was successful in having blacks selected to NYA posts at the national, state, and local levels. But she also wanted a black presence throughout the federal government. It was "very necessary that something outstanding be done for my people," she wrote Williams in 1939, "to assure them of the gains" which they had achieved under the New Deal. She suggested the appointment of Negro judges in a number of northern states; more black chaplains and engineers in the CCC; representation in the FHA, the Home Owners' Loan Corporation, and the Social Security Administration; and the addition of a black woman to the Women's Bureau of the Department of Labor.[28] At the beginning of the war she joined other

---

and Negro Youth," *Proceedings of the Sixteenth Annual Conference of the Presidents of Negro Land Grant Colleges*, Nov. 1938, 61-62; "Certain Unalienable Rights," in Rayford W. Logan, ed. *What the Negro Wants* (Chapel Hill, 1944), 249-258; her remarks before the 1937 and 1939 conferences of the "Negro and Negro Youth," *Report . . . Conferences on the Problems of the Negro*, 1937, and *Proceedings of Second Conference*, 1939, 31-33.

26. Bethune, "Certain Unalienable Rights," 257; 255-56.

27. See correspondence, Division of Negro Affairs, NYA, NARG 119; also Kifer, "Negro Under the New Deal," 83-85; Rawick, "New Deal and Youth," 234-35; Motz, "Black Cabinet," 36-39; Ross, "Mary McLeod Bethune and the National Youth Administration," 6, 22.

28. Kifer, "The Negro Under the New Deal," 77-83; Bunche, "Political Status of the Negro," Carnegie-Myrdal Study, 1421-24. Ross, "Mary McLeod Bethune and the National Youth Administration," 14-24, indicates Williams' support of Bethune but also his continued doubts regarding the Division of Negro Affairs, which he feared would give support to segregationist sentiment. Comment in Bethune to Williams, NARG 119.

black leaders in demanding appointments to the Selective Service Board and to the Department of Army, and she was instrumental in 1941 in securing Earl Dickerson's membership on the Fair Employment Practices Committee.[29] By 1944, she was still making appeals for black representation in "all public programs, federal, state and local" and "in policy-making and administrative posts as well as rank and file jobs."[30]

Because the Roosevelt administration refused to challenge southern segregation directly, Bethune and other black advisers were forced to accept a "separate but equal" philosophy in order to gain federal assistance for blacks in the South. On the grounds that more money meant additional jobs for Negroes and greater opportunities for quality education, Mrs. Bethune thus supported the NYA's separate southern educational and youth programs.[31] And she was able to persuade a reluctant Aubrey Williams to establish a Special Negro Fund, which she personally administered, providing financial resources to many black students. Over a seven-year period, she spent some $610,000 aiding nearly 4,000 Negro undergraduates and graduates and increasing salary levels of black elementary and grammar school teachers.[32] Certainly aware that her activities did not alter the segregated status of blacks, Bethune held that federal aid would further the cause of integration in the future by providing black youth with critical skills and training. In the Northern cities, NYA money was enormously important in the survival of community schools and youth programs which were devastated by the Depression.[33]

Nevertheless, despite her forceful personality, support from Aubrey Williams, and personal contacts within the administration, Bethune came up against considerable difficulty in her endeavors to help her people. Though blacks were appointed to administrative

29. See ER to Bethune, Feb. 2, 1941; Bethune to ER, Mar. 4, 1941, ER Papers, Box 1589.

30. Bethune, "Certain Unalienable Rights," 253.

31. Ross, "Mary McLeod Bethune and the National Youth Administration," 6, 12-13. See also Kifer, "The Negro Under the New Deal," 136-38; Rawick, "The New Deal and Youth," 231-38.

32. Kifer, "The Negro Under the New Deal," 136-38; Rawick, "The New Deal and Youth," 250.

33. Melvin Reubin Maskin, "Black Education and the New Deal" (Ph.D. diss., New York Univ., 1973), argues that in a number of major northern cities, including New York, Philadelphia, and Chicago, the NYA's contribution to black education and black youth was considerable.

positions throughout the NYA system, they never gained representation commensurate with their numbers, nor were they paid salaries equal to their white couterparts. As was frequently the case in other government agencies and departments, local NYA committees, which were crucial in implementing Youth Administration programs, remained white-dominated, particularly in the South.[34] And as hard as Bethune struggled to see that black concerns were brought to her personal attention, white state and local administrators, often with support from national officers, bypassed her and reported directly to their immediate superiors. That was also true for black NYA officials, who felt pressure from whites not to communicate with the Division of Negro Affairs. A recent study of Bethune's experience with the Youth Administration indicates little evidence that "Negro state assistants regularly corresponded, either officially or unofficially, with Mrs. Bethune or her division."[35]

With other black New Deal advisers whose authority was considerably less than hers, Bethune also found the government's bureaucratic structure a serious impediment to her effectiveness as an administrator. Assuring blacks an equitable portion of federal funds and access to important NYA programs was made even more difficult, in view of the prevailing system, when there did not exist strong pressure from black communities. The result then, according to one student's careful analysis of her activities, was that despite her pragmatic acceptance of "separate but equal" benefits, Bethune often had to accept "less than equal consideration for her people."[36]

Frustrated by the personal obstacles she was forced to confront and by the persistence of racial hostilities in American life, Bethune's optimism at times gave way to bitterness. In 1938, addressing the Association for the Study of Negro Life and History, which she served as president for a number of years, she exclaimed that black Americans cried out like

> . . . children lost in the wilderness. Hemmed in by a careless world, we are losing our homes and our farms and our jobs. We see vast numbers of us on the land sunk into the degradation of peonage and virtual slavery. In the cities, our workers are barred from the unions, forced to "scab" and often to fight with their lives for work. About us cling the evertightening tentacles of poor wages, economic insecurity, sordid homes, labor by

34. Ross, "Mary McLeod Bethune and the National Youth Administration," 13-20.
35. *Ibid.*, 25.
36. *Ibid.*, 13.

women and children, broken homes, ill health, delinquency and crime. Our children are choked by denied opportunity for health, for education, for work, for recreation, and thwarted with their ideas and ambitions still a-borning. We are scorned of men; they spit in our faces and laugh. We cry out in this awesome darkness.[37]

Later, noting the Detroit and Harlem riots in 1943, she wrote in Rayford Logan's collection *What the Negro Wants* that there was "rumbling of anger and resentment impelled by all the anger and all the resentment of all colored Americans in all black ghettos in all cities in America—the resentment against the mistreatment of Negroes in uniform, against restriction and oppression and discrimination."[38] Racial tension existed in the United States because of the "growing internal pressure of the Negro masses to break through the wall of restriction which restrains them from full citizenship" and the "unwillingness of white America to allow any appreciable breach" in that wall. The immediate cause of racial conflict in 1943 and 1944, she felt, resulted from the treatment of black armed servicemen, from the "failure of their government to protect and provide" for them, and from the "frustrated efforts of Negroes to find a place in war production." Yet such frustrations were simply part of the nation's "historical hangover, . . . a product of the half-hearted and timorous manner in which we have traditionally faced the Negro problem in America." Even when the American people did recognize that the black man was hungry and in need of food, because he was a Negro, "they suggest that a half meal will suffice." This was clearly unsatisfactory, and in 1944 she called for the federal government, led by the President, to "initiate a sound program carried out through appropriate federal agencies to indicate the importance of race" and for the news media to "replace caricature and slander with realistic interpretations of sound racial relations"; she pressed for integration into the armed forces, full protection of civil rights, "universal adult suffrage," expansion of federal programs in health, social security, education, and relief, and the elimination of union discrimination through strong government controls.[39]

Bethune thus indicated considerable dissatisfaction when she believed the pace of black progress was too slow or when she felt white leaders and the government were not extending the necessary help

37. Bethune, "Clarifying Our Vision with the Facts," *Journal of Negro History* 23 (Jan. 1938), 11.
38. Bethune, "Certain Unalienable Rights," 249.
39. *Ibid.*, 250-51, 253-56.

and assistance required to aid the cause of black liberation. Although she cautioned Negroes to be more patient and understanding in their insistence on equality, she nevertheless as a sensitive black woman and race leader reacted forcefully when she felt that Negro patience had been tried beyond its logical and humane bounds. She constantly affirmed the need for Roosevelt and the New Deal to do "something very outstanding" in order for blacks to sustain their hope. To inspire greater black faith was one of the reasons she traveled so extensively to black communities, carrying the message of the NYA's contributions.

But even in her moments of despair, Bethune never lost hope that Franklin Roosevelt might ultimately launch "bold offensives against bigotry and Jim Crow everywhere."[40] She was willing, therefore, to accept certain compromises and partial solutions that someone with less faith than hers might have found difficult to reconcile. Bethune was one of the few black New Dealers, for example, who openly supported A. Philip Randolph's March on Washington in 1940. But once FDR issued his FEPC order, she was unwilling to sanction any further action. In 1941 she wrote Mrs. Roosevelt that she was "happy that we were able to ward off the March on Washington," and she praised the President's FEPC order as the most "memorable day" since Lincoln signed the Emancipation Proclamation.[41]

Bethune looked for symbols to inspire black confidence in the government; and the FEPC, she believed, represented an important commitment by the administration—"something" blacks could look to for hope. She was highly sensitive to any movement that could jeopardize what she considered to be Negro gains under the New Deal or that could give comfort to those unsympathetic to the cause of racial justice. In October 1939 she told Aubrey Williams that she hesitated to call a third conference on the "Problems of the Negro and Negro Youth" until the administration took "immediate action . . . upon recommendations of the two preceding conferences."[42] If early proposals were not implemented, she observed, black New Dealers would be forced to "answer many embarrassing questions which are already being posed by persons who look to us for guidance and leadership." To call a third conference under such condi-

40. Bethune, "My Secret Talks," 56.

41. Bethune to ER, July 10, 1941, ER Papers, Box 1589. For discussion of her involvement with the March and the FEPC, see Herbert Garfinkel, *When Negroes March: The March on Washington Movement in the Organizational Politics for FEPC* (Glencoe, Ill., 1959), 38; Motz, "Black Cabinet," 46-47, 94.

42. Memorandum, Bethune to Williams, Oct. 17, 1939, NARG 119.

tions, particularly on the eve of a national election, was unwise; already, she told Williams, the Republican National Committee in charge of the Negro press was focusing attention "upon the deficiencies" pointed to in the first two conferences. "We do not have sufficient ground to stand upon," she concluded, "to ward off the bombardment from the opposition. They see clearly the inadequacies in the numerous federal departments. If we can get something outstanding done for the Negro, it will furnish us with ammunition which we do not now have."[43]

Though recognizing the weakness in the Roosevelt administration's response to Negro needs, Mary Bethune ultimately emerged as a black partisan champion of the New Deal during the 1930s and 1940s. Her strong advocacy of administration policies and programs was predicated on a number of factors: her assessment of the low status of black Americans during the Depression years; her faith in the willingness of some liberal whites to work for the inclusion of blacks in the government's reform and recovery measures; her conviction that only massive federal aid could lift the Negro from the depths of his economic and social degradation; and her belief that the thirties and forties were producing a more self-aware and self-assured black population. Like a number of her white friends in the government, Bethune assumed that the preservation of democracy and black people's "full integration into the benefits and the responsibilities" of American life were inextricably tied together. Where whites believed it necessary to expand the general basis of equality, primarily economic, to assure Afro-Americans ultimate participation, Bethune emphasized as the first necessity the winning of equal opportunity specifically for blacks, assuming that if this were accomplished, greater equality for the rest of the population would follow. She was convinced that, with the help of a friendly government, a militant, aggressive "New Negro" would emerge out of the devastation of depression and war.[44] It would be this "New Negro" who would "save America from itself," who would lead America toward the full realization of its democratic ideas. Thus, although she placed

43. *Ibid.* Ralph J. Bunche argues that Emmett J. Scott, who was a delegate to both NYA conferences, was indeed using the conference's "criticisms as Republican propaganda"; see Bunche, "Political Status of the Negro," 1451.

44. Bethune, "The New Negro," *Interracial Review* 15 (July 1942), 106. August Meier notes how the "New Negro" theme has been a familiar feature of black thought since the late 19th century, *Negro Thought in America*, 256-60, 270-71, 277-78. For a creative analysis of this same theme, see Fullinwider, *Mind and Mood of Black America, passim.*

a different priority on the role of blacks in the struggle for the "New Democracy" compared with her white supporters, she nevertheless agreed with them regarding the basic outlines of that struggle. Assuming that racial progress and New Deal progress were interdependent, she remained loyal to the administration while she strove to convince others that American democracy could not be preserved with a population "nine-tenths free and one-tenth oppressed."

Robert Weaver, almost forty years younger than his female black colleague, chose like Bethune to work for blacks within the existing political system. In respect to his holding significant administrative posts and in the autonomy and influence he acquired in the 1930s and 1940s, he was probably the most powerful black adviser in the New Deal.[45]

In contrast to Bethune, Weaver came from an urban middle-class background and was educated in the finest schools, earning his Ph.D. degree in economics from Harvard University, where he was a fellow student of William Hastie and Ralph Bunche. Weaver's involvement with New Deal policies began outside the government, however, when he and John P. Davis organized the Negro Industrial League and later merged it with the Joint Committee on National Recovery. With Davis, Weaver appeared on behalf of Negroes at early NRA wage and hour hearings, arguing for fairer treatment of black workers and attacking specifically wage differentials based on race.[46] In November 1933 Clark Foreman announced Weaver's appointment as his chief assistant to the Interior Department. In accepting the offer, Weaver noted that he was leaving the Joint Committee not out of dissatisfaction with its role but because of his belief that he could provide better service to black people within the administration.[47]

Throughout his ten-year stint with the New Deal, Weaver restricted his service to two major black concerns—housing and employment. From 1935, after Foreman left, until 1938, he was Harold

45. See, for instance, Bunche, "Political Status of the Negro," 1414-18; Motz, "Black Cabinet," 13-14, 17, 20, 22, 27-28, 45; Kifer, "The Negro Under the New Deal," 230-32. For biographical data on Weaver, see *Current Biography* (1961), 474-76, and "National Defense Labor Problems: The Weaver Appointment," *Crisis* 47 (Oct. 1940), 319.

46. Wolters, *Negroes and the Great Depression*, 110-11; "The Negro Industrial League," undated ms., NNC Papers, NYPL (Schomburg Collection), Box 1. The Industrial League was the forerunner of the Joint Committee and was organized by John P. Davis and Robert Weaver.

47. Pittsburgh *Courier*, Nov. 18, 1933.

Ickes' chief racial assistant in Interior and PWA. In 1938, he joined the newly created United States Housing Authority as its race relations adviser. During the war, from 1940 to 1942, he was an adviser in the labor division of the Office of Production Management. Later he became chief of Negro Employment and Training in the labor branch of the War Production Board and finally, from 1943-44, director of the Negro Manpower Service for the War Manpower Commission. He left the government in 1944 to become executive director of the Chicago Mayor's Committee on Race Relations.

Weaver perceived his role as an adviser during this time in somewhat more limited terms than did Mrs. Bethune. Although with his friend and colleague William Hastie he helped force the integration of the Interior Department's lunchroom facilities, he was never the political or civil rights activist of the Bethune type.[48] Seldom did he express himself on the subject of the "Negro problem" in the sweeping, moralistic manner for which she was noted; nor did he reflect her extreme states of euphoric optimism or bitter disillusionment. Weaver's strength was his efficiency and self-control. His friend Will Alexander considered him a "first-class administrator," extremely cooperative, a man "with no emotional or other racial biases."[49] Weaver made his appeal not to the moral conscience of America but to its rationality. Statistics were his weapon, whether he was writing about the nature of black housing or labor conditions for essentially Negro audiences in *Crisis* and *Opportunity*, or for a wider readership in the *Journal of Political Economy*. One of his most lasting contributions while in the New Deal was the publication of a two-volume study on the *Urban Negro Worker in the United States, 1925-1936*, which along with his numerous later analyses became an important statistical source for future government and scholarly reference to black labor conditions.[50]

Weaver's concentration on housing and employment problems did not stem entirely from the fact that they were the two most pressing and obvious issues confronting blacks in the Depression and war years nor from his background as a trained economist. These two areas were, for Weaver, the keys to all the other problems

---

48. Birnie, "Black Brain Trust," 95.

49. Alexander to E.X. Mohr, Feb. 2, 1946, Rosenwald Fund Archives, Box 132.

50. Herbert R. Northrup's study on *Organized Labor and the Negro* (New York, 1944), was especially indebted to Weaver's work, published by the Department of Interior in 1939. Many of Weaver's articles written in the 1930s and 1940s were included in his books, *Negro Labor* (1946) and *The Negro Ghetto* (1948).

confronting the black population; dealing successfully with them would represent a solution to the "Negro problem."[51] The history of black oppression in America could be clearly understood in the statistical data which showed the exclusion of blacks from decent jobs and housing. The Depression, he argued, had simply underlined the already marginal level of Negro existence.[52] Prior to 1929, blacks had been employed primarily as unskilled laborers, domestics, and tenant farmers; what gains they had made since World War I were destroyed by the collapse of 1929. Traditionally assigned the most menial employment tasks in both the South and North and excluded from labor organizations by the AFL, Afro-Americans had become fundamentally separated from the economic mainstream of American life.[53] Without adequate jobs, they had little choice except to live in the most undesirable dwellings, where ill health, delinquency, and crime were inevitable. Even worse, such segregation historically undermined black people's hope of ever obtaining the skills, work, and living habits required to make it in an increasingly industrialized and urbanized society.[54]

Weaver saw the New Deal's importance in terms of its potential for transforming and helping uplift the status of black Americans. The integration of Negroes into the American economic system, through expanded federally financed employment and housing opportunities, would not only create a better environment for developing necessary skills among blacks and facilitating their entry into a growing industrial society, it would also improve the climate of race relations. The low standard of living for Negroes in America had more than an economic implication; it tended to affirm in white minds the general undersirability of all black people. The more

51. See particularly Weaver, "The New Deal and the Negro: A Look at the Facts," *Opportunity* 13 (July 1935), 200-03; "An Experiment in Negro Labor," *Opportunity* 14 (Oct. 1936), 295-98; "Training Negroes for Occupational Opportunities," *Journal of Negro Education* 7 (Oct. 1938), 486-87; "The Negro in a Program of Public Housing," *Opportunity* 16 (July 1938), 198-203; "Racial Policy in Public Housing," *Phylon* 1 (Second Quarter 1940), 149-57; "Federal Aid, Local Control and Negro Participation," *Journal of Negro Education* 11 (Jan. 1942), 47-59.

52. Weaver, "The New Deal and the Negro," 200; "With the Negro's Help," *Atlantic Monthly* 169 (June 1942), 697; *Negro Labor*, 8-15.

53. Weaver, "The New Deal and the Negro," 200; "Defense Industries and the Negro," *The Annals* 223 (Sept. 1942), 60; "Recent Events in Negro Union Relationships," *Journal of Political Economy* 52 (Sept. 1944), 235; "The Efficiency of Negro Labor," *American Federationist* 41 (Dec. 1934), 1327-31.

54. Weaver, "The Negro in a Program of Public Housing," 199; "Training Negroes," 497; "Defense Industries and the Negro," 60; "War-Time Employment Gains," *Negro Digest* 2 (May 1944) 33-34.

blacks remained restricted from actual participation in business, labor, and government, the more white people were convinced that every black was lazy and shiftless. The worst feature of the wage differential, Weaver noted in 1934, was that it encouraged the "tendency to judge all Negroes by the least able colored person." A "racial differential" signified that industrial efficiency was "based on race, and [that] the individual black worker—because he is a Negro—is less efficient." This blanket characterization of an entire group was the "most damnable feature of racial prejudice in America."[55]

In this connection, Weaver believed that the racist policies of the AFL in excluding Negroes from the trade unions had simply strengthened in the minds of white workers the feeling that every black laborer was unqualified and inefficient. But, in reality, it had been the existence of organized labor's exclusionist posture that was largely responsible for undermining the early skilled status of black workers prior to the late nineteenth century.[56] One could not judge Negroes by white standards when the opportunities were not the same for both groups. Since "Negro workers do not enjoy equal working conditions in American industry," Weaver wrote in the *American Federationist*, there was not "direct evidence to refute or prove this assertion of relative inefficiency." Black workers' efficiency and productivity, he reminded labor, varied "in proportion to the favorableness of their working conditions."[57]

The same principle applied elsewhere. In supporting federally financed low-income housing, Weaver maintained that the "whole theory behind public housing is that the individual is affected greatly by his environment. Not only does the person develop more fully if he is given better surroundings, but society benefits because a better citizen is produced. . . . To stress environmental factors is to open new doors of opportunity and hope to colored Americans."[58]

If the federal government provided a better environment for black equal opportunity, it would help remove some of the obvious symbols with which whites rationalized racial inferiority, and it would give black people a new desire to raise their own standards of living. This sense of black hope was especially necessary in light of

55. Weaver, "A Wage Differential Based on Race," *Crisis* 41 (Aug. 1934), 238; see also "War-Time Employment Gains," 33-34.
56. "With the Negro's Help," 697.
57. "The Efficiency of Negro Labor," 1327, 1330.
58. "The New Deal and the Negro," 200.

the changes occurring in American society in the thirties and forties. The "urbanization of Negroes," Weaver pointed out in 1938, involved the development of entirely "new occupational patterns." This called for "new skills and new expression of old ones," for the entrance of blacks at the "bottom of the industrial ladder and the perfection of methods which facilitated advancement." World War II provided such an opportunity, and it was "important that the Negro worker feel that his services are wanted." The black man, like any one else, "must have faith and belief in his opportunity to participate so that he will be eager for training and will be anxious to go into war industries." That faith was as significant in peacetime as it was when the nation was at war; the greatest threat to democracy existed when a minority believed they were not wanted.[59]

Years of feeling unwanted, of being relegated to the lowest levels of American social and economic life, had produced certain effects within the Afro-American community. Writing in 1963, Weaver argued that a black "sub-culture" had been created as a result of generations of existing "outside the mainstream of our society" with little hope of entering.[60] That "sub-culture" often gave expression to a "lack of motivation and . . . anti-social behavior," and in 1944 he observed that "in our society the deficiencies of the black worker" would continue to "haunt him in the future."[61] It was necessary to realize, he later stated, that America was a "middle-class society and those who fail to evidence most of its values and behavior are headed toward difficulties."[62] But, at the same time, it was equally important to recognize that no people, traditionally assigned to an "inferior status," could be expected overnight to assume middle-class values and behavior. The "current deficiencies of the Negro worker," Weaver wrote toward the end of the war, were "largely the result of his experiences in a society dominated by white America; and any effective program for improving [his] habits must address itself to modifying this society." It was perhaps possible, as many argued, for Negroes who had achieved certain middle-class standards to be examples to others of their race. Yet it was far more important in the long run that America provide the black masses with a meaningful

59. "Training Negroes," 497, and "With the Negro's Help," 706.
60. "The Negro As an American," *Center for the Study of Democratic Institutions* (1963), reprinted in Ned E. Hoopes, ed., *Who Am I? Essays on the Alienated* (New York, 1969), 95, 98.
61. "War-Time Employment Gains," 34, and "The Negro As an American," 98.
62. "The Negro As an American," 95-96.

stake in the system, with a real sense of economic and social security. No program for improving the black condition would be successful until it was recognized "why people act the way they do." What was essential was a campaign "designed to give new hope and higher aspirations to colored citizens." It was a project, he concluded in 1944, "for white and black America to accomplish together; neither can do it alone."[63]

These ideas, expressed in the period after Weaver's ten-year service with the New Deal, give some indication of the philosophical basis for many of his earlier activities and his rationale as to the importance of Negroes working within the federal government. For Weaver, black and white habits and values were deeply embedded throughout American life: traditional economic segregation reinforced the social and political separation of the races. The Depression served to illuminate the depth of black destitution and increase the urgency for immediate black assistance. The only institution capable under these circumstances of responding to the conditions of black people, he believed, was the federal government. Only the national state possessed the power and the machinery required to modify social institutions and provide blacks and other minorities with the material and spiritual aid necessary to assure their ultimate integration into the American mainstream. Private action, whether it emanated from white or black communities, was simply impotent to overcome the depth and the complexity of the problems confronting Negro Americans. In line with his various duties as race relations adviser during the 1930s and 1940s, Weaver did strive to persuade private business and labor organizations to expand opportunities for blacks, and in addition he encouraged Negroes to organize within their own communities and establish meaningful programs of self-help.

But these activities were considered supplementary to actions taken by the New Deal; the initiative for change, the programs, and the execution of those programs had to originate in the federal government. For this reason, Weaver believed it was particularly important that blacks be consulted in developing government policies affecting the lives of black people. He was not always happy with the efforts of the New Deal in this regard. In 1940 he noted that too often the Negro, having been excluded from policy planning, found himself "shunted from the main line. He has little voice in administration and development of the activity and often receives

63. "War-Time Employment Gains," 33-34.

126

.

but paltry benefits. The opportunity to feel that he is an essential factor has been denied him." Thus, in many areas, programs that reached the black were "usually brought to him by persons working for him rather than by persons working cooperatively with him." It was "little wonder that the Negro's response is frequently less than enthusiastic."[64]

The significance of having black advisers like Weaver in the New Deal rested with their being able to influence federal programs which took in the "needs and specific problems" of black people. "Social programs initiated or supported by the Federal Government," he pointed out, "must involve racial policy." What might appear as "no racial policy" was "in fact, a most dangerous one, since it frequently implies ignoring colored Americans. The Negro is too often not considered an integral part of the body politic."[65] The racial labor quotas established by the PWA were an example of sound racial planning. In this instance, the federal government had "done more than make a gesture in the direction of effectively preventing discriminations against colored workers. Here is a program which does not correct an abuse after the project is completed—as is usually the case when Negroes' rights are being protected—but . . . sets up a criterion which is *prima facie* evidence of discrimination."[66]

What increased the importance of the labor quota program was not only its ability to open up certain jobs for blacks but also its potential for establishing policy which could be utilized in the future to modify the traditional labor practices of private employers and unions.[67] In an essay in 1937 on the "Value of Federal Employment to Negroes," Weaver maintained that the employment of blacks in every phase of federal service, but particularly in public works, was extremely important "principally because of its numerical possibilities for directly affording occupational opportunities and because of its values in establishing precedents for other employers throughout the nation."[68] Summarizing the housing policies of the New Deal in 1942, he asserted that the PWA and the USHA had shown how it was

64. "Racial Policy in Public Housing," 149. See also "Federal Aid, Local Control," 58-59.
65. "Racial Policy in Public Housing," 149, and "Federal Aid, Local Control," 59.
66. "An Experiment in Negro Labor," 298. See also Kruman, "Quotas for Blacks," 37-49.
67. "The New Deal and the Negro," 202-3; "An Experiment in Negro Labor," 295-98; "Want a Job in Housing?" *Opportunity* 17 (Mar. 1939), 73.
68. "The Value of Federal Employment to Negroes," *Opportunity* 15 (Apr. 1937), 107.

possible for government agencies to "establish effective safeguards for Negro labor"; mechanisms could be created which would "facilitate employment for colored skilled workers and not destroy unions in the building trades."[69]

Based on his assessment of the black condition and the responsiveness of agencies like the PWA and the USHA, Weaver concluded in 1946 that the New Deal did have a "profound effect upon the economic status of Negroes." Despite "certain discriminations" by the relief agencies, the FERA and the WPA had "benefited hundreds of thousands of colored Americans." A more significant New Deal legacy "was the fact that vast numbers of Negroes were enabled to retain work habits and a minimum of health as a result of federal aid. Programs of the National Youth Administration and the Civilian Conservation Corps had similar effects upon Negro youth." Even the much-criticized NRA, he argued, "had its good influences." Although some displacement of black workers occurred, the "extent of it was much less than had been prophesied, since in the average establishment it is expensive and troublesome to replace a group of workers who have been employed for some time. More important, however, was the fact that NRA initiated a trend toward weakening the wage differentials based on race."[70] Earlier, in 1935, appraising the New Deal's two-year contribution to blacks in housing, employment, and education, he concluded that there had occurred a "definite break from the status quo in governmental activity, method and policy." As far as it represented "an extension of governmental activity into the economic sphere," the New Deal was "a departure which can do much to reach the Negro citizens."[71]

It was what he considered the "break from the status quo in governmental activity" and its "extension . . . into the economic sphere" which therefore ultimately determined Weaver's favorable assessment of the New Deal and his continued loyalty to it during the 1930s and 1940s. The central problem confronting Negro people was economic in nature and national in scope; only the federal government, through wise and conscious planning, could overcome that problem. Yet the success of this for Weaver, as well as for other black advisers who shared his ideas, rested on a number of considerations which they did not always have control over. Whether the federal government pursued policies that actually assisted blacks

69. "Federal Aid, Local Control," 58, and "Experiment in Negro Labor," 298.
70. *Negro Labor*, 14.
71. "The New Deal and the Negro," 201, 202.

depended in part on whether those policies took into account the "needs and specific problems" of black people. Because its power was so extensive, government could do even more harm to the black community's welfare by following ill-conceived policies than by taking no action at all. Weaver noted this possibility himself in discussing the expansion of low-income housing projects in black ghettos, observing that it would "not be easy to change the type of racial occupancy if a definite pattern of separate facilities has been established, for such a pattern creates vested interests which resist change."[72]

Moreover, a situation which allowed the federal government to finance segregated low-income housing could not be avoided simply by having in the administration black advisers with some influence and responsibility. That might help, but other factors were involved which complicated the efforts of New Deal blacks like Weaver. Confronted in the thirties with demands from the black community for immediate relief, Weaver, like Bethune, accepted the necessity of supporting certain emergency programs on a segregated basis in order to assure Negroes some "equity" in the New Deal recovery program. But he was extremely conscious of the possible long-term ill effects of this approach. In arguing against fellow blacks who believed racial differentials were necessary to maintain black employment in many southern industries, he pointed out that much more was involved than simply "arresting . . . Negro displacement. In it are elements which combine to establish the whole industrial position of colored Americans." Institutionalizing wage and hour differentials through NRA codes would "brand black workers as a less efficient and submarginal group"; it would "increase . . . ill-will and friction between white and colored workers," destroy any possibility of ever forming "a strong and effective labor movement in the nation," and ultimately "relegate Negroes into a low wage caste and place the federal stamp of approval upon their being in such a position."[73]

Weaver feared any policy that tended to put a "federal stamp of approval" on the separation of blacks from the dominant institutions of American society. There was always that possibility, of course, if

---

72. "Racial Policy in Public Housing," 156. Charles Abrams, *Forbidden Neighbors: A Study of Prejudice in Housing* (New York, 1955), argues that Weaver's earlier fears were fully realized, as New Deal housing programs in effect expanded residential segregation. See also Wye, "The New Deal and the Negro Community," 621-39.

73. Weaver, "Wage Differential Based on Race," 238.

care was not taken at the highest levels of government planning and if black people refused to accept Weaver's thesis that at times their immediate and long-term needs were not always identical. There were occasions when the nonsegregation goals of Weaver and other black advisers ran directly into conflict with Negroes who sought, under any conditions, better housing and more jobs.[74]

Yet even when guidelines were established for black participation in administration reform and recovery measures, Weaver maintained that much of the final success rested on the response of the black community. The full achievement of black integration in federal housing and employment programs depended on whether "local leadership assumes its responsibilities, cooperates with local authorities and fights to protect the Negro's participation."[75] And that depended in large degree on the unified strength of local blacks, on their awareness of federal programs, and on their ability to assume leadership in ensuring the "Negro's participation."

Along with his attempt to translate complex federal programs to the black rank and file so they might then take advantage of them, Weaver maintained close communication with organizations like the NAACP, the National Urban League, and the Rosenwald Fund. On occasion, he appealed to his friends outside the government to assist the passage of some program he considered of particular benefit to Negroes by encouraging a strong public response on its behalf. In February 1935, for example, he asked those at Rosenwald to have civil rights organizations and prominent individuals in the community write Harold Ickes urging him "to make it mandatory for contractors on the Federal Housing Projects in Chicago . . . to hire skilled and unskilled Negroes."[76]

Robert Weaver left the Roosevelt administration in 1944 believing that he no longer had any real influence as a racial adviser.[77] Yet he continued to support the New Deal because he was convinced that black equal opportunity was possible only through the kind of government intervention the New Deal represented. Unlike many,

74. Motz, "Black Cabinet," *passim*, discusses this and other conflicts.
75. Weaver, "Federal Aid, Local Control," 47.
76. Memo, Feb. 8, 1935, Rosenwald Fund Archives, Box 152.
77. Motz, "Black Cabinet," 32, quoting a black colleague of Weaver's, states that Weaver left the War Manpower Commission because he was " 'being enmeshed in the maze of irrelevant, unimportant functions' by Commissioner Paul McNutt and embroiled in disagreement with the Fair Employment Practices Committee regarding techniques, policies and divisions of responsibilities, and felt increasingly hopeless in the face of the growing power of congressional opponents."

he had faith that the existing political system could accomplish what he felt were the long-term objectives of Negro Americans. But success or failure in this regard was never entirely in Weaver's hands; it depended on the ability of federal policies to alter traditional customs and habits of both white and black and on the development within the black community of an understanding that New Deal programs were not ends in themselves but simply the starting point from which they might build a better life.

III.

Not every black New Dealer was able to share the optimism of Bethune or Weaver as to the administration's real or potential benefit to black America. For some race advisers, the Negro's relationship to the expanding welfare state and the Democratic party of Roosevelt created new problems that posed a serious threat to the immediate and future status of their people.

When Robert L. Vann arrived in Washington in 1933, he was filled with the sense of his past contributions to race progress and certain that those contributions had finally received a just recognition. He looked to his new position with the Justice Department as an opportunity to ensure for Negro Americans a prominent place in Roosevelt's New Deal and within the Democratic party. Yet after two years the publisher and editor of the influential black weekly, the Pittsburgh *Courier*, was disillusioned with life in the nation's capital, and in early 1936 he officially resigned from the government. Vann's experience offers an interesting contrast to that of Bethune and Weaver, not just because of the brevity of his New Deal affiliation but because of the political reasons which led the black journalist to break with the administration.

Politics was central to Vann's entire career. Until recently, historians have remembered him primarily for his famous remark, made during the 1932 campaign, that black people should turn the portrait of "Abraham Lincoln to the wall," declare their debts to Republicanism paid, and join the party of Roosevelt. But Vann had been a powerful spokesman for Negro political interests long before 1932.[78]

78. Vann's statement came in a speech he gave in Pittsburgh, Sept. 11, 1932, printed in the Pittsburgh *Courier*, Sept. 17, 1932, as "The Patriot and the Partisan." Comment on Vann's frequently quoted reference to Lincoln is noted in Schlesinger, *Politics of Upheaval*, 430; William E. Leuchtenburg, *Franklin D. Roosevelt and the New*

Born in North Carolina, possibly illegitimate, and educated in Virginia, Vann came to Pittsburgh in 1903 to an established black community. Working at various jobs, he continued his education and received a law degree from Western University of Pennsylvania, later known as the University of Pittsburgh. Almost from the start, Vann jumped into local Pittsburgh politics. In 1910 he took over as editor of the fledgling Pittsburgh *Courier*, and while turning it into one of the leading national black newspapers, he also built up a solid legal and political reputation.[79]

Vann was proud, egocentric, and always independent, and his political and social philosophy is difficult to categorize. During the 1920s, he endeared himself to a number of prominent Pennsylvania Republicans; and in the presidential campaigns of Harding, Coolidge, and Hoover, he directed Republican publicity for the black news media. Yet, until a personal feud ended their relationship, Vann was also one of the few Negro editors in the 1920s who supported A. Philip Randolph and the struggle to win union recognition for the Brotherhood of Sleeping Car Porters. And when no one else seemed to care, the *Courier* publisher provided his newspaper as a vehicle for the deported Marcus Garvey to publicize his nationalist ideology.[80]

Certainly personal ambition and political strategy were inseparable in Robert Vann's activities. In part, it was his sense of neglect at the hands of the Republican party that led him to leave the GOP and take up the cause of the Democrats. Failure to receive political appointments from either Herbert Hoover in 1928 or, two years later, Pennsylvania Governor Gifford Pinchot deeply disturbed him. So also did political divisions within the Pennsylvania Republican organization and the unwillingness or inability of Hoover to provide strong leadership in the early Depression years. By 1932 Vann had developed a close friendship with Joseph Guffey, who was a chief strategist for Franklin Roosevelt in Pennsylvania and in charge of reorganizing the state Democratic party. The Guffey relationship, combined with his political snubbing and· Hoover's Depression

Deal, 1932-1940 (New York, 1963, 87. Andrew Buni's *Robert L. Vann*, cited previously, has now provided us with a thoughtful and intelligent understanding of Vann's career. An early analysis of Vann's thought and political philosophy is James H. Brewer, "Robert Lee Vann, Democrat or Republican: An Experiment in Loose Leaf Politics," *Negro History Bulletin* 21 (Feb. 1958), 100-103.

79. Buni, *Robert L. Vann*, chs. 1-5; Brewer, "Robert Lee Vann," 100-103.

80. Buni, *Robert L. Vann*, 161-71, 230-34. Ch. 8 is a good discussion of Vann's involvement in Republican politics during the 1920s, nationally and in Pennsylvania.

policies, convinced him that his future—and his race's—no longer remained with the Republicans.[81]

Thus, it was politics that brought Vann to the New Deal. His efforts on behalf of the Democrats and his ability to swing a number of black votes to Roosevelt in 1932 (though he always exaggerated its importance) won him praise from party figures like Democratic national secretary James A. Farley. Under Vann, the first effective Negro division of the Democratic party was established; and his work here and elsewhere was instrumental in aiding the dramatic shift in black support for the New Deal in 1934 and 1936.[82]

Vann was never given, however, the kind of political authority (especially patronage power) that he felt was owed him in view of his partisan contributions and the position he held within the administration. Though bombarded from the start by individuals and numerous black organizations for job requests, he got little satisfaction from Farley or other Democratic officials. Of even greater disappointment to him were his limited responsibilities as assistant to Attorney General Homer Cummings. Not only did he have no contact with Cummings, he was seldom given an assignment of any significance and was often treated disrespectfully by the Attorney Generals's staff. The Pittsburgh publisher and editor therefore accomplished little if anything in his role as special assistant; and while he served in the Justice Department demands for federal anti-lynching legislation and guarantees for black civil and political rights, particularly in the South, were generally ignored.[83]

Initially, like other black New Dealers, Vann attempted to use his government post to help guide the administration toward greater recognition of Afro-American needs. Serving as chairman of the Interdepartmental Group Concerned with the Special Problems of Negroes, Vann participated in the Group's debates and its abortive efforts to influence the NRA and other New Deal departments and agencies considered neglectful of black interests. His political allegiance to the Democrats did not deter him from criticizing the administration's programs or its apparent unwillingness to include

81. Buni, *Robert L. Vann*, 180-202; Brewer, "Robert Lee Vann," 101-102; Moon, *Balance of Power*, 17-18; Schlesinger, *Politics of Upheaval*, 430-36.

83. Bunche, "Political Status of the Negro," Carnegie-Myrdal Study, 1443; Moon, *Balance of Power*, 17-18; Schlesinger, *Politics of Upheaval*, 430, 436.

83. On patronage requests and Vann's frustrations with Farley and others, Buni, *Robert L. Vann*, 203-205. Analysis of the Justice Department's racial unresponsiveness during Vann's tenure is discussed in Walter White, "U.S. Department of (White) Justice," *Crisis* 42 (Oct. 1935), 309-10; also Buni, 204-206.

more blacks within the government. He maintained that the federal government had a basic responsibility to protect black workers against discrimination from both organized labor and management. And he became particularly incensed when he believed the administration did not show proper concern for black feelings, as evidenced by the leadership he assumed in attacking New Deal officials involved in the dismissal of a black woman, Mabel Byrd, from the staff of the National Recovery Administration.[84]

As was often the case in his career, Vann operated as an outsider during his years in the Roosevelt administration. Ignored by his white superiors, he was not especially well received by other black advisers who, like Robert Weaver, perceived him as a professional politician with little distinctive expertise. His recent biographer, Andrew Buni, concludes that "Vann's situation in Washington was full of sad irony. He had started his education late, had been driven by the idea that he had a limited amount of time in which to prove himself, and had worked doubly hard to keep up with the rapidly advancing clock. Now he found himself not too old, as he had feared, but passé among blacks in his outlook and methods. An old-line political race leader like Vann was somewhat anachronistic in FDR's Washington."[85] Even before he left in 1936, he was already spending much of his time on *Courier* business and local affairs. Thus Vann resigned from the New Deal, one writer later noted, "because he had become convinced that it offered him no field in which to serve his race."[86]

But the "field" Vann always considered most fruitful for himself and his race was politics. Had he been given the "latitude" and autonomy granted a Bethune or a Weaver, it is unlikely he would have remained in the New Deal any longer than he did, and personal rebuff alone did not drive Vann away from Washington in 1936, or

84. Kifer, "The Negro Under the New Deal," 221; Motz, "Black Cabinet," 17; "Minutes of the Interdepartmental Group Concerned with the Special Problems of Negroes," Mar. 2, 30, 1934, NARG 48; Pittsburgh *Courier*, Feb. 17, 1934; Buni, *Robert L. Vann*, 207-11. On Vann's response to the Mabel Byrd affair, see Robert Vann to Louis Howe, Sept. 15, 1933, FDRL, OF 93. Vann called the firing "unpardonable" and expressed hope that New Dealers who had participated in Byrd's dismissal would become better informed about black needs as well as black feelings. For discussion of the Byrd affair, see also Wolters, *Negroes and the Great Depression*, 140-42.

85. Buni, *Robert L. Vann*, 207.

86. Quoted in Pittsburgh *Courier*, Nov. 2, 1940. For a similar view expressed by George S. Schuyler, the black writer and friend of Vann during the 1920s and 1930s, see George S. Schuyler (Columbia Oral History Collection, 1960), 390.

ultimately away from the New Deal and the Democrats. Beyond his personal fortunes or misfortunes, there was a consistent theme extending throughout his political life. What Vann sought was Afro-American political independence. He understood better perhaps than Robert Weaver that it was power that shaped policy; professional expertise was fine, but political muscle determined results.

For Vann, there would be no equal opportunity—economic, social, or political—until black people were in a position to influence directly the decisions of government on their own behalf. That influence would not come simply by having Negro advisers in the New Deal; it would come when blacks had the independence and power to force government to recognize their needs. His pursuit of this objective best explains his resignation from the Roosevelt administration and his later opposition to it.

In the early thirties, Vann was in agreement with Harold Ickes that the historical oppression of black people was a result of their political domination, specifically, their domination by the Republican party. In his famous speech in 1932, which marked his break with Republicanism, he argued that during the Reconstruction era, "under the guise of justice and political equality" and "clothed with the appearances of humanitarianism and philanthropy, the Republican party went into the South and sealed our doom for fifty years." Black people had been propagandized into believing in the legend of Lincoln, of viewing the emancipator as "Jesus Christ himself"; as a result, decade after decade, "without rhyme or reason," the black man "swore by the Republican party and swore at everything else. . . . The Negro literally sold his soul to the Republican party." But Negroes had failed to understand, Vann stated, that the "abolition of slavery was brought about through a political issue purely and solely to relieve an economic crisis." Once slavery was terminated and, more importantly, once the Republican party had assured its political and economic hold on the country, it "no longer invited Negro support. It no longer gave Negroes political recognition. It no longer invited the black man into its councils."[87]

Only with the Depression did even such staunch supporters of Republicanism as Vann see clearly their past folly. When Herbert Hoover nominated Judge John J. Parker to the Supreme Court, which Vann claimed was "designed to destroy for all time both the

---

87. Pittsburgh *Courier*, Sept. 17, 1932; Brewer, "Robert Lee Vann," 102.

hopes, as well as the legally constituted protection, of the American Negro," it was obvious that black Americans and the Republican party must part company. "Deceived and prostituted, bought and commercialized, until we have lost our self-respect in a bland search for a political utopia," it was time for political realism.[88] The "only true political philosophy dictates that the Negro must select his party"; he must not wait for a party to say it wanted him but must "say whether I want the party." It might mean, Vann speculated in a symposium in *Crisis*, that blacks would even support the Socialist and Communist parties.[89] But he felt that these organizations were not strong enough in 1932 to "overthrow the oligarchy now enthroned at Washington." The issue of the hour, he asserted, was "the eating cancer of Hooverism." From his perspective, the only political group capable of overcoming Hooverism was the Democratic party, which had the organization, the experience in government, and the "leaders imbued with the ideals of the people." In 1932, at least, he concluded he would join blacks who were determined to "form a part of that new deal" to help the "forgotten man."[90]

To this point, Vann's analysis in 1932 remained consistent with Ickes'. But at the time the Interior Secretary was carrying this message to black audiences, Vann was moving in another political direction. Unlike Ickes, he was less certain that the New Deal and in particular the Democratic party would afford blacks the necessary political independence denied them in the past. After working for Roosevelt in 1936, Vann stated in a post-election editorial, "And We Are Still Negroes," that the election indicated how black people could not lose because "for the first time, we were in both parties taking our chances along with all other Americans." It was not FDR's or the Democrats' success in 1936 that was important; what counted was that black Americans were now included in both national political organizations. For a "people who have been slaves to one party for over a half century," this was a momentous occasion. Now that the election was over, it was significant to realize that "we are still Negroes." For blacks in the victorious party, there was the responsibility for "securing something for the Negroes of this country . . ."; the party that won at the polls "must face the plain duty of keeping faith with the people—all the people." It was necessary, in this

88. Pittsburgh *Courier*, Sept. 17, 1932.

89. "Negro Editors on Communism: A Symposium of the American Negro Press," *Crisis* 39 (May 1932), 154.

90. Pittsburgh *Courier*, Sept. 17, 1932.

regard, that "some of us must be able to touch" the government in Washington "as often as is necessary for the good of all our people."[91]

But the Negro should also remain in the Republican organization, since the "black man must so divide his vote that he will be in line regardless of what party wins at the polls." Ultimately, Vann concluded, after any political battle, blacks must "come back to ourselves. We are our own best bet. We cannot afford to fall out with each other over any white man. White men are not going to fall out with each other over us." Like white people who returned after their political struggle, blacks must also return "to a common fireside for conference and counsel."[92]

Vann thus sought an autonomous political base for black people. The guiding principle supporting that base was racial unity; "no one," he stated, could or would fight for Negro political and economic freedom "but ourselves."[93] The ultimate objective was for blacks to use their political strength to force concessions from whatever party in power. As late as 1937, he felt that blacks were still in a position to do this within the New Deal since the "Democratic party leaders as well as the President are aware that about three million or more Negroes supported President Roosevelt" in 1936.[94] But increasingly he came to fear that New Deal relief and public works measures were enticing the Negro to follow blindly the Democratic party.[95]

Accordingly, from 1936 until his death in 1940, he attempted to move blacks to a position independent of the administration and the Democrats. Unless they were to repeat their mistakes of the past, it was necessary for both black Americans and the New Deal not to take one another for granted. To prove Vann's point, in 1938 the *Courier* inaugurated a vigorous campaign for an all-black Army division, which led frequently to harsh attacks against Roosevelt and the United States Congress. Though a separate black division was opposed by the NAACP's Walter White as being contrary to the Association's struggle for total armed forces integration, other NAACP

---

91. Editorial, Pittsburgh *Courier*, Nov. 7, 1936.

92. *Ibid.*

93. The affirmation of "race unity" was a theme which ran throughout Vann's life as a politician, as a lawyer, and especially as an editor and publisher of a black newspaper. See Buni, *Robert L. Vann*, *passim*.

94. Vann, "What Should We Expect of the National Administration?" *Opportunity* 15 (Jan. 1937), 14.

95. Brewer, "Robert Lee Vann," 102; Buni, *Robert L. Vann*, 290, 297-98.

officials, including Roy Wilkins and Charles Houston, applauded Vann's efforts.[96]

To gain more backing for his cause, Vann joined forces with Republican Congressman Hamilton Fish, Jr., an outspoken conservative and opponent of the New Deal.[97] The same year, he came out in support of Republican Arthur H. James as governor of Pennsylvania, an action which won him public rebuke from his old friend Joseph Guffey as well as from many Pennsylvania blacks.[98] From 1938 until 1940, *Courier* editorials and news articles stressed the Roosevelt administration's failure to combat discrimination both in and outside the government. Publicity was given to black protests over segregation in the TVA and the Federal Housing Authority. The *Courier* backed wage-and-hour legislation in 1938, but it demanded that Negroes be placed on national and local boards which administered the new law. Without black involvement, the paper saw little hope that the Negro would secure lasting benefits.[99]

Vann's fear of growing black dependence on the New Deal and the Democratic party ultimately led him in October 1940, just prior to his death, to favor Wendell L. Wilkie over FDR. In a front-page editorial in the *Courier*, he argued that Roosevelt had "strayed afar from his original principles and policy." Though his comments gave evidence of an increased economic conservatism, his central attack on Roosevelt was political. The Democratic party, he asserted, was dominated in the Congress by white southerners who controlled all the key legislative committees; that domination would ensure that racist attitudes continued to destroy the hopes of Negro workers, farmers, and servicemen. Roosevelt was not interested, he was convinced, in changing this condition, but simply in maintaining his and the Democrats' power. Vann concluded that under these circumstances there would be no future liberation of black people, whatever the short-term benefits might be in relief and WPA measures.[100]

Robert Vann's central concern throughout the 1930s was that

96. See, e.g., Pittsburgh *Courier*, Feb. 19, Apr. 2, 9, 26, 27, May 7, 1938, July 21, Sept. 28, Oct. 12, 1940. White and NAACP noted in Buni, *Robert L. Vann*, 306-309.

97. Pittsburgh *Courier*, Apr. 2, 9, 1938; New York *Times*, Apr. 27, 1938; Buni, *Robert L. Vann*, 305-12.

98. Buni, *Robert L. Vann*, 290-94; "Black Purge," *Time* 32 (Oct. 31, 1938), 13-14.

99. For examples of views, see Pittsburgh *Courier*, Aug. 20, Sept. 3, Oct. 22, Nov. 11, 1938; on wage and hour legislation, Editorial, Pittsburgh *Courier*, Aug. 13, 1938.

100. Pittsburgh *Courier*, Oct. 26, 1940. Also, after his death, Pittsburgh *Courier* editorial, "The Negro Vote," Nov. 2, 1940; Buni, *Robert L. Vann*, 316-19.

blacks must never lose sight of their need to secure independence; without independence, which emanated from the unity of all black Americans, they stood little chance of gaining economic and social equality. As long as he felt that the New Deal and the Democratic party offered tangible opportunities for blacks, he supported them. But he increasingly came to doubt the commitment of the President and the New Deal. He feared, moreover, that economic and political dependence on the federal government and the Democrats presented the real likelihood of politically re-enslaving the Negro just as it happened during and after Reconstruction. In 1937 he noted in an article written for *Opportunity* that "too much legislation requested for us as Negroes because we are Negroes may prove our undoing in later years."[101] The issue was not just the setting of bad policy precedents, as Weaver and other Negroes sometimes viewed it, but the dependence of black people on a government and party whose commitment to their welfare was limited and beyond their power to influence.

Forrester Washington was, in contrast to Vann, more typical of black advisers chosen in the early New Deal. The same age as Vann, Washington was born in Salem, Massachusetts, and educated at Tufts, Harvard, and Columbia, where he received an M.A. degree in social work; he served as an organizer for the National Urban League during the 1920s. In 1927, he became dean of the Atlanta School of Social Work. He was known, North and South, in the words of Will Alexander, as a "man who can render constructive service in meeting the practical problems" confronting black social workers.[102]

It was through the personal recommendation of Alexander that Washington came to the Federal Emergency Relief Administration as its race adviser in February 1934. Alexander was particularly impressed with Washington's work at the Atlanta School, his contacts with blacks in higher education, his relationship with northern philanthropic foundations, and above all his racial independence and his ability to view the "problems of Negroes with the minimum of racial feeling."[103] Fairly prominent then as a race leader, his selection

101. Vann, "What Should We Expect?" 16.
102. *Who's Who in Colored America: A Biographical Dictionary of Notable Living Persons of African Descent in America* (5th ed.: Brooklyn, 1940), 542. On Washington's earlier career as executive secretary of the Detroit Urban League see Parris and Brooks, *Blacks in the City*, 77, 79, 89-92. Also see Strickland, *History of the Chicago Urban League*, 51-53. Alexander comment in Alexander to Aubrey Williams, Jan. 16, 1935, CWA, NA Box 83.
103. Alexander to Williams, Jan. 16, Jan. 25, 1934, NA Box 83.

was considered a favorable sign by the Negro community. Floyd C. Covington, executive secretary of the Los Angeles Urban League, wrote Harry Hopkins that Washington's appointment was "certainly an indication not only of your own interest in the Negro group in America, but that of the entire Administration in striving to really achieve a 'New Deal' era."[104]

While serving the FERA as race adviser and taking part in the activities of the Interdepartmental Group, Washington early expressed faith that he would be able to help find solutions to some of the pressing problems confronting black people. But within six months he had submitted his resignation to Hopkins and returned to Atlanta, where, he stated, he could be "of the most service to the needy of my race."[105] His speedy departure was widely commented on by segments of the black press. The Pittsburgh *Courier* stated that his resignation "shocked political and social circles." A writer for the Chicago *Defender* maintained that he had left because of the "indifference and complete apathy on the part of the Administration toward doing anything tangible for the masses of the Colored people, despite numerous recommendations and surveys." And the Kansas City *Call* noted that Washington was simply no longer willing to serve as "merely window dressing" for the New Deal.[106]

Actually, Washington's decision to return to private social work was more complex. Like Vann, he was convinced by his brief service with the government and his inability to influence administration policies that the Negro stood in real danger of becoming a ward of the federal government. In contrast to Vann's, Washington's concern was less with the political consequences of this dependence than with its social and economic manifestations. But the result, to a large extent, was the same.

On July 1, 1934, just prior to his resignation, Washington submitted a report to the Civil Works Administration in which he pointed to the disproportionate number of blacks on FERA relief rolls. Beside the three major problem areas the FERA was focusing on—

104. Covington to Hopkins, Feb. 13, 1934, CWA, "Interracial Correspondence," NARG 69; see also Kifer, "The Negro Under the New Deal," 232-33.

105. "Minutes of the Interdepartmental Group," Mar. 2, 30, 1934, NARG 48; Kifer, "The Negro Under the New Deal," 233; Wolters, *Negroes and the Great Depression*, 143-44; Washington to Harry L. Hopkins, July 30, 1934, FERA, Old Subject File, NARG 69, Box 19.

106. Pittsburgh *Courier*, Sept. 8, 1934; Chicago *Defender*, Aug. 25, 1934; Kansas City *Call*, quoted in Kifer, "The Negro Under the New Deal," 233.

"Distressed Families in Rural Areas, Stranded Populations, and the Unemployed in Large Cities"—there was immediate need for "special planning" to "prevent the development of a fourth major problem," something that he termed "Negro chronic dependency."[107] This "chronic dependency," he told a conference of social workers in May 1934, was due "largely to factors which can be controlled, but which are not in the control of the Negro."[108] To the NAACP's Walter White, who passed on his report to Eleanor Roosevelt, Washington noted that he had pointed out to Harry Hopkins and Aubrey Williams that the "reason the Negro bulks large on the relief rolls of the FERA so much out of proportion to his numbers in the population is due to a number of factors, some of which could be dealt with by the Administration."[109]

The problem, according to Washington, was the lack of black economic opportunity at every class level. Black people had been forced out of meaningful employment not only by the Depression but as a result of certain activities which had their origins before 1929. In some southern states, such as Florida and Georgia, vigilante groups like the Black Shirts and Blue Shirts had pressured employers to replace Negroes with white workers. For years black agricultural laborers had suffered from the "lay-off" practices of large landowners, and throughout the twenties manufacturers, North and South, had maintained color bars which excluded black employment. The discriminatory policies of the American Federation of Labor had simply aggravated the situation, and finally, with the Depression, the minimal gains some blacks had made after World War I were completely wiped out.[110]

Thus, by the early 1930s, the black man saw no opportunity for a "secure place in industry"; his "death rate, which had been declining," was now rising, and "crime within his group increased." Instead of improving his deplorable conditions, the NRA and AAA had worsened them. The AAA's cotton reduction program, Washington argued, failed to provide controls which would have forced landowners to keep blacks employed and, at the same time, would have

---

107. Report of Forrester Washington, July 1, 1934, CWA, "Interracial Correspondence," NARG 69.

108. Washington, "The Negro and Relief," *Proceedings*, National Conference of Social Work, 61st Annual Session, Kansas City, Mo., May 20-26, 1934, 178.

109. Washington to White, Dec. 11, 1934, NAACP Papers, File C-383. See also Washington to White, Nov. 28, 1934, White to Washington, Dec. 3, 1934, memo, White to Roy Wilkins, Jan. 7, 1935, *ibid*.

110. Washington, "The Negro and Relief," 178-79, 186.

given them an equitable proportion of federal assistance. Although both black and white tenant farmers suffered as a result of AAA failures, it was the Negro who suffered most because white landowners had "less to fear from him and from public sentiment." Similarly, under NRA unwise codes resulted in the "discharge and forcing on relief of many Negro workers"; without adequate federal enforcement policies, white employers continued their "blind allegiance to the mores" of the past, which meant discrimination and hardship for black Americans. In the North as well as the South, Washington maintained, black men and women were being displaced by whites in their traditional jobs as elevator operators, maids, porters, and domestics, for example.[111]

As was fairly obvious to those who were aware, all this meant that the Negro had become the "worst victim of the depression," leading directly to his being placed on the relief rolls "in numbers all out of proportion to his numbers in the general population." Unless the federal government did something to change the basic employment conditions in the country, besides simply giving relief, there was the immediate likelihood that black people would never get off welfare. It was not, Washington tried to make clear, that Negroes were ungrateful for the assistance which the New Deal had so far provided them. In many respects, the black masses would "hardly have survived" without it. For many, FERA was literally a "godsend," and ironically it had brought to "some Negroes a standard of living superior to that to which they had been accustomed before the depression."[112]

But relief, Washington argued, dealt only with the symptoms of the black dilemma, not with its cause, which was industrial and agricultural unemployment created by years of discrimination and exploitation. Although relief helped the masses at the lowest level, it did little for other black classes—"the Negro mechanic, the Negro technician, the Negro of the profession, and the Negro business man." The FERA had, in effect, "seriously neglected all Negroes above the lowest socio-economic class."[113] The opportunities for these groups of people were there; indeed, they existed within the FERA itself, in every administrative and occupational category. In his report to the CWA, Washington listed job vacancies for engineers, statisticians, economists, architects, home planners, field and office

111. *Ibid.*, 181-83.
112. *Ibid.*, 184, 189, 190.
113. *Ibid.*, 189, 188.

workers; "unemployed Negroes" were "available for every one of the . . . positions, and should be considered for placement."[114]

The basic reason for the "lowest socio-economic class" of blacks being consigned to a relief status and other Negroes being denied work opportunities which they had the ability to fulfill was the New Deal's failure to utilize its full powers. The black man, Washington argued, could "not lift himself up by his boot straps. The cards are stacked against him," and the "only source to which the Negro can look for real aid is the United States government." It was not that individuals like Harry Hopkins or Aubrey Williams, who were at the highest levels of administration, did not care about blacks or were unaware of their predicament; these were men, he was satisfied, who were "eminently fair," who truly wanted to see the benefits of the "recovery program extended to every citizen." But such a lofty "ideal" was frequently "neutralized in many local communities" where discrimination against the hiring of blacks in CWA programs ranged "from that which might be called slight to that which amounted practically to criminal malfeasance in office." It was not "much consolation to a Negro white-collar worker in a local community to know that the national office of the FERA is opposed to discrimination if he or she is unable to obtain a white-collar job in his local community because he is a Negro."[115]

Washington believed that the New Deal had to confront the issue of race prejudice openly and assume control over every facet of relief and work programs within each community. The federal government had to make certain that "the right kind of administrators are appointed in various local communities"; that Negroes were "placed on all committees having to do with the distribution of government funds intended for the rehabilitation of victims of the unemployment crisis"; that "colored workers be used throughout the relief organization in communities where there is a considerable Negro population"; and that blacks be fully integrated into the FERA's "work program" in order to "preserve the industrial stability and morale of Negro labor, which private industry is destroying."[116] Further, it was necessary that the Roosevelt administration embark on a massive and positive educational program directed to the white population of the country. "The President, or some public power almost as important," must "impress upon the employing class, both

---

114. Report, July 1, 1934, NARG 69.
115. Washington, "The Negro and Relief," 187, 191, 189.
116. *Ibid.*, 193-94; Report, July 1 1934, NARG 69.

in the North and in the South, that they are committing not only a social injustice but a civic blunder in deliberately throwing the support of the Negro labor on the relief arm of the federal government." This same "public power" should also be brought to "bear upon local political officeholders who have used their legislative or executive power or the influence of their position to encourage the discharge of Negro labor." Some "sort of federal curb" should be directed against "certain private organizations . . . who have been definitely organized for the purpose of ousting Negroes from industrial employment," and, finally, organized labor must be "compelled to remove the bans that are set up against Negro membership in the . . . craft unions." Those unions, Washington concluded, which continued to exclude blacks should "not be allowed to have any preferential treatment from the NRA, the PWA, or any other agency which expends funds of the federal government."[117]

Forrester Washington called his proposal for an expanded New Deal authority one of "moderate and modernized, centralized control." Although his ideas were far-reaching in their implications, he was not a militant; his ideas evolved more out of what he considered to be the only real guarantee that black people would be provided a "fair chance for rehabilitation now, during the depression, and in the future."[118] Belief that the New Deal would not carry out such a program of "centralized control" led to his ultimate departure from government after only six months of service. As late as 1939, as a participant in the NYA conference on the "Problems of the Negro and Negro Youth," he argued that existing government programs were essentially irrelevant to the kinds of issues facing black Americans. It was ridiculous to talk "about vocational education alone, vocational rehabilitation and that sort of thing when there aren't any jobs to direct the Negroes to." What black people and the New Deal should be discussing, he concluded, is "something more fundamental"—that is, devising "something to protect Negroes, to see that there are jobs to guide them to."[119]

The failure of the federal government to protect the Negro in every phase of the New Deal's relief and recovery program contained, Washington believed, ominous implications. It signified that the black masses would continue to be prohibited from gaining a foothold as unskilled and semiskilled workers and that black artisans

117. Washington, "The Negro and Relief," 193-94.
118. Ibid., 194.
119. Washington, Proceedings of Second Conference, 1939, 104.

and white-collar professionals would be precluded from developing and exercising their skills. The only recourse left to blacks would then be federal welfare, the expansion and perpetuation of what he feared would be known as "Negro relief." That, in turn, would endanger further the future of black-white relations by causing "racial friction through creating resentment on the part of the majority public against the presence of so many Negroes on the relief rolls."[120] It would thus have the effect of reinforcing racist doctrines regarding the inferiority and inefficiency of all Negroes. In the end, the greatest danger would be that of making the "Negro, as a race, a chronic dependent," destroying his initiative, his independence, and his hope for equal status in American life.

Washington and Robert Vann were not political radicals; neither was identified in the thirties with the black militant expressions of individuals like John P. Davis or Ralph Bunche. As a former National Urban League official and later dean of a prominent black school in the deep South, Washington was accustomed to compromising with conservative whites and relying on them for advice and support. And Vann, whose Booker T. Washington–style economic orthodoxy went unchanged throughout his life, no doubt was suspicious of even Forrester Washington's proposal for "moderate and modernized, centralized control." Both Washington and Vann, however, recognized the need for immediate federal support to blacks hard hit by the Depression; and they acknowledged the benefits their race had received as a result of government assistance.

But they believed also that given the limited efforts of the Roosevelt administration in areas of race discrimination and segregation and the still weak political voice of blacks, a real danger existed that the Negro might become economically and politically dependent on the federal government and a single political party. The inherent power of an expanding federal welfare state, a power many saw as offering the only salvation for Negroes, symbolized to Vann and Washington a potentially new form of slavery, more humane than the former but no less destructive of black self-esteem.

IV.

In 1939, William H. Hastie, who held New Deal appointments in the thirties and forties as an assistant solicitor in the Interior De-

---

120. Washington, "The Negro and Relief," 185.

partment, federal judge in the Virgin Islands, and civilian aide in the Department of War, outlined to an NAACP convention the impact and the implications of six years of Roosevelt administration policies. "Since 1932," he noted,

> the Federal Government has entered into the economic life of the nation and has undertaken to perform social services to an extent and over an area much larger than could have been foreseen. Spending billions to furnish jobs, housing, and recreation, to improve health, to provide credit, to subsidize education, to pension the aged, the Federal Government has come to a position of enormous influence in the entire life of the nation. Not only the existence of employment, but also its conditions— wages, hours, preferences, the treatment of labor unions, attitudes toward racial and religious minorities—can be and are being influenced profoundly by the Federal Government. Federal policies could and can contribute largely to the improving of the disadvantaged status of labor generally and to the lessening of discrimination against Negro labor in particular. Racial attitudes reflected in Government-financed enterprises of various types are potentially significant for the modification of the pattern of American life.[121]

Hastie's analysis suggested the enormous influence that the New Deal had assumed in many areas considered of vital significance to black welfare. That influence, reflected in the ideas and activities of Bethune, Weaver, Vann, and Washington, produced ambivalent and conflicting reactions which derived not only from the ethnic or racial duality of the historic black experience but in the comprehensiveness of the administration programs and the Negro New Dealer's special role in the government.

As Hastie noted in his speech, "countless projects" in employment, housing, health, education, and recreation "represented problems of a variety and complexity" which staggered the imagination. "The job of keeping track of new proposals and analyzing them; the problems of learning the administrative procedures of a great many independent agencies; the bringing of pressure while administrative policies are in their formative stages; and the effort to correct abuses and injustices as varied as the ingenuity of man, make up a tremendous undertaking."[122]

Part of the responsibility for that "undertaking" obviously rested with the black advisers. Roy Wilkins stated that the presence of so many black experts "had never existed before. The Negro had never

121. William H. Hastie, "A Look at the NAACP," *Crisis* 46 (Sept. 1939), 263-64.
122. *Ibid.*, 264.

146

... had this penetration into the government that he had under Roosevelt."[123] Yet differences in responsibility and authority, in personal attitude and training complicated any determination as to what that "penetration" ultimately meant for black Americans. Certainly black advisers in the thirties and forties established important trends for the future involvement of Negroes in the federal government; and most contributed an awareness of black needs which would have been absent in the administration without their presence.

But if a Bethune or a Weaver received considerable freedom to pursue his or her objectives, often with the active encouragement of those in higher positions, many other advisers did not. Robert Vann was clearly an example of the latter, as was Edgar Brown, who worked for the Civilian Conservation Corps. And unlike Vann or National Urban League secretary Eugene Kinckle Jones, both of whom were appointed for political considerations but had certain qualifications, Brown was "an obscure newspaper man who was able to obtain employment . . . apparently through the intercession of Irwin H. McDuffie, who was President Roosevelt's valet and Brown's brother-in-law."[124]

Brown, of course, was the exception, since most black New Dealers, as already noted, were well trained and qualified in some manner to represent the black perspective. As a group, however, they never constituted a real "Black Cabinet" in the sense of articulating a unified or even a consistent point of view. Some, like Bethune, Weaver, and Hastie, agreed on basic issues and met together frequently to discuss possible strategy. But Robert Vann was seldom included, and labor adviser Lawrence Oxley appeared to have as many conflicts with his black colleagues in the government as he had with white administrators.[125] Moreover, the most powerful among them were seldom consulted on policy matters in their "formative stages." One student who has studied their activities concludes that "their influence on the official process of decision-making at a high level was almost non-existent"; in effect, most of the Negro advisers' achievements were "preventative" rather than innovative.[126]

123. Roy Wilkins, Columbia Oral History, 68.
124. Calvin W. Gower, "The Struggle for Leadership in the Civilian Conservation Corps: 1933-1952," *Journal of Negro History* 61 (Apr. 1976), 131.
125. Buni, Robert L. Vann, 206-7; on Oxley, see "Minutes of the Interdepartmental Group," June 1, 1934, NARG 48.
126. Motz, "Black Cabinet," 80.

An added problem for all was the decentralized structure of many administrative programs. Even in cases where they were able to shape policies at the top level, it was never certain that those policies would be enforced or carried out at state and local levels as they were originally conceived. And as Forrester Washington argued, the lack of central control and enforcement "neutralized" most of the efforts of advisers like himself, efforts aimed at assuring blacks "equity" and participation in the government's programs. Robert Weaver pointed to the same problem in connection with his activities in the USHA, which maintained less federal supervision over housing programs than its predecessor, the PWA. In 1937 and 1939, the NYA-sponsored conferences on the "Problems of the Negro and Negro Youth" considered decentralization one of the most pressing black concerns.[127]

In many respects, the success of black advisers was dependent not only on liberal white support within the government but on activities in the Negro community. Henry Lee Moon, who served for a while with Weaver in the USHA, noted later that "whatever value was accomplished by . . . advisers was incalculably aided by the organized pressure of Negro groups, both national and local, and the Negro press."[128] One adviser, speaking to a group of black leaders in 1941, observed that "when a *Courier* or *Defender* gives me hell in an editorial or Walter White writes me a stinging letter, I take it in to my chief and tell him that I won't be any use to the agency unless I can produce or if Negroes think I'm an Uncle Tom. Then I can usually get some concessions that I have been after for weeks. I tell you the only way we can operate in Washington is for you to keep putting plenty of pressure on us."[129] Involvement of blacks outside the government was also essential in ensuring the participation of the Negro in federal programs at the local levels. This involvement was especially crucial considering the decentralization of New Deal programs, and it explains why Weaver, Bethune, and other advisers spent so much time popularizing and explaining administrative

127. Weaver, "The Negro in a Program of Public Housing," 198-203; "Federal Aid, Local Control," 47-59; Wye, "The New Deal and the Negro Community," *passim*; Ross, "Mary McLeod Bethune and the National Youth Administration," 20-26; *Report . . . Conference on the Problems of the Negro,* 1937, *passim,* and *Proceedings of Second Conference, 1939, passim*; Bunche, "Political Status of the Negro," 1414-15.
128. Moon, *Balance of Power,* 30.   ·
129. Quoted in Lawrence, "Negro Organizations in Crisis," 217-18; see also Motz, "Black Cabinet," 56-62.

policies to blacks around the country and, on occasion, orchestrating their own pressure with help from black and civil rights groups.

But any successful interrelationship between Negro New Dealers and the black community was predicated on the existence of some degree of organization in local areas and certain agreement as to what policies were in the best interests of Negro Americans. During the thirties, neither of these conditions prevailed to any great extent. Armed forces desegregation and defense employment did help to unify black opinion in the war years and gave impetus to A. Philip Randolph's March on Washington Movement in its early stages. During the "formative" period of reform and recovery in the 1930s, however, that kind of unity was rarely present, though the NAACP, the National Urban League, and other organizations did keep close scrutiny over government policies and attempted to influence their direction.

Black advisers themselves were often divided over the proper position to take regarding certain New Deal proposals. Community demands for immediate assistance, regardless of the racial implications, conflicted with the view of many black New Dealers that such assistance would help to foster a federally sanctioned policy of race segregation. With the federal government assuming such an "enormous influence in the entire life of the nation," as Hastie pointed out, the stakes were very great. Ill-conceived programs, no matter how attractive their present benefits might appear, could possibly create far worse conditions for blacks in the future. Ralph Bunche expressed what many Negro advisers were consciously or unconsciously afraid of when he wrote for the Gunnar Myrdal study in 1939 that there was a "danger, not too widely recognized perhaps, that excessive centralization and bureaucracy in the national government might tend to cement the Negro in a permanent position of segregated inferiority in the society."[130] That "danger" particularly distressed individuals like Washington and Vann; but the conflict between the priorities of immediate equity and long-term economic, political, and social integration involved every black New Dealer. At the same time, the problems associated with the decentralized administration of New Deal programs often led even those who feared Negro dependence on a powerful federal government, such as Forrester Washington, to advocate greater governmental centralization.

In 1943 Henry Moon, generally sympathetic to the New Deal's

130. Bunche, "Political Status of the Negro," 1525.

efforts on behalf of blacks, noted a number of weaknesses in its approach to racial questions. Too often, he maintained, there was a tendency by both black and white in the government to engage in "make-shift efforts" in the "vain hope of remedying a malevolent condition which might well have been averted had a continuing and understanding relationship been maintained providing a two-way flow of information, attitudes and influences" between the New Deal agencies and groups they were supposed to be helping. Generally, in regard to the policies of those agencies, there existed a conflict between the claims of the Negro and the white community; and when that occurred, black people's needs were seldom met. Too often, vacillation and inaction were the common practice; "too frequently, federal agencies and their administrations yield to local prejudice and bias." A classic example was the Sojourner Truth crisis in Detroit, where conflicting federal housing policies ultimately led to violence between blacks and whites. Finally, there was the failure of New Deal administrators to deal directly with race prejudice within the government itself, particularly as manifested in the Congress. Instead of forcing congressional "race baiters" into the open, Moon argued, New Deal policy had been a "hush-hush" one, in which the "tragic and ironic consequence" was "not merely that the Negro [was] quietly sacrificed but that the whole program" was seriously impaired.[131]

A "make-shift" effort, a yielding to "local prejudice and bias," and a "hush-hush" approach to political "race baiters" were determined by the political and economic priorities which New Dealers placed on the government's commitment to blacks, the innumerable needs of the black community, and the racial environment in which blacks and whites operated in the 1930s and 1940s. Essentially, New Deal blacks were forced to follow the lead on racial matters outlined by their white liberal supporters and superiors in the Roosevelt administration because of their own lack of authority, the conflicting demands over immediate and long-term assistance, and the absence of unified opinion among black Americans. How long they followed that lead depended on their assessment of the Negro condition, their basic faith in the reform philosophy of the New Deal and liberal whites, and their perception of their own effectiveness within the federal government.

There was always a tendency to return to the black community in order to find a means of supplementing and expanding efforts car-

131. Moon, "Racial Aspects of Federal Public Relations," 68-71.

ried on by the administration. Hastie's speech to the NAACP was an appeal to that traditional civil rights organization to take account of the new conditions, to engage in programs which would help local branches understand how New Deal agencies "work and how the citizen may approach the problem of their functioning in his community." Hastie called for an expansion of NAACP activities concentrating on the basic economic conditions confronting blacks, on bringing Negroes into the labor movement, and on building up alliances between poor blacks and whites around economic, political, and educational issues affecting both races.[132] Confronted by the extensiveness of federal activity and its uncertain implications for blacks, Hastie and other Negro New Dealers increasingly saw the need to develop a power base outside the government to affect administration policies. That awareness reflected the extent of the government's influence and the impotence of blacks within the government system, and led Robert Vann and Forrester Washington to resign their positions in the mid-1930s. In 1943, William Hastie took the same step, leaving his post as civilian aide to the Department of War. It was, he noted, the "only course" which he felt would "bring results"; public opinion was "still the strongest force in American life."[133]

Whether public opinion could be effectively channeled into a force capable of improving the status of black Americans was open to considerable debate. Still, the experience of Negroes in the government clearly suggested that their success was often linked to the ability of black leaders and organizations outside the system to organize opinion and pressure in support of meaningful programs. How that might be accomplished was a topic of much discussion among black and civil rights groups.

---

132. Hastie, "A Look at the NAACP," 264.
133. Hastie, "Why I Resigned," Chicago *Defender*, Feb. 2, 1943.

SEVEN

Pressure From the Outside

THE POLITICAL STRUGGLE

I.

In many respects it was as difficult for blacks outside the Roosevelt administration as for those within it to get a firm hold on New Deal policies and policy makers and to move them in the directions they thought best for the Afro-American community. There were differing reasons for this: the complex nature of government programs; the absence of Negro influence in the Democratic party, especially in the early 1930s; the lack of any unified or consistent strategy among black and pro–civil rights groups; and their frequent competition in representing the masses of black people.

As was true for many whites, the combined forces of Depression and New Deal reform pushed black political activity and thought in a leftward direction during the Roosevelt years. Like their white counterparts, a number of black reformers were affected by Marxist and non-Marxist class theories and by the dominant economic tone of New Deal recovery efforts.[1] Communist party involvement in the thirties, and to a lesser extent that of the Socialists, gave added emphasis to the leftist drift of black protest.

How much the Communists and their fellow travelers influenced black thought and the Negro's response to the New Deal is still not clear. Less bothered about historical consistency than its Socialist rivals, the Communist party passed through numerous ideological shifts in the 1930s while endeavoring to win black converts. It

---

1. Discussion of these influences can be found in a variety of sources: James O. Young, *Black Writers of the Thirties* (Baton Rouge, 1973); August Meier and Elliott Rudwick, "The Origins of Nonviolent Direct Action in Afro-American Protest: A Note on Historical Discontinuities," in Meier and Rudwick, *Along the Color Line*, 314-53; Harvard Sitkoff, "Emergence of Civil Rights as a National Issue," *passim*; Wolters, *Negroes and the Great Depression*, 219-384; Lawrence, "Negro Organizations in Crisis," *passim*; Bunche, "Programs, Ideologies, and Tactics," Carnegie-Myrdal Study, *passim*, and "The Programs of Organizations Devoted to the Improvement of the Status of the American Negro," *Journal of Negro Education* 8 (July 1939), 539-50; James A. Harrell, "Negro Leadership in the Election Year 1936," *Journal of Southern History* 34 (Nov. 1968), 546-64.

probably won its strongest Negro support after 1935, when it discarded its earlier public denunciation of interracial groups like the NAACP and the National Urban League, as well as the New Deal, and worked in a less overtly hostile manner to push the cause of race equality and Communist philosophy.[2]

However one judges their motives, Communists were often at the front in the battle for black rights. During the thirties they attacked race discrimination in the federal government and the later cutback of New Deal public works programs, challenged racist attitudes and policies of organized labor, and led the celebrated legal struggles in the Scottsboro and Angelo Herndon cases. The Communist party's nomination of James Ford, a black man, as its vice presidential candidate, its elevation of blacks to key positions within the party (including young writers like Richard Wright), and its willingness to risk physical harm and arrest, especially in the South, in the fight for race equality won it praise from even such staunch anti-Communists as the Negro press.[3]

Communist militancy and the direct-action agitations pursued by blacks within local communities, such as the "Don't-Buy-Where-You-Can't-Work" campaigns, often forced established civil rights groups to examine their own philosophies and strategies more closely. The creation of national movements like the National Negro Congress and Randolph's March on Washington provided additional challenges for them.[4]

Of course, neither the NAACP nor the NUL was immune to the economic and political emphases of the thirties and forties. Within the ranks of both organizations were individuals ready to see them embark upon a more militant course of economic and social action. Young intellectuals like Abram Harris, E. Franklin Frazier, and

2. In addition to studies previously noted, see esp. Sitkoff, "Emergence of Civil Rights as a National Issue," ch. 6; Record, *The Negro and the Communist Party* and *Race and Radicalism*; Nolan, *Communism Versus the Negro*. See also Harold Cruse, *Crisis of the Negro Intellectual: From Its Origins to the Present* (New York, 1967), esp. 174–89.

3. An honest and beautifully written account of what the Communist party represented to one sensitive and searching black writer in the mid-1930s is Richard Wright's posthumously published autobiography, *American Hunger* (New York, 1977). A recent study of the Angelo Herndon episode and the involvement of the Communist party is Charles H. Martin, *The Angelo Herndon Case and Southern Justice* (Baton Rouge, 1976). For a general analysis of some of the above involvements of Communists, see Sitkoff, "Emergence of Civil Rights as a National Issue," ch. 6 and chs. 7, 8, and 11, *passim*.

4. For a discussion of "Don't-Buy" campaigns and the role of Communists and others, see Meier and Rudwick, "Origins of Nonviolent Direct Action," 314–44.

Ralph J. Bunche pressed the NAACP to involve itself directly in class-related issues and to develop a comprehensive economic program. William Hastie's speech in 1939, noted in the previous chapter, suggested how far the NAACP had traveled since 1929 and indicated the direction at least one of its younger supporters hoped it would go in the future.[5] Though political agitation continued mainly as the purview of the National Association, the Urban League did move beyond its previous political neutrality and lobbied for federal programs considered important to black Americans. With the addition of Lester Granger to its staff in the thirties and the creation of community-based workers' councils, the League also increased its pro-union and labor education efforts.[6]

While both the NAACP and the NUL criticized the Roosevelt administration for its failures in adequately addressing the needs of Negroes, they also maintained close ties with individual New Dealers, black and white. Indeed, a number of race advisers were recruited directly from their ranks, including William Hastie and Henry Moon of the NAACP, and Eugene Kinckle Jones, Ira de A. Reid, and T. Arnold Hill of the Urban League. Other black New Dealers, like Bethune, Weaver, and Vann, had connections with one or both interracial organizations. Roy Wilkins recalled that NAACP officials "spent all our waking hours working. . . to get Negroes into government," and the black writer George Schuyler noted with some sarcasm that the New Deal was packed with Walter White's "cronies."[7]

Central to NAACP and Urban League strategy was developing direct links to the government by seeking and nurturing personal friendships and by encouraging the appointment of advisers friendly to their point of view. A critical part of that strategy also involved maintaining sufficient independence to attack New Deal policies

5. Hastie was considered one of the spokesmen for the younger militants in the NAACP during the 1930s, and August Meier and Francis L. Broderick have seen Hastie's speech as heralding a "shift in NAACP viewpoint," particularly in respect to black relations with industrial unions. See Broderick and Meier, eds., *Negro Protest Thought in the Twentieth Century* (Indianapolis, 1965), 190. Also see Bunche, "Programs, Ideologies, Tactics," Carnegie-Myrdal Study, 23-203; Wolters, *Negroes and the Great Depression*, 230-52; Lawrence, "Negro Organizations in Crisis," 219-94; Ross, J.E. Spingarn, 178-85, 218-45.

6. Weiss, *National Urban League*, chs. 17-18; Bunche, "Programs, Ideologies, Tactics," 217-300; Lawrence, "Negro Organizations in Crisis," 259-65; "Report on the Activities of the Workers' Councils During Their Four Years of Existence," National Urban League Publication, July 1, 1938, Rosenwald Fund Archives, Box 306.

7. Roy Wilkins, Columbia Oral History, 69; George S. Schuyler, *ibid.*, 602.

when these were considered contrary to the interests of black people. Such an approach often worked well from the standpoint of the NAACP and the Urban League, but it was not one without problems.

One immediate difficulty was that many blacks found unacceptable as well as uninspiring the NAACP and NUL dual approach of both advocating and criticizing reform liberalism. Many held that an expanded federal authority in the economy and the centralization of power in Washington under the New Deal required new strategies and more radical responses by blacks. Discouraged by what they felt was an inability or unwillingness of established black rights and welfare groups to provide that, they thus turned to the creation of other organizational means and the building of alliances with other groups. But if the means they employed were different, the essential objective was often that of the NAACP and Urban League: to force the New Deal and its liberal supporters into extending and expanding the scope of its reform ventures and embracing more completely the black American perspective.

II.

One who traveled that difficult road in seeking new or different ways for blacks to respond to the economic and political challenges of the 1930s and 1940s was John P. Davis. Trained at Harvard Law School, where he came to know Robert Weaver, William Hastie, and Ralph Bunche, Davis' own political priorities underwent considerable transformation during the Roosevelt era from an early sympathy with Republicans to a close relationship with the Communist party by the late 1930s. During that time he was an energetic political organizer, heading the Joint Committee on National Recovery from 1933 to 1935 and, after 1935, serving as national secretary of the National Negro Congress. During the forties he was active in Clark Foreman's Southern Conference for Human Welfare, and in 1943 he joined the late Robert Vann's Pittsburgh *Courier* as a political correspondent.[8]

These and other involvements placed him at the center of black social and political activity. And, perhaps more than that of any other

8. Davis' activities during the 1930s are discussed by Wolters, *Negroes and the Great Depression*, 61-64, 125, 127-29, 139, 141, 152-53, and esp. 354-76. Also Krueger, *And Promises to Keep*, 91, 116-17; Pittsburgh *Courier*, Sept. 16, 1944; John P. Davis, "What Price National Recovery?" *Crisis* 40 (Dec. 1933), 271-72; Bunche, "Programs, Ideologies, Tactics," 319-71.

Negro leader of his time, Davis' passionate advocacy of a black "united front" and of an alliance with the Negro's white allies provided for him a vast range of contacts that included black spokesmen, government officials, and white interracialists of differing political persuasions.

Davis' first venture into building a coordinated struggle of Negro and civil rights groups came with his leadership as executive secretary of the Joint Committee on National Recovery, an umbrella organization that involved a number of interests concerned with black welfare, including the NAACP. Formed during the summer of 1933, the Joint Committee grew out of the concerns of Davis and Robert Weaver, who had earlier established the Negro Industrial League to keep tabs on New Deal legislation during the "Hundred Days." The Negro League never consisted of more than the personal efforts of Davis and Weaver, who attended congressional hearings dealing with proposed legislation and tried to express the interests of black people.[9] In July 1933, therefore, Davis proposed to the NAACP, the National Urban League, and other groups the creation of an "organization or agency which can speak with authority for the major organized forces among Negroes, that can speak quickly and intelligently."[10]

Although the Joint Committee never fulfilled his hopes, what Davis had in mind—and what guided his thinking throughout the years—was set forth in a statement written in the summer of 1933. A "change of national administrations," he maintained, "has seen vast changes wrought in the methods used to bring about national recovery. Vast power has been vested in the President and the mode of attack on the problem caused by the depression has shifted from cumbersome legislative action to swift administrative control. This change has made necessary a different set of tactics for Negro

9. "The Negro Industrial League," undated ms., NNC Papers, NYPL (Schomburg Collection), Box 2. This paper indicates that the idea for the Industrial League orginated with a group of black graduate students in the East, primarily those attending Harvard University; "at the time of the hearings on the proposed codes for fair competition at Washington, there seemed to be no Negro organization ready to represent the interests of the race in these new economic arrangements." Also, for discussion of Davis and Weaver activities, see Wolters, *Negroes and the Great Depression,* 110-11, and Ross, *J.E. Spingarn*, 152-53.

10. Davis, "Suggested Plan for Coordination of Negro Organizations for the Purpose of Integrating Interests of the Negro in All Federal Recovery Projects," July 10, 1933, NNC Papers, Box 1.

organizations engaged in advancing the welfare of the American Negro."[11]

Davis did not propose in 1933—nor did he suggest publicly at any time in the thirties or forties—that existing organizations should give up their special identities or functions and merge under the banner of a new movement. What concerned him was that the "duplication of effort, the working at cross-purposes, the multiplication of expenditure for the same purposes is apt to be a great hindrance to the securing for the Negro of his proper place in the scheme of national recovery." So "multifaceted are the plans now in operation to bring about this recovery," he concluded, "that it seems essential that all organizations pool their strength in order that the fight can be carried on all fronts at the same time."[12]

Despite some support for Davis' scheme of a coordinated involvement of all groups concerned with seeing that the interests of Negro Americans were properly addressed by the Roosevelt administration, his committee was beset with problems from the start. The National Urban League refused in 1933 to back it and instead created its own watchdog committee, the Emergency Advisory Council (EAC), which in effect duplicated Davis' work.[13] Furious with the League, Davis claimed that the EAC was simply a paper organization, "an after-thought of those persons who, having every opportunity to cooperate with us, have chosen to play the field alone."[14]

Both the NAACP and the Rosenwald Fund were instrumental initially in providing the Joint Committee with crucial financial assistance; but by 1934 the Fund turned to other projects and was no

11. *Ibid.*

12. *Ibid.*

13. "Plan of Organization for the Emergency Advisory Council for Negroes," National Urban League, Aug. 28, 1933, Rosenwald Fund Archives, Box 306; T. Arnold Hill to Edwin Embree, Aug. 11, 1933, in which Hill indicates that pressure on the League came from its local branches to establish something like the EAC. Also see Parris and Brooks, *Blacks in the City*, ch. 25, and Weiss, *National Urban League*, 277-79.

14. John P. Davis to Frances Williams, Sept. 11, 1933, NAACP Papers, File C-311. Will Alexander also expressed disappointment at the League's unwillingness to support the Joint Committee, noting that he supposed it was "impossible to keep these organizations from functioning as organizations in relation to this situation in Washington. There is little glory to be gotten from having someone representing the organization in Washington." Alexander to Edwin Embree, July 6, 1933, Rosenwald Fund Archives, Box 94.

longer willing to accept the financial burden of Davis' salary, which it had assumed during the first three months of the Joint Committee's operation.[15] When Edwin Embree, Will Alexander, and Charles Johnson secured a $50,000 grant in 1934 from the Rockefeller Foundation to carry out their own investigation of "various government activities in connection with economic reconstruction," a project that led to publication of *The Collapse of Cotton Tenancy*, Joint Committee supporters saw another example of "playing the field alone." George E. Haynes, who was president of the Joint Committee on National Recovery and a prominent black sociologist, a former Urban League official, and director of the Race Relations Department for the Federal Council of Churches, complained to Will Alexander that the Joint Committee, given its purpose and financial needs, could have put the Rockefeller money to much greater use. Haynes predicted that the Rosenwald Fund investigation would simply lead to more unread publications.[16]

Of all the contributions to the work of the Joint Committee, that of the NAACP was the most important and the most sustained. Yet the National Association's working relationship with the committee was never congenial. NAACP national secretary Walter White respected Davis' abilities but resented what he felt were his personal and political ambitions and his unwillingness to accept NAACP advice on tactical and strategic matters.[17] Making the relationship more

15. The Rosenwald Fund paid Davis $200 a month from Nov. 1933 to Jan. 1934, granting him a special "fellowship"; Edwin Embree to Davis, Oct. 30, 1933, Rosenwald Fund Archives, Box 406. For termination of the Fund's assistance, see Embree to Davis, Jan. 12, 1934; Davis to Embree, Jan. 13, 1934, Embree to Davis, Jan. 31, 1934, *ibid.*; Davis to George R. Arthur, Feb. 15, 1934, *ibid.*, Box 561. As he did frequently, Embree consulted with Alexander and Charles S. Johnson regarding their views on ending Fund support for Davis; see Embree to Alexander, June 4, 1934, *ibid.*, Box 105.

16. Memorandum, "Study of Negroes and Economic Reconstruction," Jan. 28, 1934, Charles S. Johnson Papers, Fisk Univ., Box 78; Will Alexander to Stacy May, Dec. 26, 1934, and Jan. 24, 1935, Rosenwald Fund Archives, Box 309. As noted elsewhere, May was an official of the Rockefeller Foundation. Haynes to Will Alexander, Mar. 29, 1934, Charles S. Johnson Papers, Box 309; also see Alexander to Haynes, Apr. 11, 1934; Alexander to Charles S. Johnson, June 9, 1934; Edwin Embree to Johnson, Apr. 18, 1934; Embree to Alexander, Apr. 14, 1934; Embree to Johnson, June 7, 1934, *ibid.*, Box 78.

17. From the beginning of the Joint Committee, the NAACP saw its financial assistance and the committee itself as temporary. White wrote to George E. Haynes, Sept. 14, 1933, NAACP Papers, File C-311, that the "NAACP has agreed to date to cooperate in this joint effort only for the period necessary for examination of the various codes being submitted to the NRA, up to the approval of these by the

difficult was that from 1933 to 1935 the NAACP was embroiled in its own internal controversies stemming from the race "segregation" debate, the resignation of W.E.B. Du Bois, and the Abram Harris "Report" which called for redefining the Association's racial philosophy and its organizational structure. As early as 1934 some NAACP members suggested incorporating the Joint Committee's functions within the Association, but White considered the idea sound only so far as it might allow greater NAACP control over the committee's activities, and that was unacceptable to Davis. By 1935, when the Joint Committee collapsed from lack of support, NAACP interest in its operations had already declined.[18]

Despite the financial backing given it, the Joint Committee's work essentially consisted of the singular efforts of John Davis. After Robert Weaver left the committee to join Clark Foreman's staff, it was Davis who functioned as chief researcher, organizer, and public spokesman and who endeavored to fulfill the committee's objectives of disseminating information to contributing organizations about New Deal programs and representing those groups before congressional hearings.[19] With characteristic tenacity, the executive secretary pursued the Negroes' case by testifying at NRA and other agency hearings and by publishing accounts of the effect on blacks of the Recovery Administration's wage differentials, the Agricultural Adjustment Administration's cotton subsidy policies, discrimination in relief and public works progress, and restrictions in federal hiring practices. Though his criticisms of New Deal programs won him, on occasion, the scorn of some officials, even those friendly to the

President. At the present time, we do not anticipate that this period need be longer than the estimated six months set forth in the tentative budget dating from August 1, 1933." In respect to White's attitude toward Davis, see White to William Hastie, Dec. 5, 1933, Feb. 9, 1934; White to Frances Williams, June 2, 1934; White to Hastie, July 5, 1935; White to Charles Houston, July 5, 1935, NAACP Papers, File C-311. Also see discussion by Wolters, *Negroes and the Great Depression*, 331-34; Roy Wilkins, Columbia Oral History, 65-66.

18. Abram Harris is one who suggested making the Joint Committee a direct part of the NAACP; see Wolters, *Negroes and the Great Depression*, 333.

19. The number of organizations supporting the Joint Committee ranged from 18 in 1933 to 24 in 1935, though the only organization of national importance and strength was the NAACP. On the origins and goals of the Joint Committee, see Davis, "What Price National Recovery"; "Report of Executive Secretary, Joint Committee on National Recovery Memorandum," June 2, 1934, NNC Papers, Box 3; Davis, "Report of the Joint Committee on National Recovery," *Senate Misc. Docs.* no. 217, 74th Cong., 2d sess., 10016, 41; Davis to Frances Williams, Sept. 11, 1933, NAACP Papers, File C-311.

Negro, Davis' objectives were not very different in the early 1930s from those of white liberals in the administration.[20]

By 1935, however, he had become more pessimistic about the New Deal's potential contribution to blacks and the ability of the Joint Committee on National Recovery to do much to change the situation. The Joint Committee had no real power to act on its own. It had no constituency and no resources beyond those provided by the organizations which gave it a reason to exist in the first place. It had to rely on both the willingness and the ability of the member groups to provide information Davis collected to rank-and-file Negroes and to put pressure on the government.

But with the possible exception of the NAACP, that pressure seldom materialized, at least not to the satisfaction of Davis. Few organizations supporting the Joint Committee's work had either the will or the capability to pursue such activity. When Frances Williams, a YWCA official, confidante of Walter White, and budget director for the Joint Committee, complained to White in 1934 that the committee was failing to "increase the Negro's awareness of what is happening to him," White had to acknowledge that the failure perhaps lay elsewhere. The fact was, he told Williams, "participating organizations . . . have not transmitted to our constituencies as we should have the information those constituencies needed about the work of the Committee." Knowing the " 'brother' as you do," White added, "you have an understanding of how great a task it is to stir him up on

20. One incident involving Davis and the New Deal created considerable discussion in the black press and led to some tense relations between Davis and race liberals like Harold Ickes. This concerned Davis' public disclosure of the minutes of a meeting involving Ickes, Frances Perkins, and NRA officials which indicated the reluctance of the New Dealers to send Mabel Byrd, a black woman, into the South to investigate charges of race discrimination. As noted earlier, Byrd was ultimately fired from her post, but Perkins and Ickes were incensed by Davis' disclosure, and the Interior Secretary sent an investigator to Davis to determine the source of the "leak." See Perkins to Ickes, Dec. 16, 1933; Ickes to Perkins, Jan. 2, 1934; Clark Foreman to Ickes, Dec. 13, 1933, NARG 48; Chicago *Defender*, Dec. 23, 30, 1933; Pittsburgh *Courier*, Dec. 23, 30, 1933. Many of Davis' investigations were published in *Crisis* and other journals; for a sampling see Davis, "Blue Eagles and Black Workers," *New Republic* 81 (Nov. 14, 1934), 7-9; "NRA Codifies Wage Slavery," *Crisis* 41 (Oct. 1934), 298-99, 304; "The Plight of the Negro in the Tennessee Valley," *Crisis* 42 (Oct. 1935), 294-95, 314-15; "A Survey of the Problems of the Negro Under the New Deal," *Journal of Negro Education* 5 (Jan. 1936), 11-12; Charles Houston and John P. Davis, "TVA: Lily-White Construction," *Crisis* 41 (Oct. 1934), 290-91, 311; and Davis' testimony in U.S. Congress, Senate, Committee on Finance, *National Recovery Administration, Hearings,* on S. Res. 79, 74th Cong., 1st sess., 1935, 2139-60.

non-dramatic issues even though they are so close at hand as in the matter of jobs, food, shelter, and the like."[21]

In the winter of 1935 Davis joined with Ralph Bunche, then chairman of Howard University's political science department and, like Davis, a strong critic of the New Deal and existing civil rights organizations, to inaugurate a new movement aimed at winning black and white support for the "non-dramatic issues" confronting black America. In May 1935 the two sponsored a conference at Howard designed, as they put it, not as another "talkfest" but as a gathering of people who "see in the social and economic problems facing the Negro the germs of national catastrophe," individuals who had worked on "some particular aspect of these problems" and were intent on "putting into operation . . . programs for solution."[22]

For three days, representatives from government, labor, the NAACP, and the NUL, along with Communists and Socialists, participated in sessions detailing the innumerable "problems" of black Americans and the failings of the national government. Though some, like Kelly Miller, maintained that little was accomplished other than denunciation of the New Deal, the NAACP's Charles Houston disagreed, reporting to Walter White that "John had a swell conference. Don't let anybody fool you. The speeches of the experts were informative and objective on the whole." Both assessments may have been correct, but Miller was right in noting that in spite of the broad range of opinions voiced at the gathering, most were extremely critical of the Roosevelt administration.[23]

21. White to Williams, June 2, 1934, NAACP Papers, File C-311. Williams in effect operated as a private source of information for White concerning the activities of the Joint Committee, esp. Davis' tactics and philosophy. At times she seemed impressed with Davis, but she also appeared to fear him apparently for both political and personal reasons. See the correspondence between Williams and White and Williams and Davis in NAACP Papers, File C-311.

22. John P. Davis and Ralph Bunche to Charles Houston, Feb. 25, 1935, NAACP Papers, Post-1940 File 138; also form letter, Davis and Bunche, Mar. 1935, "The Position of the Negro in Our National Economic Crisis," NNC Papers, Box 1. For general discussion on the background of the Howard Conference, see Wolters, *Negroes and the Great Depression*, 354-58.

23. Houston to White, May 23, 1935, NAACP Papers, File C-62; on Kelly Miller's views, Chicago *Defender*, June 8, 1935. For some of the papers presented at the conference, including those of Davis and Bunche, see *Journal of Negro Education* 5 (Jan. 1936), which devoted its entire issue to the event. The presence of radicals such as James Ford of the Communist party and Socialist Norman Thomas prompted a congressional investigation. See U.S. Congress, Senate, *Senate Misc. Docs.* 217, 74th

No one was more critical than Davis, who proclaimed at Howard and elsewhere that at every level the New Deal had failed to address even minimally the basic concerns of Negro people. Perhaps the best indication of the "effect of the New Deal on the Negro," he noted, was the increase of blacks on relief from slightly over two million in 1933 to three and one-half million by January 1935. Some might consider it a sign that the administration was "more charitable" than its predecessors; but, like Forrester Washington, Davis was inclined to view it as a failure of the New Deal to provide real security and employment opportunity for black people.[24] In October he argued that, in the "last six years of an extraordinary economic crisis," Negroes had been "made to feel the full brunt of exploitation. Every day since has swept larger and larger numbers of Negro Americans into the ranks of the jobless, the starving"; today, twelve million Americans "find themselves disrespected and victims of double exploitation; as Negroes and as workers."[25]

Inherent within the Roosevelt administration reform plans, he told those at Howard, was the "well-defined philosophy that Negroes must be left to develop in a ghetto of their own quite apart from the white population." On every hand the New Deal had used "slogans for the raw deal." Since 1933 the status of black workers, skilled and unskilled, had steadily deteriorated; as of December 1934, the black industrial unemployment rate had risen to almost 900,000.[26] The NRA-sanctioned wage differentials had increased the "inferior" position of black laborers, while PWA's equal wage order was a "paper ruling" and "enforced in only rare cases." Adding further to the workers' predicament were the Jim Crow policies of trade unions, which the New Deal did nothing to curb, and discrimi-

Cong., 2d sess., 10016. Nothing came of the investigation other than a harassment of Howard University president Mordecai Johnson. On the other hand, George Haynes was disturbed that Davis was pushing a "Negro Congress" prior to the Howard Conference while he was still officially executive secretary of the Joint Committee. Although Haynes agreed that there was need for "Negroes to help themselves out of their present plight through concerted political action," he nevertheless felt that Davis' "proposal is quite beyond the purpose and the policy of the Joint Committee and its officers," Haynes to Davis, Apr. 27, 1935, NAACP Papers, File C-311; Haynes was quite right, of course, since that was clearly what Davis had in mind.

24. Davis, "A Black Inventory of the New Deal," *Crisis* 42 (May 1935), 141-42; also "Survey of the Problems," 5.

25. Davis, *Let Us Build a National Negro Congress* (Washington, D.C., 1935), 5.

26. "Survey of the Problems," 9-11; also *Let Us Build*, 6, 9-12, and "Black Inventory of the New Deal," 141.

nation in federal relief and public works agencies, for which the government was directly responsible.[27]

In agriculture, the same bleak picture emerged. The AAA cotton subsidies had driven black farmers from the land, while the courts had stripped them of any legal redress against oppressive land-lords.[28] Davis argued that the Bankhead bill, intended to provide relief and assistance to Negro and white tenants and sharecroppers, would not afford "protection to sharecroppers against discrimination because of race, color, organization affiliation or . . . political beliefs." Such a proposal would instead "be used to drive a deeper wedge into the race prejudice which separates Negro and white on the same economic level."[29]

Hardly anywhere did he find in 1935 that New Deal reforms brought comfort to black Americans. Social security was a fine idea, but it excluded the largest group of Negro workers, household domestics and farm laborers; the CCC discriminated against black applicants and segregated the majority of those it admitted into its program; and the NYA helped a "few thousand college youth" but did nothing for the masses of poor young blacks. The administration, particularly the Justice Department, ignored the civil liberties and civil rights of blacks in the South, who were denied voting privileges by "Lilly-white primaries" and threatened by constant fear of lynch mobs. To be a Negro in America in 1935, Davis stated, "is to be robbed of the protection of law. Daily, black citizens are slugged and beaten by thugs wearing the badges of officers of the law. They are dragged into the courts whose 'justice' is a mockery to democracy. White juries, from which Negroes are systematically excluded, cry 'guilty' with utmost ease. White judges fix inhuman penalties, which white chain gang bosses execute like fiends."[30]

Davis concluded that the "present burdens" borne by blacks in the "period of national economic crisis might find some excuse if there emerged promises of a more equitable treatment of the Negro in the future." But unlike many New Deal blacks, he did not believe that likely, especially for a people who had "no voice in the government." When one viewed the "future plans of the New Deal, the plight of the Negro" looked as "dismal" as it had in the past. And "hardly anywhere in America does there exist for Negroes an effective

27. "Black Inventory of the New Deal," 142, and *Let Us Build*, 9-12.
28. *Let Us Build*, 14-16, and "Black Inventory of the New Deal," 142.
29. "Survey of the Problems," 8.
30. *Let Us Build*, 17-20, 24-27.

weapon to compel respect and justice from the government under which they live." Economically unorganized and politically impotent, black people were left at the exploitive mercy of the "employer group and an employer-dominated national and local government."[31]

To overcome economic disorganization, political impotence, and the lack of a "voice in the government," and to "compel respect and justice," Davis turned in 1935 to the creation of a National Negro Congress; and for the next seven years most of his energies were directed toward making the Congress into the united black movement he had envisaged for the Joint Committee. "Having spent nearly two years in close touch with the federal recovery administration," he stated in April 1935, "I am convinced of the necessity for the widest possible cooperation of Negro leaders and Negro organizations in an effort to win real economic and social gains for the Negro population in America."[32] Later in the year, in a pamphlet entitled "Let Us Build a National Negro Congress," he repeated his contention that "no single organization alone" could help the Negro's dilemma; the present situation demanded "united action of every form of organizational life among Negroes." The goal of a Negro Congress would not be to "usurp the work" of others but to bring "unity of action of already existing organizations on issues which are the property and concern of every Negro in the nation" and to "work for the solutions of basic problems facing the Negro."[33]

Initially, the hope of Davis, Bunche, and A. Philip Randolph, the dynamic leader of the Pullman Porters' Union who became the NNC's first president in 1936, was to build a nationally based, unified movement on two levels: first, making use of existing race and civil rights organizations and organizing rank and file blacks within Negro communities, and second, securing alliances with progressive white groups, especially labor, who shared common economic and political concerns with blacks. A coalition of blacks and whites was considered possible, according to Davis and others, because the "inequalities experienced by the Negro masses under the New Deal stem from economic and not racial causes"; and the "processes affecting Negro workers and farmers have their counterpart in the

---

31. "Survey of the Problems," 11, and *Let Us Build*, 5.

32. Form letter, John P. Davis, Apr. 18, 1935, NNC Papers, Box 1. It was this letter, written on Joint Committee stationery and sent to various individuals and organizations prior to the Howard Conference, that George Haynes objected to (see note 23).

33. *Let Us Build*, 30.

lives of the white working class."[34] But the goal was the construction of a mass struggle which encompassed the "broadest numbers of Negro organizations and individuals and such mixed and white organizations that are willing to join in the fight for the rights of Negroes."[35]

It was a tall order, and one which ultimately could not be filled—not, however, because of lack of commitment on Davis' part. As he had with the Joint Committee, he poured his energies and talents into trying to realize the ambitions of the NNC. With Randolph ill or devoting his time to other endeavors, it was Davis who planned most NNC strategies and carried out the difficult organizing duties.[36]

During the first year, as he had earlier, he emphasized black political unity. The first two conventions of the Negro Congress, in Chicago in 1936 and a year later in Philadelphia, suggested a fairly broad representation of black leaders and organizations. A number of NAACP and National Urban League members, some from the national offices of the two organizations, openly praised the goals of the Congress, and a few even served on the NNC's national board. Lester Granger of the Urban League was especially close to Davis in the early stages of the Congress and was a member of its board in 1936. Davis also kept the lines of communication open to blacks within the New Deal, informing advisers like Mary McLeod Bethune and Robert Weaver of Negro Congress activities and soliciting the New Dealers' support.[37]

Nor, during the first few years, was the black community slighted. Local NNC councils were established across the country, and accord-

---

34. "Survey of the Problems," 12.

35. *Let Us Build*, 29.

36. The papers of the National Negro Congress indicate little consistent involvement by Randolph in NNC affairs. Correspondence between Davis and Randolph was confined generally to suggestions by Randolph regarding individuals, particularly those in the labor movement, whom Davis might contact for personal or financial support.

37. *Official Proceedings of the National Negro Congress, Feb. 14-16, 1936* (Chicago, 1936); *Proceedings, 2nd National Negro Congress, Oct. 15-17, 1937* (Philadelphia, 1937); Bunche, "Programs, Ideologies, Tactics," Carnegie-Myrdal Study, 320-46; Bethune to Davis, Sept. 28, 1936, Nov. 24, 1936; Davis to Bethune, Nov. 25, 1936, Dec. 23, 1936, NNC Papers, Box 4; Davis to Bethune, Feb. 15, 1939, *ibid.*, Box 16; Davis to Weaver, Apr. 2, 1936, *ibid.*, Box 8; Davis to Granger, Nov. 27, 1935, Sept. 12, 1936, Aug. 11, 1936; Granger to Davis, Aug. 6, 1935, July 29, 1935, Nov. 13, 1935, Sept. 18, 1936, *ibid.*, Box 5. Listed as members of the NNC's National Executive Council at the 1936 Convention, besides Granger, were William Hastie and Henry Lee Moon, both affiliated with the NAACP. See also Lawrence S. Wittner, "The National Negro Congress: A Reassessment," *American Quarterly* 22 (Winter 1970), 883-901.

ing to a report Davis wrote in June 1936 some twenty-six community organizations had been already established, with another thirty in their developing stages. As might have been expected, the strongest councils were in northern cities where there was a heavy black concentration—in Chicago, New York, Washington, D.C., Baltimore, and Oakland, California.[38]

Yet despite Davis' efforts, the "united action" he and others believed possible in 1935 never materialized. NAACP official William Pickens commented shortly after the Negro Congress idea was raised that it was a "miracle of God to make twelve Negroes pull in the same direction," and it would be a "miracle beyond God to bring all Negro and pro-Negro organizations under one direction." Indeed, neither Pickens nor any other prominent leader of the NAACP gave support to the Congress, particularly after 1936, when even those who had indicated an early sympathy for the movement lost interest.[39] Neither the NAACP nor the National Urban League ever endorsed the Negro Congress, and the NAACP's powerful national secretary, Walter White, was suspicious of Davis and the philosophy of the Congress from the start. As he had done during the years the Joint Committee on National Recovery was functioning with Davis as its head, White suspected his younger colleague of personal and political opportunism. When in 1937 and 1938 the Congress made anti-lynching and wage and hour legislation two of its major concerns, the NAACP secretary was convinced that Davis was out to destroy the National Association rather than construct a united action campaign. White claimed in 1938 that Lester Granger had resigned from the NNC's national board for the same reason—namely, Granger's belief that Davis and others were pushing issues like anti-lynching simply to build support for the Negro Congress.[40]

As late as 1940, when it was clear to everyone, probably including Davis, that there was absolutely no hope for black unity through the efforts of a National Negro Congress, Davis still argued that the NNC's future depended on the "degree of unity and collaboration

38. Report of the National Secretary, Cleveland, Ohio, June 19-20, 1936, NNC Papers, Box 2.
39. Quoted in Young, *Black Writers of the Thirties*, 237; on Pickens and the NNC, see Wolters, *Negroes and the Great Depression*, 365.
40. See White to John P. Davis, Apr. 1, 21, 1938; Davis to White, Apr. 30, 1938; memo, White to Roy Wilkins and Charles Houston, Mar. 8, 1938; White to Leon A. Ramson, Mar. 4, 1938, NAACP Papers, File C-383.

which we can create amongst the Negro people and their organizations on the basis of a common unifying program."[41]

In part because that could not be achieved, but also because Davis
continued to hold that a broad-based, nationally organized movement representing the economic and political needs of all blacks was
essential to gain Negroes a voice in government and effect changes
in New Deal policies, he came to rely increasingly on alliances with
organized white groups. By 1937 and early 1938, the two most
highly organized political movements that showed an interest in the
National Negro Congress were the American Communist party and
John L. Lewis' Congress of Industrial Organizations. In December
1936 Davis wrote to a friend that "because we realize that lack of
organization lay at the bottom of the joblessness of Negro workers
we have thrown ourselves into the most significant of organization
campaigns: the steel drive."[42] A year later, he thanked Lewis for the
CIO's "confidence in our work" and their "substantial contribution."
Urging Lewis to appoint a black labor leader as an executive assistant
in the CIO's national office, he maintained that such an appointment
would strengthen the Negro Congress "in our attempt to win the
Negro workers to the industrial unions of the CIO."[43]

In a speech to the National Convention of Social Workers in
1936, Davis had attacked W.E.B. Du Bois' economic segregation
philosophy, arguing that attempts by "some Negro leaders to envi-
sion a separate Negro economic order . . . is a vision doomed to be
wrecked on the shoals of economic reality." The "only hope of the
Negro to effect any meaningful improvement of his social and
economic status," he concluded, "is through his alignment with the
progressive forces of organized labor."[44] By 1940, as others have
often noted, the alignment of the NNC with not only these forces but
with the Communist party as well had become so complete that
there was little trace of the early emphasis given to black unity. At
the NNC's 1940 convention, Randolph concluded that it was no
longer a "Negro" Congress and dramatically resigned the presi-

41. Report of John P. Davis, National Negro Congress, Apr. 27, 1940, NNC
Papers, Box 21.
42. Davis to Marcus Goldman, Dec. 29, 1936, *ibid.,* Box 5.
43. Davis to John L. Lewis, Oct. 19, 1937, *ibid.*, Box 11. See also Wolters, *Negroes
and the Great Depression*, 367-68.
44. Speech, National Convention of Social Workers, Atlantic City, N.J., May 25,
1936, NNC Papers, Box 15.

dency. A few years later, Davis also left the Congress to become a writer for the Pittsburgh *Courier*.[45]

What had happened? Why did the National Negro Congress fail to live up to the ambitions even political realists like Ralph Bunche originally hoped it might achieve in 1935? The argument that John Davis' cozy relationship with the Communists and with industrial unions doomed the NNC and destroyed its legitimacy as a representative of black people is somewhat misdirected.[46] It was true, certainly, that by the late 1930s the Communist party had assumed considerable influence with Davis and in the Congress, and that as early as 1936 the NNC national secretary's strong backing of the steel workers had led Lester Granger to write that he feared the Congress might become a "temporary subsidiary of the S. W. O. C. rather than a national organization for education and correlation of Negro effort."[47] But Davis' reliance on Communists, as well as on industrial unions like the steelworkers, came only after the theme of black unity appeared to him to have little possibility of success. It may well have been that Davis was too impatient, that he failed to give enough time or attention to organizing the black grass roots and to developing a confident working relationship with established black rights organizations.

But the initial response from groups like the NAACP and NUL to the NNC's "united action" appeals was not encouraging, and the lack of financial support for its organizing efforts and the difficulty involved in inspiring Negro interest in what White had called the "non-dramatic issues" further weakened the Congress. From Davis' perspective, given the urgencies of the time, black people simply had to be organized. When he was unable to achieve this through black leaders and black organizations themselves, he turned to those he thought could accomplish the task—Communists and labor. Yet

---

45. Bunche, "Programs, Ideologies, Tactics," 353-71; Wittner, "National Negro Congress," 897-901; Record, *The Negro and the Communist Party*, 191-99, 154-59; and Wolters, *Negroes and the Great Depression*, 368-72, all discuss the last years of the NNC and the 1940 convention, though often with different emphases.

46. That was the view of A. Philip Randolph, of course, and has been best stated in Cruse, *Crisis of the Negro Intellectual*, 171-80; Record, *The Negro and the Communist Party*, 191-99; Bunche, "Programs, Ideologies, Tactics," 319-71. The interpretation expressed in these pages follows from an analysis of the NNC Papers and fits more closely the analysis of Wolters, *Negroes and the Great Depression*, 353-82, and Wittner, "National Negro Congress," esp. 897-99.

47. Granger to Davis, Aug. 10, 1936, Sept. 18, 1936, NNC Papers, Box 5.

by that time it was too late, and when the stress shifted to class rather than race alliances, Randolph and others were correct in assuming that blacks no longer determined NNC priorities.

More important, however, it was the New Deal which had much to do with the NNC's failures. The Congress' ultimate purpose was to organize black people and to organize political coalitions to bring about what Robert Vann, in a less radical way, also sought—black political independence. At its 1936 convention, Davis and others asserted that it was the responsibility of the Negro Congress to "articulate the demands of Negro voters to candidates on both a national and local scale. . . . We must make the Negro question a vital issue in the election campaigns."[48] After Roosevelt's landslide victory in 1936, he noted that the election might signify a "decline in indignities heaped on Negroes," but "we know unless substantial pressure is exerted on Congress, on the President, on state legislatures, this hope will go unfilled."[49]

The pursuit of black political independence came at an inopportune time, however; Franklin Roosevelt and the Democratic party were at the height of their popularity, and black voters—where they existed—were turning their support to the New Deal. Davis and the NNC were confronted, then, with a difficulty like that faced by Norman Thomas and the Socialists, especially when it came to the "bread and butter" or the "non-dramatic issues": whatever the limits of the New Deal's reforms, they did provide some real benefits to many blacks which were far more attractive than the theoretical hopes held out by a Negro Congress or a Socialist party.

Unable to organize the black community against New Deal shortcomings, the NNC shifted its emphasis from racial to economic coalitions, affirming the "common interests" of black and white; but that, in turn, drew it farther into the orbit of New Deal racial reform philosophy. Thus, by 1938, Davis was asking Harold Ickes to address a Negro Congress conference in Baltimore, praising the Secretary for his efforts on behalf of Negroes, and assuring him that the NNC had "consistently supported the politics of the Roosevelt administration, both foreign and domestic." Two years later, Davis wrote a political draft intended for NNC supporters entitled "The Negro Vote and the New Deal," in which he urged the Congress to

48. Quoted in Bunche, "Programs, Ideologies, Tactics," 357-358. See also *Official Proceedings of the National Negro Congress, 1936* for political resolutions.
49. Davis to Marcus Goldman, Dec. 29, 1936, NNC Papers, Box 5.

help "win the Negro vote to support of the New Deal . . . in the general election."[50]

In the end, despite his long efforts, Davis was unable to construct a "united action" movement which provided a serious challenge to either existing black rights organizations or to the Roosevelt administration. By the late 1930s, the philosophy and activity of the National Negro Congress led to simply attacking the New Deal for not going far enough in its reform program, and this, in effect, put it in the same company as the moderate NAACP and blacks working within the administration. The demise of the NNC as a potentially powerful expression of black sentiment and of Davis as a potentially forceful spokesman against race and class oppression came long before both were absorbed by the Communist party and industrial unionists.

The difficulties encountered by the Joint Committee on National Recovery, the National Negro Congress, and John P. Davis in trying to give rise to an independent black political movement during the thirties and forties were experienced also by Davis' one-time ally, A. Philip Randolph. The activities of Randolph from 1917, when he and Chandler Owens founded the *Messenger*—"the Only Radical Negro Magazine in America"—through the 1920s and 1930s, when he headed the Brotherhood of Sleeping Car Porters and was president of the Negro Congress, followed by his leadership of the March on Washington Movement in the 1940s, made him, in the words of Lewis Killian, "*the* Negro leader in America."[51]

Randolph, in effect, attempted to capitalize on his immense popularity, as well as his previous experiences, to transform what was initially in 1940 a proposed "march" to secure blacks opportunities in the armed forces and the national defense industries into a full-scale "movement" to achieve political and economic reform for the Negro masses. Many historians, indeed, have seen the March on

50. Davis to Ickes, Nov. 15, 1938, *ibid.*, Box 13; Davis, "The Negro Vote and the New Deal," draft of paper, 1940, *ibid.*, Box 16.
51. Killian, in introduction to Herbert Garfinkel, *When Negroes March: The March on Washington Movement in the Organizational Politics for FEPC* (1968 ed., New York). For discussion of various aspects of Randolph's career, see Garfinkel; Theodore Kornweibel, Jr., "*No Crystal Stair": Black Life and the Messenger, 1917-1928* (Westport, Conn., 1975); Jervis Anderson, *A. Philip Randolph: A Biographical Portrait* (New York, 1973). Also, especially for MOWM and the 1940s, Louis C. Kesselman, *The Social Politics of FEPC: A Study in Reform Pressure Movements* (Chapel Hill, 1948); Richard M. Dalfiume, *Fighting on Two Fronts: Desegregation of the Armed Forces, 1939-1953* (Columbus, Mo., 1969), and "The 'Forgotten Years' of the Negro Revolution," *Journal of American History* 55 (June 1968), 90-116. A recent discussion of some of Randolph's ideas during the 1930s is found in Young, *Black Writers of the Thirties*, 65-76.

Washington Movement as representing "something different in black protest," something that symbolized the beginning of the "Negro revolution" that emerged in the late 1950s and early 1960s.[52]

In part, what they have perceived as distinguishing MOWM from earlier protest struggles, including that of the Negro Congress, was Randolph's conscious policy of excluding whites from his organization, thereby ensuring that the movement would be black-led and black-organized. That was certainly the case, but there were also some basic similarities between the MOWM and the NNC. Both were attempts at building a mass structure which would allow Negroes effectively to pressure government, political parties, business, and labor groups into responding more directly to black needs. Both the MOWM and the NNC considered integration as the ultimate objective of the black American, and whatever the different means employed, they worked consciously for that end.[53]

It was Randolph's involvement as a Socialist and labor organizer in the twenties and his analysis of the Roosevelt administration in the thirties, as well as his experience with the Negro Congress, that determined his approach to the MOWM and his attempt to separate it from other struggles. Theodore Kornweibel, Jr., who has studied his career with the *Messenger* and the Sleeping Car Porters, concludes that the "twenties had taught Randolph that economic and political issues were inextricably intertwined, but that no political solution was likely until the race, primarily through its own efforts, gained a measure of economic security and power. This was the thrust of the Brotherhood, a grass roots organization depending solely on black support, black idealism, and black will to struggle."[54]

His criticisms of the New Deal, in spite of the Pullman Porters being direct beneficiaries of the administration's labor policies, led him in 1935 and for a brief period thereafter to identify the "thrust of the Brotherhood" with that of the National Negro Congress. Like other blacks who rejected New Deal liberalism, Randolph considered it both politically and psychologically dangerous for the Negro to depend on the Roosevelt government or its white supporters to alter the circumstances of race and class oppression. The New Deal,

---

52. Dalfiume, "The 'Forgotten Years,'" 99; Garfinkel, *When Negroes March*, 8.
53. For analysis of the MOWM's goals and strategies, see Garfinkel, *When Negroes March*, 102-49.
54. Kornweibel, Jr., *"No Crystal Stair,"* 261. For earlier analysis of Randolph's involvement with the Pullman Porters' Union, see Brailsford R. Brazeal, *The Brotherhood of Sleeping Car Porters: Its Origins and Development* (New York, 1946).

he stated in 1936, was "no remedy" for black people; it did not "seek to change the profit system," nor did it "place human rights above property rights"; it simply gave to "business interests the support of the state."[55]

Whatever benefits blacks might receive from the federal government's relief and public works program, it was foolish to believe that politically Roosevelt or the Democratic party would do much to alter the environment responsible for the oppression facing the majority of black Americans. Randolph was not surprised that FDR refused to support federal anti-lynching legislation since, as he noted in 1942, the "South is in the saddle in the Nation's Capitol," and all the "ranking secretaries of the President are Southerners. The chairmen of the most powerful committees of the House and Senate are Southerners." And it was "naive" to assume that the President would "stick his neck out, unless they [blacks] have political power and sympathy to counterbalance the Solid South, which fights every effort to deal more justly with the Negro."[56] The Democrats, he argued in the thirties, were no different from the Republicans, and both were the "political committees of Wall Street and are constructed to serve the profit-making agencies."[57]

A government dependent for its power upon racist southerners and corporate business interests simply could not address the problems of black people. That kind of government, he affirmed, could not "tell trade unions and business that they should not jim-crow and discriminate against Negroes when it jim-crows and discriminates against Negroes itself."[58]

Randolph concluded, then, that blacks should neither rely on the New Deal nor "place their problems for solution down at the feet of their white sympathetic allies, which has been and is the common fashion of the old school of Negro leadership." In the final analysis, he stated in his first speech as president of the NNC, "the salvation of the Negro, like the workers, must come from within."[59] The following year, he told Negro Congress delegates meeting in Philadelphia that it was "more and more becoming correctly understood that the

55. Speech to the 1936 NNC convention (which was read in Randolph's absence), *Official Proceedings of the National Negro Congress, 1936*, 2-3.

56. Randolph, "Government Sets Pattern of Jim-Crow," *Interracial Review* 15 (July 1942), 101; Lawrence, "Negro Organizations in Crisis," 347.

57. Quoted in Young, *Black Writers of the Thirties*, 70.

58. Randolph, "Government Sets Pattern," 101.

59. Randolph, "Why a National Negro Congress," introduction to Davis, *Let Us Build*, 4.

task of realizing full citizenship for the Negro people is largely in the hands of the Negro people themselves. . . . True liberation," he added, "can be acquired and maintained only when the Negro people possess power, and power is the product and flower of organization—organization of the masses, the masses in the mills and mines, on the farms, in the factories."[60]

It was not only the inadequacy of the New Deal and the white liberal response to the Negro's needs that bothered Randolph but the state of dependence, politically and otherwise, that existed when blacks did not carry on their own struggle for equality. In 1943 he wrote that it was necessary for black people to cooperate with "mixed organizations" such as the NAACP and at times join forces with "white liberals and labor" in the "fight against Jim Crow . . ."; but the initiative for that fight must come from Negroes. No matter how much liberals and labor sympathized "with the Negro's fight against Jim Crow," they were "not going to lead the fight. They never have and they never will."[61] And when John Davis gave up on the idea of organizing the black community through black efforts, A. Philip Randolph gave up on the National Negro Congress. Black dependence on the CIO or the Communist party was no better, and perhaps it was even worse since there were no direct benefits assured, than dependence on the New Deal and liberal reformism.

Thus when Randolph laid plans for his campaign in 1940 and 1941 to open up the defense industries to black workers and desegregate the armed forces, he was determined to make the MOWM an all-black organization. In 1941 he stated that MOWM leaders do not call "upon our white friends to march with us. There are some things Negroes must do alone. This is our fight and we must see it through."[62] A year later in Detroit, speaking to MOWM supporters, he emphasized again the need for Negroes to acquire faith in their own leaders and their own abilities. An all-black movement, he maintained, "develops a sense of self-reliance with Negroes depending on Negroes in vital matters. It helps break down the slavery pyschology and inferiority complex in Negroes which comes and is nourished with Negroes relying on white people for direction and support."[63]

60. Speech, Second National Negro Congress, Oct. 1937, NNC Papers, Box 11; also *Official Proceedings, Second National Negro Congress*.

61. Randolph, "March on Washington Movement Presents Program for the Negro," in Logan, ed., *What the Negro Wants*, 155.

62. Randolph, "Let the Negro Masses Speak," *The Black Worker*, March, 1941.

63. Randolph, "Keynote Address to the Policy Conference of the March on Washington Movement," in *March on Washington Movement: Proceedings of Conference*

Randolph's fear of black dependence was similar to that expressed by Robert Vann and Forrester Washington. But it was one thing to articulate that fear; it was something else to channel it into a constructive movement of black independence. The Washington March did, of course, achieve some immediate results: the creation of the Fair Employment Practices Committee and certain initiatives by the government toward improving conditions for black servicemen. But the unified support from black leaders and rights organizations that existed in 1940 and early 1941 faded quickly following President Roosevelt's executive order establishing the FEPC and Randolph's decision to build a permanent grass-roots organization through the MOWM. By 1942, Randolph was listing eight major objectives for his new movement, including the elimination of "Jim Crow in education, in housing, in transportation and in every other social, economic and political privilege"; enforcement of the Fourteenth and Fifteenth Amendments guaranteeing Negroes "due process of law"; abolition of all suffrage limitations and restrictions; the end of discrimination in every area of employment, both private and government; and expansion of black representation in "all administrative agencies," as well as at world peace conferences. These were, Randolph argued, the "full works of citizenship," and Negroes were willing to accept nothing less.[64]

But Randolph and the MOWM were forced to accept much less. Richard M. Dalfiume, who has studied the war years closely, concludes that even FEPC must be considered a marginal success when balanced with the other demands made by the MOWM and Randolph's hopes for a permanent organization. Ultimately, Dalfiume states, the FEPC was more a victory for Roosevelt than for Randolph; in issuing the order, the President successfully weakened black opposition to his war policies and to the administration's handling of racial matters.[65] Relfecting upon the goals of the MOWM, Roy Wilkins has argued that there was nothing to differentiate it "from the NAACP—indeed, from the Urban League—and so it quietly died."[66]

Held in Detroit, Sept. 26-27, 1942, reprinted in Broderick and Meier, eds., *Negro Protest Thought in the Twentieth Century*, 204. See also Young, *Black Writers of the Thirties*, 70-73.

64. Goals stated in Randolph, "Why Should We March?" *Survey Graphic* 31 (Nov. 1942), 489; also Randolph, "March on Washington Movement Presents," 133-62.

65. Dalfiume, *Fighting on Two Fronts*, 121.

66. Roy Wilkins, Columbia Oral History, 82.

That may have been true, but MOWM strategy was different, and it was that strategy which failed to take hold.[67] Like the Negro Congress, the MOWM and Randolph's hopes for it were doomed by the power of the Roosevelt administration to make partial concessions to black demands and the unwillingness of other organizations and black interests such as the NAACP to support a "united action" campaign. Randolph continued to be revered by black Americans for his ability to express their aspirations; but the mass movement concept in which he put so much faith as a vehicle for the realization of those aspirations failed to survive the war years.

III.

John P. Davis was certainly one of the more energetic black leaders during the thirties and forties, and A. Philip Randolph was unquestionably one of the most popular. But the Negro spokesman who had the greatest influence in the New Deal was the NAACP's Walter White. Light-skinned, blond and blue-eyed, born and educated in Atlanta, socially and economically middle-class, White joined the national office staff of the NAACP in 1918 and became its national secretary in 1931 following the resignation of James Weldon Johnson. For the next twenty-four years, during Depression, New Deal, World War II, and Supreme Court desegregation, White dominated not only the affairs of the NAACP but most of the headlines in the black and white press. Egocentric, at times vindictive when he believed his authority was being questioned, White could be also kind, gracious, and even self-deprecating when the circumstances seemed to require it. Though often disliked by both blacks and whites, he was a man who commanded respect for his tenacious commitment to causes like anti-lynching and the articulate manner in which he voiced the concerns of many Negroes.[68]

67. Garfinkel, *When Negroes March*, chs. 4-6, is an excellent study of the difficulties Randolph's MOWM confronted from both established organizations like the NAACP as well as the Negro masses once he endeavored to build a permanent, grass-roots struggle rather than simply a protest march. Garfinkel, 107-59, 183, also discusses the single-mass-movement approach—its limitations and its emphasis on the single leadership. Also Lawrence, "Negro Organizations in Crisis," 350-51.

68. At present there is no full-length biography of Walter White, but for an understanding of certain aspects of his background and career see Ross, *J.E. Spingarn*, 113-238, *passim*; Wolters, *Negroes and the Great Depression, passim*; Embree, *13 Against the Odds*, 71-96; Walter White, *A Man Called White* (New York, 1948), and *How Far the Promised Land* (New York, 1955).

White's importance to black Americans during the Roosevelt era was predicated on two major considerations: his leadership of the NAACP, the oldest and still the most highly recognized black rights organization of its time, and his close association with public officials and with other powerful interests in American society. To a great extent it was his interpretation of NAACP philosophy and his link to persons of influence that determined the direction of his leadership and his response to the conditions of the 1930s and 1940s.

In spite of its financial difficulties, internal quarrels, and declining membership in the thirties, the NAACP demanded attention, if for no other reason than its past record in the struggle for race justice and the continuing support it received from important white leaders and philanthropic organizations. As further testimony to its significance, many young black intellectuals of the time, like Abram Harris, E. Franklin Frazier, Ralph Bunche, and William Hastie, directed their efforts toward trying to influence the NAACP's policies, and John Davis and Philip Randolph were obliged to accommodate the association in their struggles. By 1935 the NAACP and Walter White had survived two major challenges: the "segregation" issue raised by White's long-time antagonist, W.E.B. Du Bois, and in 1934 the internal report concerning the NAACP prepared by Abram Harris' committee.[69]

Du Bois and the segregation debate are discussed briefly in the following chapter. But the most immediate result of the controversy was Du Bois' resignation from the NAACP, a personal victory for White. The philosophy of black economic self-determination—the building of a "Negro Nation Within the Nation"—won for Du Bois few backers, even from those who were close to the veteran civil rights advocate and scholar.[70]

But that was not the case with the Harris report. Harris, a professor of economics at Howard University and an NAACP board member, was put in charge in July 1934 of a special committee to assess the "Future Plan and Program of the NAACP." Though much was incorporated in the committee's final recommendations, Harris

69. Both Ross and Wolters provide a good discussion of the issues and tensions affecting the NAACP in the Depression and New Deal years. See Ross, *J.E. Spingarn*, chs. 6-8, and Wolters, *Negroes and the Great Depression, passim*, but esp. 230-52 in respect to Du Bois and the Harris report. Also on Du Bois, see Young, *Black Writers of the Thirties*, 19-29.

70. For criticisms of Du Bois' ideas, Wolters, *Negroes and the Great Depression*, 249-58; Young, *Black Writers of the Thirties*, ch. 2. For a particularly strong attack on Du Bois by a young militant, see E. Franklin Frazier, "The Du Bois Program in the Present Crisis," *Race* I (Winter 1935-36), 11-13.

and a number of his colleagues gave primary emphasis to the need to decentralize power within the National Association, develop more direct action, build grass-roots political strategies, and formulate an economic program that might encourage class and labor alliances between blacks and whites. Many of the assumptions reflected in the Harris report had been expressed earlier, especially at the Second Amenia conference in 1933; and though neither White nor the NAACP board accepted the major proposals, the ideas continued to have support from younger black spokesmen throughout the 1930s and early 1940s. Some of those who identified with Harris' recommendations participated in the Davis-Bunche Howard University conference in 1935, and for a time they looked to the National Negro Congress as fulfilling their concerns.[71]

White's response to these challenges, as well as to the New Deal, was essentially to keep the NAACP committed to its traditional legal, political, and educational integrationist priorities while he pursued, especially after 1935, the quest for federal anti-lynching legislation. This did not mean, however, that either White or the NAACP ignored those fundamental economic issues that were central to New Deal reform and to the lives of black Americans. The ability of the NAACP to survive the Depression years and to grow in strength during the 1940s rested in part on White's ability to involve the association in economic and other critical matters. But how he did that seldom satisfied critics such as Harris, John Davis, and W.E.B. Du Bois.

It was, nevertheless, the investigations conducted by John P. Davis on behalf of the Joint Committee on National Recovery that provided much of the data used by White in formulating his own critique of the Roosevelt administration's programs and their limited assistance to black Americans.[72] Even if he disliked Davis, White realized the value of much of his work, and he continued to urge NAACP support of the Joint Committee through 1934, acknowledging that the "Negro would have been far worse off, bad as his present

71. On the Harris report, see "Future Plan and Program of the N.A.A.C.P.," esp. "Introductory Statement," 1-5, NAACP Papers, File A-29. Also Ross, *J.E. Spingarn*, 218-41; Wolters, *Negroes and the Great Depression*, ch. 12, for analysis of the report and reaction within and outside the NAACP.

72. Through Frances Williams, previously mentioned, and in direct communication with Davis himself, White was close to the Joint Committee's investigations and Davis' work. Also, as noted, Davis published many of his findings in the pages of the *Crisis*. For correspondence, see NAACP Papers, File C-311; on the various activities of White in response to early New Deal programs, see Wolters, *Negroes and the Great Depression*, 46-50, 61-64, 100, 111, 127-29, 179, 181, 185, 207, 330-36.

lot is, had not the Joint Committee been in existence."[73] Armed with Davis' analyses, White attempted in 1935 to secure approval from philanthropic foundations and others to have a congressional investigation determine the "discrimination against the Negro under the 'New Deal.' " In one of many letters he wrote to foundations soliciting their financial assistance, White offered his most complete criticism of the New Deal up to that time, a criticism which placed him in the same company as many of his more militant opponents.

"Through a variety of reasons," he wrote, "chief among them discrimination by local officials, no racial group in the United States is so disadvantaged, even during a period of attempted recovery, as the Negro." The plight of the "Negro industrial, agricultural and domestic worker" had "steadily worsened through wage and other differentials under NRA codes, through the reduction of acreage devoted to cotton-raising, and through discrimination by labor unions, which have prevented qualified Negro workers from obtaining employment even on federal-financed projects." The shortsightedness of AAA and NRA planners had worsened the already precarious status of black farmers and laborers; the FERA had failed to provide safeguards which might halt local relief discrimination practiced openly by southern racists like Georgia's Governor Eugene Talmadge. One of the most obvious manifestations of the administration's inability to protect blacks was the rise in the black unemployment rate, particularly in northern urban centers; it was almost twice that of whites. The effect of such joblessness and the absence of any real hope that things would be better was largely responsible, White believed, for the Harlem "riot" in March 1935; and it was "easily conceivable and almost certain that other riots" would occur "in New York City and other places unless public attention can be aroused and made effective in correcting these conditions.[74]

It was to arouse public interest in these questions that White apparently thought a congressional investigation would be helpful. The NAACP, he stated to potential backers of the idea, had been assured that once a resolution on government discrimination was introduced into the House of Representatives, the House Labor Committee would provide as much "latitude as possible . . . for the

73. White to Williams, June 2, 1934, NAACP Papers, File C-311.
74. NAACP Application to the Maurice and Laura Falk Foundation, Apr. 8, 1935, *ibid.*, File C-278. Besides the Falk Foundation, White also wrote the Twentieth Century Fund, the Rosenwald Fund, the Rackham Fund, and the Carnegie Foundation.

introduction of factual material."[75] To support that "factual material," White hoped to call upon sympathetic New Deal officials like Harold Ickes and Harry Hopkins, black critics John Davis, Forrester Washington, and the NAACP's Charles Houston, and black industrial and agricultural laborers who would "be presented as samples of those of their various classes which have suffered acutely" from government neglect and discrimination. He was convinced that if such an investigation were conducted, it would result in the "ending of at least some of the discrimination which now exists" and would "materially better the economic condition of many Negroes now in distress."[76]

Whether he believed such a study would actually accomplish those changes or whether it was his desire simply to increase political pressure on the New Deal and neutralize conservative influence within the administration is uncertain. No doubt White's need to affirm his own leadership and that of the NAACP as the leading advocates of black interests influenced his thinking, especially given the criticisms coming from the Harris report and the Howard University conference. In any event, despite the willingness of many to testify at the anticipated congressional hearing, foundation assistance never materialized, and by late 1935 White had dropped the plan.[77]

White continued, nevertheless, to challenge the New Deal in the thirties and forties for its failure, as he saw it, to support the economic and social needs of black Americans. In 1938, he urged President Roosevelt to include in his forthcoming "State of the Union" message legislation extending social security benefits to agricultural and domestic workers, expanding the Wage and Hours Act, increasing federal aid to segregated black schools in the South, and amending the National Labor Relations Act to prohibit labor union discrimination.[78] At the same time, he encouraged NAACP support of the CIO's organizing activities and gave his blessings to the

75. Falk Foundation Application, *ibid*. The NAACP had drawn up a sample resolution to be introduced into Congress; see "Resolution for Senate Investigation of Discrimination Against the Negro under the New Deal," Draft (n.d.), *ibid*.

76. Falk Foundation Application, *ibid*.; see also White to Forrester Washington, Mar. 11, 1935; White to Gardner Jackson, Mar. 22, 1935; memo on "Proposed Congressional Investigation of economic status of the Negro under the New Deal," Mar. 11, 1935, *ibid*.

77. White to Roy Ellis, Aug. 14, 1935, *ibid*.; Wolters, *Negroes and the Great Depression*, 336.

78. White to FDR, Dec. 23, 1938, copy included in letter of White to ER, Dec. 23, 1938, ER Papers, Box 1532.

National Association's legal staff to initiate lawsuits against wage differentials which affected countless blacks. In analyzing White's leadership during the 1930s,[79] Ralph Bunche, one of his most persistent critics, concluded that under his direction the National Association had become far more responsive to a number of major economic questions confronting Negro Americans than one might have expected given the NAACP's traditional approach to such issues.[80]

Yet it was also White's influence that limited the NAACP's ability to be more "mass oriented" in its appeal to blacks and determined its refusal to support those who did seek to develop a more broadly based, grass-roots struggle. Despite the urgings of William Hastie and, initially, Roy Wilkins that he do so, White never endorsed the National Negro Congress or provided it with much cooperation. In reporting to White and the NAACP on the NNC's first convention in 1936, Wilkins acknowledged that there was considerable criticism of the NAACP, but he saw the convention as "impressive" and argued that "criticism . . . would intensify a hundredfold if we held off and refused to take any part in this movement."[81] But White did hold off. In writing to Eleanor Roosevelt, he noted that the NAACP had not endorsed the NNC "first because we were not given sufficient information about its sponsorship, program, or purposes, and second, because there were too many rumors that it was being pushed in some respects by Communists and in others by Republicans."[82]

Communists figured in a different way in the support White did give to Randolph's March on Washington in 1940 and 1941. It was partly because of his fear that the Communists might "capitalize" on the tensions between blacks and the Roosevelt administration regarding the defense employment and armed forces desegregation

79. White discusses the NAACP's legal activities and support of the CIO in a letter to Guy Johnson, a southern white liberal, Mar. 15, 1941, NAACP Papers, unprocessed File B-220. Also Sitkoff, "Emergence of Civil Rights as a National Issue," 284-85.

80. Bunche, "Programs, Ideologies, Tactics," Carnegie-Myrdal Study, 167. White's letter to Guy Johnson was a response to Bunche's critique of the NAACP presented to the Myrdal project. Though he thought Bunche did a good job, he concluded that the Howard professor was not enough of a "realist" to understand the NAACP's difficulties or why it approached issues in the manner that it did; White to Johnson, Mar. 15, 1941, NAACP Papers, unprocessed File B-220.

81. Memorandum of Roy Wilkins to NAACP Board of Directors, Mar. 9, 1936, *ibid.*, File C-383. In his report, Wilkins refers to Hastie's belief that the NAACP should involve itself with the work of the Negro Congress. See also Wolters, *Negroes and the Great Depression*, 364-65.

82. White to ER, Feb. 28, 1936, ER Box 1362.

issues that he joined Randolph and others.[83] White, moreover, felt he had been betrayed earlier by the President after he, Randolph, and the Urban League's T. Arnold Hill had met with Roosevelt to discuss the future of blacks in the armed forces. Following their meeting, the White House issued a press release that implied the three black leaders had consented to the continued segregation of Negro servicemen; and White, like the others, found himself being denounced by many of his own race who feared he had sold them out. But once FDR created the Fair Employment Practices Committee in 1941 and Randolph showed signs of turning the March into a permanent movement, White's admiration for Roosevelt increased and his support for Randolph diminished.[84]

It was his personal desire to be seen as the administration's main source of information and advice concerning the welfare of black people and his promotion of the NAACP as the leading organization in the civil rights field that, as much as anything, determined White's response to racial and political events in the 1930s and 1940s. Critical as he was at times of the New Deal, White identified with its basic assumptions. Unlike many black leftists and race nationalists, he did not disagree with the economic or social objectives that guided the administration's recovery and reform program. And like his New Deal friends Harold Ickes and Eleanor Roosevelt, he was convinced that if blacks were properly included, their lives would greatly improve as the New Deal ideals were fully realized. As a committed integrationist, White also believed that liberal reform, whatever its limitations, offered the surest guarantee for the ultimate creation of a racially just society.

In addition, it was hard for White to ignore the fact that those who most often attacked him and the NAACP, black as well as white, were frequently the same individuals and groups who attacked Franklin D. Roosevelt and the New Deal. There was a fundamental connection in his mind between the social vision he and the NAACP held and that of the New Deal; and that connection remained intact despite instances, as in 1940, when he felt momentarily let down by

83. Garfinkel, *When Negroes March*, 39, includes a statement by White regarding Communists and why the NAACP supported the Randolph march.

84. White wrote to New York Mayor Fiorello H. La Guardia regarding the early meeting with Roosevelt and the effect of the White House news release, noting that "persons who are independent and non-partial and honest are flinging in my teeth that this unscrupulous thing has been done to me by the White House where I was naive enough to believe that we had friends"; White to La Guardia, Oct. 12, 1940, NAACP Papers, File X-36; see also Garfinkel, *When Negroes March*, 34-38. Garfinkel, 97-114, discusses White's and the NAACP's break with the MOWM after 1941.

Roosevelt and the government. White endeavored, in effect, to shape NAACP philosophy and strategy in accordance not only with past Association principles but also with contemporary reform liberalism. Robert Zangrando has noted that it was not just an increase in lynching that led him after 1935 to renew his anti-lynching crusade but that "New Deal liberalism, the expansion of interracial cooperation throughout the South, and recent victories within the Senate all augured well for the attempt."[85]

Strengthening White's identification with the New Deal and sustaining his faith in its racial commitment was his association with government leaders like Ickes and Eleanor Roosevelt and New Deal supporters such as Edwin Embree and Will Alexander. Alexander recalled that not only were he and White "good friends," there was never "a time when we didn't cooperate. Walter always knew what I was doing, and I knew what he was doing."[86] Embree was a source for both financial assistance and advice to White on matters involving the NAACP. In June 1935, for example, White sent the Rosenwald president a copy of the Harris report and requested his "critical appraisal" and "personal opinion"; Embree responded with a lengthy analysis that supported most of White's own views on the issues raised by Harris.[87]

But his relationship with Mrs. Roosevelt was special, and it was through the First Lady that he attempted to secure his political influence in the Roosevelt government. As did Mary McLeod Bethune, White frequently advised Mrs. Roosevelt about black concerns and particularly about how the NAACP felt on critical questions. Also, like Bethune and others close to Mrs. Roosevelt, he relied on her to convey his ideas directly to the President. In attempting to convince either the President or his wife of the importance of a particular issue, White often evoked the significance of the Negro vote to the Democratic party.[88]

Prior to the 1934 elections, he wrote Mrs. Roosevelt that blacks

85. Quote from Wolters, *Negroes and the Great Depression*, 351. See also Robert L. Zangrando, "The NAACP and a Federal Anti-Lynching Bill, 1934-1940," *Journal of Negro History* 50 (Apr. 1965), 106-17, which is based on his more extensive treatment in his Ph.D. diss. on the same subject but covering the years 1920-40.

86. "Reminiscences of Will Alexander," Columbia Oral History, 260.

87. White to Embree, June 19, 1935; Embree to White, June 24, 1935, Rosenwald Fund Archives, Box 302.

88. Both in the NAACP Papers and in Eleanor Roosevelt's correspondence, ER Papers, are countless letters between White and Mrs. Roosevelt covering numerous topics dealing with race matters. Also see White correspondence to other New Deal officials in NARG 69.

held the "balance of power" in many northern and border states; and if the Congress, with the President's backing, passed an anti-lynching law, it would provide a "valuable weapon" for the administration in suggesting that "what Republican Congresses failed to do a Democratic Congress had done."[89] In 1940, he passed on to Eleanor Roosevelt a Republican National Committee news release that showed 140 Republican congressmen supporting the Gavagan-Fish anti-lynching bill pending in the House of Representatives.[90] Later in the same year, after the bill had gone down to defeat, he provided Mrs. Roosevelt with a copy of a recent speech where he attacked both political parties for their failure on lynching but came down particularly hard on the Democrats. "We wonder if the Democrats," he stated, "have become so drunk with power that they are going to make the same mistake" as had the Republicans in ignoring black needs, thus driving the Negro back into the opposition party.[91]

White was not only trying to persuade the administration to be more receptive to black concerns or suffer the political consequences, he was suggesting that if the New Deal did not respond to moderate critics like the NAACP, it would possibly have to face a more radical opposition. To help the government understand that, in his correspondence with Mrs. Roosevelt and other New Deal liberals White kept them informed on the energetic involvement of Communists in black rights activities. Indicating in 1936 why the NAACP had not given its backing to the Negro Congress, he not only raised the issue of possible Communist and Republican influence in the Congress but noted that NNC statements were "especially critical of the NAACP, to the effect that we have been promising action against lynching and failed to show any results."[92] The message was obvious.

White's political strategy in relation to the Roosevelt administration was one of "loyal opposition." But his ability, and that of the NAACP, to command a strong political following among blacks was minimal. Quite often it amounted to little more than White's own personal protest when government policies appeared antithetical to Negro needs; and though he could be very articulate and persuasive in expressing his views on certain matters, he did not represent a

---

89. White to ER, Apr. 20, 1934, ER Papers, Box 1325. This letter prompted the First Lady to set up a meeting between White and the President.

90. White to ER, Jan. 29, 1940, *ibid.*, Box 1584.

91. White speech, June 23, 1940, in letter of White to ER, June 24, 1940, *ibid.*, Box 1584.

92. White to ER, Feb. 28, 1936, *ibid.*, Box 1362.

serious political threat to the administration. On the eve of Franklin Roosevelt's fourth-term nomination for President, he expressed fear to Mrs. Roosevelt that the President's dumping of Henry Wallace as his running mate in 1944 and the rumored selection of a southerner as Wallace's replacement might well "drive the Negro into the Republican camp." After Missouri Senator Harry S Truman was chosen to be the Democrats' vice presidential candidate, White remained pessimistic. He was "alarmed," he wrote Mrs. Roosevelt, "by the way in which the unholy coalition of Southern Democrats and Northern Republicans are riding roughshod over men like Mr. Wallace and Mr. Willkie. The debacle at Chicago, both in the defeat of Wallace and in the inadequate planks on Negroes and other issues should be enough to stir up decent people to a realization of their peril."[93]

But White was "most of all . . . disturbed by the despair among Negroes who feel that there is little for them to hope for from either party. Their sole ray of hope is that between now and election day the Administration, and in particular the President, will by act and word demonstrate that the fight for liberalism is not only going to be continued but will be stepped up."[94] That same year White joined with, among others, Mary McLeod Bethune, A. Philip Randolph, and Max Yergen, then head of the National Negro Congress, to declare the need for black political independence and a united effort of all blacks to assure the Negro fair treatment in both national political organizations.[95]

IV.

Even after 1944, however, there was more "loyalty" to the Democrats and to the memory of New Deal liberalism than there was independent "opposition." White's own leadership during the 1930s and 1940s was partially responsible for that. Under his direction the NAACP overcame some difficult times, and in fact during the war years the organization's membership and its prestige grew. Certainly the NAACP's status was enhanced—as well as that of its national

93. White to ER, July 7, 1944, Aug. 9, 1944, *ibid.*, Box 1751.

94. *Ibid.* For similar views by White written during the war years, see White, "The Right to Fight for Democracy," *Survey Graphic* 31 (1942), 472-74; "What the Negro Thinks of the Army," *The Annals* 213 (Sept. 1942), 67-71; "Democracy for All," *Interracial Review* 15 (July 1942), 104-5.

95. "A Declaration by Negro Voters," *Crisis* 51 (Jan. 1944), 16-17; New York *Times*, Apr. 30, 1944; Chicago *Defender*, June 24, 1944.

secretary—by White's willingness to associate its cause with that of the New Deal, and by his close identification with liberal reform and reform liberals.

But there was also a price to be paid for that approach. The lack of any economic program or philosophy hampered White and the NAACP in their appeal to both the black community and the New Deal. It was not that White needed to accept the plans of Abram Harris or the theories of W.E.B. Du Bois; but a more comprehensive economic analysis was necessary as an alternative to the federal government's response to Negro needs and the problems black workers and farmers confronted and would continue to confront under the New Deal's welfare state system. White was aware of these problems as a result of the findings of the Joint Committee, information supplied him by black New Deal advisers, and his own analysis of the situation.

What complicated his willingness to embrace a distinctive black economic perspective was his disinclination to entertain an organized political struggle outside the traditional legal, educational, and personal lobbying tactics associated with the NAACP. Because he had a voice within the Roosevelt administration did not mean that most black Americans did; in fact, his closeness to Mrs. Roosevelt, Will Alexander, and other New Deal officials limited his resolve to organize an effort to increase Negro influence within the Democratic party or build the kind of independent black politics suggested by Robert Vann, John P. Davis, and A. Philip Randolph.

There were, of course, immense obstacles confronting the NAACP as well as the National Urban League and other organizations that might seek in the 1930s and 1940s to construct alternative political and economic strategies; and certainly it was not just the responsibility of a Walter White to see that the NAACP departed from its traditional civil rights emphasis and tactics in order to embark upon the risky business of a more radical approach, as many were demanding from him. Yet the NAACP's prominence in the field of black welfare and White's personal struggle to assure his own leadership affected the activities of other black leaders like Davis and Randolph and, in different ways, those of race liberals. In that respect, the influence White and the NAACP had in their relationship to the Roosevelt administration extended beyond that of one individual or organization.

Despite his criticisms of the New Deal, White's activities and ideas affirmed the racial assumptions held by liberals in the administration. He was, finally, as much a source of support for people like

185

Eleanor Roosevelt as they were to him. Given the closeness of that relationship, it was difficult for Negroes not identified with White's NAACP or its allies to build the kind of political force that William Hastie, among others, considered indispensable in furthering the civil rights cause of black Americans.

There were other reasons, of course, for that difficulty, and they stemmed from historic and existing circumstances within the black community. Perhaps the most significant of these was the argument over whether race or class constituted the proper basis for organizing black people and constructing alliances with other groups in American society. That argument certainly affected the efforts of John Davis and A. Philip Randolph and even, to a lesser extent, those of Walter White. At the heart of the debate seemed also to lie the ability of blacks to define their differences with white liberals and the New Deal's limited response to their pressing needs. Even more so than black activists, black intellectuals spent considerable time arguing the priority of race and class in determining black social and political activity.

EIGHT

Race, Class, and Reform

THE INTELLECTUAL STRUGGLE

I.

"Unless the Negro can develop, and quickly, organization and leadership endowed with broad social perspective and foresighted, analytical intelligence," Ralph J. Bunche warned in 1939, "the black citizen of America may soon face the dismal prospect of reflecting upon the tactical errors of the past from the gutters of the black ghettoes and concentration camps of the future."[1]

The responsibility for providing the sort of attitudes Bunche noted in his dramatic statement has usually fallen to the intellectual class to which Bunche himself belonged. Whatever the individual's personal preference or tendency, the American social environment has often dictated that the primary focus of the black intellectual be on race and race-related concerns. The 1930s and 1940s were no different. Profoundly affected by the general political and social ferment of the Depression years, black thinkers, unlike the majority of their white contemporaries, were absorbed in the question of the "Negro problem," and no one was more actively involved with that issue than Ralph Bunche. Yet, as his essay in 1939 indicated, by the end of the 1930s the success of the black intelligentsia in supplying the necessary "social perspective" and "analytical intelligence" required for a fruitful Negro struggle appeared no greater than were the efforts of black activists.

Nevertheless, the thirties and forties were productive years for black intellectuals, many of whom were at the beginning of promising careers. In contrast to the twenties, when it was usually the creative writer and artist who was most prominent in Negro circles, during the Roosevelt era the influential thinkers were trained professionals, attorneys, and academicians, primarily those schooled in the social science disciplines. The majority had received advanced degrees from well-known northern institutions like Harvard and the University of Chicago; and for the younger black professional who

1. Bunche, "The Programs of Organizations Devoted to the Improvement of the Status of the American Negro," *Journal of Negro Education* 8 (July 1939), 550.

graduated in the late 1920s or early 1930s, intellectual maturity coincided with the Depression and the coming of the New Deal.[2]

At the beginning of the Roosevelt period, however, not every Negro scholar was at his or her prime. Some of those who had been most active in black affairs were near the end of their careers, including Carter G. Woodson, historian; Kelly Miller, sociologist and political writer; James Weldon Johnson, novelist, poet, and former NAACP national secretary; and W.E.B. Du Bois, dean of the black intelligentsia. With the exception of Du Bois, few would be around by the time Ralph Bunche wrote in 1939.

As in the past, black intellectuals were often engaged in the struggles pursued by their activist colleagues. Attorneys Charles Houston and William Hastie joined W.E.B. Du Bois and Walter White in the NAACP in the 1930s and were naturally drawn into the political and social concerns of that organization. Hastie was also prominent as a leader of the New Negro Alliance in Washington, D.C., perhaps the most effective of the "Don't-Buy-Where-You-Can't-Work" campaigns. Ralph Bunche, of course, had assisted John P. Davis in founding the National Negro Congress; and some of Bunche's closest associates, such as Abram Harris and E. Franklin Frazier, were active political commentators and, at times, directly involved in Negro civil rights endeavors. Moreover, Bunche, Harris, and Frazier all headed major departments at Howard University in the thirties, and because of Howard's location in Washington, D.C., they stayed close to the activities of both the New Deal and the black movements.[3] Even Charles S. Johnson, perhaps the least politically engaged of the younger intellectuals, gained influence through his affiliation with the Rosenwald Fund and, in the forties, through the Southern Regional Council.

But whatever the political involvement, age, or ideological disposition of black thinkers, what dominated much of their discussion and critique of black life was the issue of race and class. That issue was not new to black thought, but the impact of the Depression, the

2. A number of the younger black scholars—Abram Harris, E. Franklin Frazier, and especially Charles S. Johnson—were fairly active in the mid and late 1920s, but their major scholarly contributions came after 1929. For a discussion of certain black intellectuals, including some discussed in this chapter, see Fullinwider, *The Mind and Mood of Black America*; Young, *Black Writers of the Thirties*. Both books are distinguished in part by their willingness to argue a particular thesis in analyzing black thought.

3. Harris was chairman of the Economics Department, Frazier of Sociology, and Bunche of Political Science. Frazier replaced Kelly Miller in 1934 as the chairman of Howard's Sociology Department.

priorities of New Deal liberalism, and the activities of black and civil rights organizations in the 1930s and early 1940s gave added importance to the race-class debate and its applicability to the Negro's struggle for justice and equality.

II.

Over the years few had given more attention to that question than the aging scholar and civil rights activist, W.E.B. Du Bois. When Franklin D. Roosevelt assumed the presidency in 1933, Du Bois was sixty-five; his long affiliation with the NAACP and other causes and his numerous published works reflected a frequent shift of emphasis on race and class considerations.[4] By the early 1930s, however, Du Bois had turned to the theme of black self-determination and racial independence, and his strong agitation for that view, especially in 1933 and 1934, gave added assurance that race and class would occupy the minds of other black leaders and thinkers.

Du Bois' reading of the Depression and the New Deal's importance to Negroes differed sharply from that of most white liberals and blacks. As a result, after 1934, when he left the NAACP, he found himself isolated from most of the reform and racial activities of the Roosevelt era. He did not return to the NAACP until after World War II (and then only for a brief time), and he played no role in the formation or direction of the National Negro Congress and the March on Washington Movement.[5]

On numerous occasions Du Bois indicated that he had not discarded his belief that integration was a noble ideal to which all men,

4. There is considerable literature on Du Bois—his life and his work—and no doubt there will be more as his papers become more available to scholars. For some early biographical studies on Du Bois and analyses of his thought, see Francis L. Broderick, *W.E.B. Du Bois: Negro Leader in Time of Crisis* (Stanford, Calif., 1959); Elliott M. Rudwick, *W.E.B. Du Bois: A Study in Minority Group Leadership* (Philadelphia, 1960); Meier, *Negro Thought in America, passim*; Fullinwider, *Mind and Mood of Black America*, ch. 3. Du Bois' autobiographies are also informative; Du Bois, *Dusk of Dawn: An Essay Toward an Autobiography of a Race Concept* (New York, 1940), and *The Autobiography of W.E.B. Du Bois: A Soliloquy on Viewing My Life from the Last Decade of Its First Century* (New York, 1968). See also Rayford W. Logan, ed., *W.E.B. Du Bois: A Profile* (New York, 1971), and the previously cited Herbert Aptheker, ed., *Correspondence of W.E.B. Du Bois, vol. I: 1877-1934; vol. II: 1934-1944*.

5. Broderick, *W.E.B. Du Bois*, 175-91. Broderick refers to Du Bois after 1934 as a "Leader Without Followers," 175. Another interpretation can be found in Wolters, *Negroes and the Great Depression*, 248-58, *passim*, who acknowledges Du Bois' critics but places a different emphasis on his "isolation" than does Broderick. See also Young, *Black Writers of the Thirties*, 19-29.

black and white, should aspire.[6] The "complete integration of the black race with the white race in America," he wrote in one of his last statements as *Crisis* editor, "with no distinction of color in political, civil or social life" was no doubt a "great end toward which humanity is tending." It was true moreover that as long as there were "artificially emphasized differences of nationality, race and color, not to mention the fundamental discriminations of economic class, there will be no real humanity."[7] That was a view to which neither Eleanor Roosevelt nor Walter White could take exception.

But Du Bois broke with them in asserting that however attractive the ideal of integration was, there was little likelihood in the 1930s, or "for a century and more probably not for ten centuries," of its being realized.[8] What precluded the creation of an integrated society was the persistence of racial prejudice. Such prejudice, Du Bois believed, was "deeply entrenched in the minds of most Americans," and neither changes in the law nor court decisions would avail "until this fundamental attitude is changed."[9] "When I was your age," he noted in 1935 to George Streator, once his protégé at the NAACP but by then one of his numerous critics, "I did not expect race prejudice to disappear, but I did think that under barrage of facts and arguments, it would in a generation noticeably decline. This has been true in some respects, but the decline has not been nearly as decisive and rapid as I had expected, and I have come to the conclusion that we have got to regard race prejudice in this country as fairly permanent for practical purposes."[10]

The NAACP's educational and civil rights protests and the militants' theories on alliance between black and white working classes were based on sensible and rational assumptions; but they failed to understand that racial prejudice was neither sensible nor rational. In his 1940 autobiography, Du Bois observed that even though an individual "may act consciously and rationally and be responsible for what he does . . ., many of his actions, and indeed, as we are coming to believe, most of his actions, are not rational and many of them arise from subconscious urges."[11]

6. For example, see Du Bois, "A Negro National Within the Nation," *Current History* 42 (June 1935), 270, and *Dusk of Dawn*, 305.

7. *Crisis* 41 (Apr. 1934), 116.

8. *Ibid.*; *Dusk of Dawn*, 305.

9. Du Bois, "The Position of the Negro in the American Social Order: Where Do We Go from Here?" *Journal of Negro Education* 8 (July 1939), 354.

10. Du Bois to George Streator, Apr. 17, 1935, in Aptheker, *Correspondence of W.E.B. Du Bois*, II, 87.

11. *Dusk of Dawn*, 171.

What distinguished Du Bois, then, from other black and white spokesmen in the 1930s and 1940s was his belief that race was seriously underestimated in the theories and strategies proposed to bring racial change. To emphasize the larger social, economic, and political questions at the expense of racial considerations was, to him, naïve and dangerous. Such an analysis implied that blacks had some real degree of choice in terms of acting as part of a racial group in relation to those larger issues. The "Negro problem" would remain "tied to race," he argued in response to critics like Ralph Bunche and Charles Johnson, "so long as the majority of white Americans believe in race and color discrimination."[12] Whatever benefits the New Deal was bringing to Americans, black and white, the government could not—and should not—be expected to confront racial beliefs deeply entrenched in the American psyche. As a result of the Depression and the response of the Roosevelt administration, he noted in 1934, government had "entered and entered for good into the social and economic organization of life. We could wish, we could pray, that this entrance could absolutely ignore lines of race and color, but we know perfectly well it does not and will not, and with the present American opinion, it cannot." Were black people then, he asked, "going to stand out and refuse the inevitable and inescapable government aid because we first want to abolish the Color Line?" If that was the case, and that was how he viewed the position of the NAACP and of groups like the Joint Committee on National Recovery, then Negroes were "not simply tilting at windmills," they were "committing race suicide."[13]

Du Bois was not, of course, opposed to the efforts of John P. Davis and Walter White or to black advisers in the administration who were seeking to eliminate discrimination in New Deal programs. "In no case," he wrote in the January 1934 issue of *Crisis*, "should there be any discrimination against whites and blacks."[14] Some months later he affirmed that both black and white must continue to protest against all laws which deprived people of their basic constitutional rights.[15] Yet he believed that one should realize there were limits to this type of protest in actually changing the immediate conditions of Afro-American life. Speaking at the 1935 Howard University conference, he pointed out that although the Joint Committee had during its two-year existence "unearthed ample proof" of New Deal

12. "The Position of the Negro," 358.
13. *Crisis* 41 (Apr. 1934), 116.
14. "Segregation," *Crisis* 41 (Jan. 1934), 20; see also *Dusk of Dawn*, 199.
15. *Crisis* 41 (Apr. 1934), 116.

discrimination, as to what black people were going to do about it the committee had "nothing to say and nothing to think."[16]

The central problem was that the Joint Committee was composed of too many diverse elements, and thus it lacked a cohesive base from which to effectively challenge the government's policies or lack of them. That same difficulty had always plagued the NAACP and the National Urban League; nor was it being remedied by the types of proposals offered by young militants at the second Amenia Conference in 1933. Even though Du Bois agreed with the militants that economic considerations were of major importance to the black masses, he no longer held, as he had earlier, that black and white class solidarity was a practical or meaningful strategy for Negroes to pursue. Commenting in 1940 on the Amenia gathering, he remarked critically that the majority of delegates were in accord "that the primary problem before us was economic, but it was equally certain that this economic problem could not be approached from the point of view of race. The only approach to it must be through the white labor masses who were supposed to accept without great reluctance the new scientific argument that there was no such thing as 'race.' "[17]

But it was exactly from the "point of view of race" that Du Bois believed it was now important for blacks to pursue their goals. How were black people supposed to convince the government, white employers, or white workers that racial discrimination was unjust and contrary to the interest of American democracy? Racial prejudice, he asserted, did not respond to "scientific argument" or to moral appeal. The power interests that controlled the decision-making processes of government, business, and labor were white; not only would they carry out their policies based on economic and political self-interest, but that self-interest would be reinforced by their irrational acceptance of racial prejudice. He was convinced that blacks could not solve the white man's "Negro problem" for him;

16. Du Bois, "Social Planning for the Negro: Past and Present," *Journal of Negro Education* 5 (Jan. 1936), 122.

17. *Dusk of Dawn*, 301. Du Bois noted in the *Crisis* 41 (Jan. 1934), 20, that it would indeed be the "class-conscious workers uniting together who will eventually emancipate labor throughout the world." But that would not occur in the immediate future, and until the time came, it would be the "race-conscious black man cooperating together in his own institutions and movements" who would eventually "emancipate the colored race."

what they could do was solve their own "problem"—lack of group unity, pride, and self respect.[18]

Du Bois proposed the formation of a black economic cooperative enterprise based on socialist principles, racial self-help, and cultural racial nationalism, which for years had been one of his constant concerns. Central to his theory was the assumption that black people as consumers held in their own hands a powerful tool which, if properly utilized, could provide a foundation for developing within the black community an independent base of power. "A people who spend . . . $185,000 a month have got economic power, and of that there can be no doubt."[19]

What was required was for blacks to cease patronizing white capitalist enterprises and turn their purchasing power to manufacturing and agricultural businesses owned by Negroes. Profits derived from increased consumer spending, Du Bois believed, could then be invested in the black community, creating new enterprises and new products. In an essay entitled "A Negro Nation Within the Nation," written in 1935, he concluded that it was essential that black Americans achieve a "new economic solidarity. There exists today a chance for the Negroes to organize a cooperative State within their own group. By letting Negro farmers feed Negro artisans, and Negro technicians build Negro home industries, and Negro thinkers plan this integration of cooperation, while Negro artists dramatize and beautify the struggle, economic independence can be achieved."[20] It would be difficult, he acknowledged to George Streator; such a program "has vast chances of failure, but I believe it has clear possibilities of success, if it is led by trained men of unselfish character, and if it eliminates the private profit motive."[21]

18. *Dusk of Dawn*, 170-72; "A Program for Negro Land Grant Colleges," *Proceedings of the Nineteenth Annual Conference of the Presidents of Negro Land Grant Colleges*, Nov. 1941, 41, 48-49; Wolters, *Negroes and the Great Depression*, 240-43.

19. Du Bois to George Streator, Apr. 24, 1935, in Aptheker, *Correspondence*, II, 91. For discussion of Du Bois' early identification with cultural race nationalism, see Meier, *Negro Thought in America*, 193-95, 204-206; Vincent Harding, "W.E.B. Du Bois and the Black Messianic Vision," *Freedomways* 9 (Winter 1969), 45-57; Broderick, *W.E.B. Du Bois*, 151-69; Fullinwider, *Mind and Mood of Black America*, ch. 3.

20. *Current History*, 269-70.

21. Du Bois to Streator, Apr. 24, 1935, in Aptheker, *Correspondence*, II, 91. Also Du Bois, *Dusk of Dawn*, 300-16, and "The Position of the Negro," 362-68, for his elaboration of these ideas. For analysis of Du Bois' economic themes, see Wolters, *Negroes and the Great Depression*, 239-44; Young, *Black Writers of the Thirties*, 23-27.

Because his scheme for a black cooperative commonwealth was predicated on community need rather than the "private profit motive," Du Bois considered his ideas distinct from the economic philosophy of Booker T. Washington. The Tuskegean had perceived every Negro as a potential capitalist and had striven to ensure for blacks a place within a free enterprise system. In contrast, Du Bois asserted that capitalism was dying, and by organizing their separate economy along socialist principles of collective ownership, blacks would not only preserve their own integrity but set a new pattern of economic democracy for all peoples in the world to follow.[22] In 1936, he noted in his "Basic American Negro Creed" that "we believe in the ultimate triumph of some form of Socialism the world over; that is, common ownership and control of the means of production and equality of income."[23]

The only way for black people to create such a system, the only way they could overcome the internal divisiveness and self-interest which had characterized their struggle in the past, was to realize their common racial bonds. There was therefore "no alternative" but for blacks to organize and act as a racial group. "Jews cannot avoid anti-semitism by changing their names or refusing to cooperate with Jews for common objects. We have got to have racial organizations and recognize the group interests of American Negroes so long as outer pressure compels this"; and there was no doubt in his mind that in the 1930s and 1940s "outer pressure" compelled such a strategy.[24]

Du Bois celebrated the expansion of federal activities under the Roosevelt administration and interpreted it as a symbol of capitalism's decline. But he argued that New Deal policies would have little significance to black Americans unless they were well organized to take advantage of the many new economic and social programs. "In the recent endeavor of the United States to redistribute capital so that some groups may get a chance for development," he wrote in 1934, "the American Negro should voluntarily and insistently demand his share."[25] Instead of sitting around, refusing the

22. Du Bois, "Social Planning for the Negro," 116; "The Position of the Negro," 364, 370; *Dusk of Dawn*, 320-21.

23. Quoted in *Dusk of Dawn*, 321. He wrote to Streator in 1935 that since leaving the NAACP "I have been striving desperately . . . to get a growing group of young, trained, fearless and unselfish Negroes to guide the American Negro in this crisis . . . toward the coming of Socialism . . . along the path of consumers' organizations." Du Bois to Streator, Apr. 24, 1935, in Aptheker, *Correspondence*, II, 92.

24. "The Position of the Negro," 358.

25. *Crisis* 41 (Jan. 1934), 20.

"inevitable and inescapable government aid because we first want to abolish the Color Line," blacks should be prepared to take it no matter what conditions were attached. "Credit unions, home mortgages, farmers' credit and even industrial capital are available for Negroes at the hands of the government. Rail if you will against the race segregation here involved and condoned, but take advantage of it by planting secure centers of Negro cooperative effort and particularly of economic power." If blacks would do this, he was certain it would "spiritually free" them for "initiative and creation in other and wider fields, and for eventually breaking down all segregation based on color or curl of hair."[26]

For Du Bois, it was futile and ultimately suicidal for any black movement to build its struggle on the premise that Roosevelt administration policies would effect change in black-white relations. Depending on white support to overcome their difficulties, whether by appeals to government officials or by alliances with the white working class, left the initiative for change with the white community, which had been the historic source of the Negro's dilemma. There might be value, he argued, in blacks cooperating with the new industrial unions. Yet he felt that the "great majority" of working people in America were "thoroughly capitalistic in their ideas and their proposals," and the "last thing they would want to do would be to unite in any movement whose object was the uplift of the mass of Negroes to essential equality with them." At best, a labor-black alliance would be slow in coming, and "in the interim, minorities, like the Negro, must do something for themselves."[27]

Like other critics, he worried about black dependence on a supposedly benevolent federal government. It was true that under Roosevelt a necessary program of aid and public works had been inaugurated, and there had been a willingness to include Negroes in its coverage. But from the "point of view of race," there was little difference for Du Bois between the New Deal and previous administrations.[28] And unless blacks were to be forever subjects of the

26. "The Position of the Negro," 368.
27. Du Bois to Streator, Apr. 24, 1935, in Aptheker, *Correspondence*, II, 91.
28. At various times, Du Bois did have some kind things to say about the New Deal and Franklin Roosevelt. See, for example, speech before the National Negro Baptist Convention, New York *Times*, Sept. 7, 1935, and Du Bois, "What He Meant to the Negro," *New Masses* 55 (Apr. 24, 1945), 9, on FDR. Also Du Bois, "The Negro Since 1900: A Progress Report," *New York Times Magazine* (Nov. 21, 1948), 24, 54-59, and *Autobiography*, 304-306.

government, they must accept the fact of their racial separation, utilize the aid the New Deal was willing to extend, and develop within their communities viable institutions and group self-respect.

> Instead of sitting, sapped of all initiative and independence; instead of drowning our originality in imitation of mediocre white folks; instead of being afraid of ourselves and cultivating the art of sulking to escape the Color Line; we have got to renounce a program that always involves humiliating self-stultifying scrambling to crawl somewhere we are not wanted; where we crouch panting like a whipped dog. We have got to stop this and learn that on such a program one cannot build manhood. No, by God, stand erect in a mud-puddle and tell the white world to go to hell, rather than lick boots in a parlor.[29]

W.E.B. Du Bois' denial of interracial cooperation, whether of a radical working-class variety or of the kind envisaged by a southern liberal like Will Alexander, his affirmation of distinctive cultural and social characteristics and the necessity of black self-help and race unity, and his assertion that race prejudice was not on a decline as a result of the Depression crisis or liberal reformism but remained a permanent feature of American life challenged the basic assumptions of most black and white thinkers of the period. As a result, few found his ideas very appealing. Walter White, of course, claimed in 1933 and 1934 that Du Bois was undermining his own past struggle for racial equality as well as the historic rationale of the National Association's integrationist philosophy.[30]

But even militant critics of White and the NAACP saw little in Du Bois' thinking to command their support. Abram Harris, Ralph Bunche, and E. Franklin Frazier argued that his black consumer scheme was visionary and opposed to meaningful race cooperation and to socialism. George Streator, who left the NAACP shortly after Du Bois' departure and was in 1935 an organizer with the Amalgamated Clothing Workers Union in Norfolk, Virginia, concluded in a lengthy exchange with Du Bois that his former mentor had not

29. *Crisis* 41 (June 1934), 182.

30. On White's views, see White, "Segregation—A Symposium," *Crisis* 41 (Mar. 1934), 81; Memorandum of Walter White to J.E. Spingarn, Arthur Spingarn, Roy Wilkins, George Schuyler, William Pickens, Mar. 21, 1934, NAACP Papers, File C-411; Ross, *J.E. Spingarn*, 187-216, for general discussion of the White and Du Bois conflict and Du Bois' resignation; also Benjamin Stolberg, "Black Chauvinism," *Nation* 140 (May 15, 1935), 570-71, and letter to the editor supporting Stolberg's attack on Du Bois from Ralph J. Bunche, Sterling Brown, Emmett E. Dorsey, and E. Franklin Frazier, *Nation* 140 (July 3, 1935), 17. For other views expressed on Du Bois' "segregation" theme in 1933 and 1934, see *Crisis* 41 (Mar. 1934) and 41 (Aug. 1934).

clearly shown that he was "working for the ultimate coming of socialism. You had me believing that once, but lately you have almost convinced me that your objectives are hardly removed from the end of your nose. . . . You want security, prestige, and the good life, and socialism without a sacrifice."[31] E. Franklin Frazier, perhaps his most vehement critic, agreed with Streator, seeing Du Bois as simply a "representative of the Talented Tenth" and a black aristocrat with little genuine interest in the Negro masses. And Harris maintained that in spite of Du Bois' denials, his economic assumptions shared the middle-class bias of Booker T. Washington.[32]

The harsh tone of Du Bois' critics, particularly the young, partly reflected their feeling of having lost a black spokesman whom they had long respected for his courage and foresight in articulating the Negro condition and the quest for racial justice. Many found it disconcerting as well that Du Bois had raised the issue at the particular time he chose when, from different perspectives, they viewed the early 1930s as offering new possibilities for racial and social change. To the radical black intellectual, a "Negro Nation Within the Nation" was antithetical to the belief in black and white working-class alliance and the restructuring of the American social and economic order. For their more moderate colleagues, Du Bois' racial emphasis was equally harmful to the hope of bringing the black masses into the mainstream of American life through the assistance of New Deal economic liberalism.[33] It was this latter concern which occupied the attention of Charles S. Johnson, like Du Bois a trained sociologist, but one whose sense of the Roosevelt years differed markedly from that of his older associate.

On one point Johnson was in agreement with Du Bois. In contrast to E. Franklin Frazier and especially Ralph Bunche, he argued that racial attitudes were not simply "myths," and that it was not only the

31. George Streator to Du Bois, Apr. 29, 1934, in Aptheker, *Correspondence*, II, 95.

32. E. Franklin Frazier, "The Du Bois Program in the Present Crisis," *Race* I (Winter 1935-1936), 11-12; Abram Harris, *The Negro as Capitalist: A Study of Banking and Business Among American Negroes* (Philadelphia, 1936), 180. Also see Wolters, *Negroes and the Great Depression*, 244-58; Broderick, *W.E.B. Du Bois*, 168-91; Young, *Black Writers of the Thirties*, ch. 2, *passim*, for general discussion of Du Bois' critics, particularly the ones noted above.

33. Wolters, *Negroes and the Great Depression*, 230-65, and Young, *Black Writers of the Thirties*, 19-29, treat Du Bois' ideas and his break with the NAACP in a balanced manner. Their views are far less critical than those found in Broderick's *W.E.B. Du Bois*, 168-91, which reflects more the attitude of Du Bois' critics of the 1930s. Wolters' conclusion is similar to the one presented here, esp. in respect to Du Bois' challenge to New Deal race and reform thought; see Wolters, 258.

black man's being "poor and underprivileged and disfranchised" that accounted for the "Negro problem." In a critical review of Bunche's book *A World View of Race*, Johnson maintained that the "problem is not so seriously one of Negroes considering themselves as a race as of other groups treating them as a race with all the special connotations presently inherent in the classification."[34]

But if Johnson affirmed that race remained an important factor in the relations of whites and blacks, unlike Du Bois, he did not wish to celebrate its persistence but looked forward to its ultimate extinction. As did E. Franklin Frazier, who like Johnson was trained under Robert Park at the University of Chicago, Johnson doubted the presence of a distinctive black culture. "The significant fact about the Negro culture," he stated in 1940, "is that it was developed out of the conditions of life found in America and out of the materials found here."[35] Discrimination and racial segregation had fostered the separation of black and white peoples; but separation did not signify different cultural characteristics of the two races. "When there is racial segregation it is not in terms of two cultures, but in terms of different planes of the same culture. The fact that there is discrimination is no way of indicating the identity of the cultures, for the term has no meaning when they are different."[36]

Johnson's analysis of the 1930s and 1940s led him to conclude that there were major forces at work undermining race separation and providing the black masses with important tools and experiences which would facilitate their entrance into the economic and social life of the nation. It was "now clear," he exclaimed in 1934, "that we are passing through one of those profoundly revolutionary periods which come at long intervals and as the crisis of long accumulating forces."[37] Of prime importance were changes in economic condi-

---

34. Charles S. Johnson review of Ralph J. Bunche, *A World View of Race* (Washington, D.C., 1937) in *Journal of Negro Education* 7 (Jan. 1938), 62.
35. Speech, "The Negro's Contributions to American Culture," Virginia Conference of Social Work, Apr. 19, 1940, Charles S. Johnson Papers, Fisk Univ. Box 168. Biographical sketches of Johnson and discussion of his sociological and political thought can be found in Embree, *13 Against the Odds*, 47-70; Fullinwider, *Mind and Mood of Black America*, 107-15; Young, *Black Writers of the Thirties*, 76-84. See also John H. Bracey, Jr., August Meier, and Elliott Rudwick, eds., *The Black Sociologists: The First Half Century* (Belmont, Calif., 1971), 7-11.
36. Speech, "Can There Be a Separate Negro Culture," Swarthmore College Institute of Race Relations, 1936, Johnson Papers, Box 158; also Johnson, "The Education of the Negro Child," *Opportunity* 14 (Feb. 1936), 38.
37. Speech, "The Present Crisis and Outlook for Negro Americans," YMCA, Mar. 3, 1934, Johnson Papers, Box 171.

tions, and any "summary of Negro status is a story of attitudes changing slowly with the steady movement of economic forces."[38]

The growth of a more interracially responsive labor movement was one of the "forces" he considered particularly encouraging. "Negro workers are now recognizing in the C.I.O. the most strategic weapon for their advance as a class." And of special comfort to the southern-bred Johnson was his sense that "this bi-racial organization in labor" was not confined to northern industrial centers but was reaching into the deep South to include "white and black sharecroppers."[39]

Where many black intellectuals viewed the labor movement as a critical step in the development of a radical alliance of black and white workers, Johnson praised the Negro's inclusion in unions for the educational and economic training afforded backward black workers and farmers. He did not want to change the American system; he simply wanted to see barriers eliminated and a situation created that would aid black people's entrance into that system. An aggressive labor movement which included blacks and sought greater equity for all workers, regardless of race, was a weapon in achieving that end.[40]

But Negroes must be prepared to take advantage of such changes; they must have the proper occupational skills and the motivation necessary to make their involvement in the economic system a success. The National Urban League's Workers' Councils were designed to help that process, but Johnson, who later became president of Fisk University, believed education had a central responsibility in that task. It was extremely important, he argued, to remake "Negro labor to fit the exigencies of the new age." If the black worker was to compete with the white worker, if the Negro was to become a vital part of the labor struggle, he must not only have the essential skills but must be "better equipped and recognize the necessity of it." When asked in 1940 what black Americans might do to assist the American defense effort, he concluded that "they can acquire through conscious, even if unglamorous, preparative training the

---

38. Johnson, *A Preface to Racial Understanding* (New York, 1936), 11.

39. Speech, "The Negro in the New South," Swarthmore College, Apr. 9, 1939, Johnson Papers, Box 167.

40. See speech, "Changing Economic Status of the Negro," National Urban League, 1942, *ibid.*, Box 158; Johnson, "The New Frontier of Negro Labor," *Opportunity* 10 (June 1932), 169, 172; also Young, *Black Writers of the Thirties*, 80-83.

basic skills so widely and urgently needed for defense industries."[41]

The New Deal's economic and social reforms, its support of labor, and its concern for the economic problems of the South were, of course, warmly applauded by Johnson. Like those of his close friend and working associate Will Alexander, Johnson's racial views were shaped by his southern experience. Despite his years at the University of Chicago and later in New York City with the Urban League, he was a southern son. Born and raised in rural Virginia, from the time he went to Fisk in 1928 his personal, political, and scholarly ideas were rooted in his southern exposure. With Alexander and other southern white liberals he argued that "it should now be fairly clear that there can be no important change in either the economics or civilization of the region without a revision of the role of the Negro population in the total economy of the South."[42]

Johnson naturally found the President's support of Clark Foreman's 1938 report documenting the South's economic difficulties encouraging. Recognition of the South's plight, he stated in 1939, "more than anything else . . . is prompting a new approach to the problems of the area, and bringing about a new order of race relations. Race problems are being viewed by the new leaders, not as a separate and lamentable phenomenon, but as an element of the total structure and situation. . . . The strength of this new conviction has been sufficient to tolerate new racial patterns of relations."[43] And, in reporting to readers of the *Crisis* on the first convention of the Southern Conference on Human Welfare, he wrote that the "strategy of the Conference was sound. It aimed at being neither a labor meeting, nor a social work body, nor a race relations assembly. It sought to present the total regional configuration, with special elements and problems in their functional setting."[44]

The changes fostered by the New Deal, the steady advance of technology and industrial capitalism, and the inclusion of both the South and the Negro within the American economy made a deep

41. Speech, "Changing Economic Status of the Negro"; speech, "The Role of the Negro in the Crisis of Democracy," Detroit, Dec. 1, 1940, Johnson Papers, Box 173. See also Johnson, "New Frontier of Negro Labor," 172, and "On the Need for Realism in Negro Education," *Journal of Negro Education* 5 (July 1936), 382.

42. Speech, "The New Order in the South," Adult Education Conference, Atlanta, Mar. 5, 1942, Johnson Papers, Box 168.

43. Speech, "New Negro in the New South," *ibid.*, Box 167.

44. Johnson, "More Southerners Discover the South," *Crisis* 46 (Jan. 1939), 14. The one thing that did bother Johnson about the SCHE's convention was the "embarrassing and regrettable" attention given to race, though he acknowledged that such attention had a value in focusing awareness on the lynching issue. *Ibid.*, 15.

impression on Johnson's thinking. The combined forces of reform and the "new technology" were forcing a "disintegration . . . of the cast structure" in the South, disrupting "old racial stratifications" and bringing "new and more satisfactory relations." And the federal government's encouragement of a universal and equitable educational system was assisting blacks in raising their "cultural standards" and their desire for "cultural assimilation."[45] Thus, whether blacks wished it or not, they could not remain separated from the rest of society. "There is not and apparently cannot be an exclusive Negro economy within the American culture; the work of Negroes is seriously proscribed, but all such work is within the American economic system."[46]

Johnson's research and writings, his close association with the Rosenwald Fund and later with the Southern Regional Council, and his advice to those in government were all designed to advance that "work." Above all a social scientist, he believed that an objective analysis of the black condition would in the long run contribute most to eliminating the Negro as a "problem." "Charlie Johnson began being a social scientist," noted his friend Edwin Embree, before "he was out of short pants."[47] At Howard University in 1941, Johnson argued that "social and human interests must be guided by the same scientific postulation of observation, comparison and tests for validity that is required in any other field in which trust is sought." It was, he concluded, the "duty of the social scientist to destroy with fuller knowledge and insights, the taboos and traditions based upon ignorance and misunderstanding; to increase the kind of knowledge that will help us deal intelligently with public problems."[48]

In contrast to black intellectuals like Du Bois and Bunche, Johnson was not a political activist; his "scientific" view of scholarship and his own personality precluded an active engagement in social and political movements. But what gave Johnson's ideas a larger audience and thus greater significance than might be expected in the case of such a scholar was his belief that scholarship should help guide public policy and his close association with individuals

45. Speech, "The Negro and the Present Crisis," n.d., Johnson Papers, Box 167; see also speech, "New Negro in the New South," *ibid.* Reference to "standards" and "assimilation" in speech, "New Negro in the New South"; also Johnson, "Education of the Negro Child," 38-39.

46. Speech, "Can There Be a Separate Negro Culture," Johnson Papers, Box 158; Young, *Black Writers of the Thirties*, 78-83.

47. Embree, *13 Against the Odds*, 47. See also Young, *Black Writers of the Thirties*, 76.

48. Speech, Howard Univ., June 13, 1941, Johnson Papers, Box 163.

who were directly involved in that endeavor. His publication with Edwin Embree and Will Alexander of *The Collapse of Cotton Tenancy* in 1935 was an example of how research might directly influence government action. Later in the thirties he also served as a consultant to the Department of Agriculture, and in the early war years he was a representative on the Labor Department's Committee on Fair Labor Standards.[49] But his relationship with men like Embree and Alexander, and often their reliance on him for an understanding of the "Negro problem," gave Johnson perhaps his strongest impact. "We worked together very well," Alexander noted, and Embree, upon leaving the Rosenwald Fund in 1948, praised Johnson for his devoted friendship: "You know how I feel about you—a feeling equally divided between fondness and admiration."[50] This admiration derived, in part, from Johnson's broad contacts with other black leaders and organizations; from his counsel to Embree and Alexander, who sought him out before making recommendations to the government on potential black advisers or on policy matters; and from his advice to his two friends in grasping some of the internal conflicts that affected the black community.[51] In the end, because his views were so similar to their own, Charles Johnson's analysis of racial conditions in America won its loudest applause—and major acceptance— from white liberals. And it was they, in turn, who in Johnson's opinion offered the greatest hope for his own race.

III.

The "broad social perspective" Ralph Bunche offered blacks during the 1930s and early 1940s lay somewhere between that of Charles S. Johnson and W.E.B. Du Bois. Like Johnson, Bunche had

49. Embree, *13 Against the Odds*, 47-70, *passim*. In a review of *The Collapse of Cotton Tenancy*, E. Franklin Frazier noted that the book was evidently written to secure support for the Bankhead Bill; Frazier, "Seventy Years Too Late," *Journal of Negro Education* 5 (Apr. 1936), 274.

50. "Reminiscences of Will Alexander," Columbia Oral History, 609; Embree to Charles S. Johnson, June 7, 1948, Rosenwald Fund Archives, Box 105. Also see Embree, *13 Against the Odds*, 47-70, *passim*.

51. See, for example, Alexander to Embree, Aug. 7, 1933, Rosenwald Fund Archives, Box 94; Johnson to Embree, July 20, 1935, and Feb. 2, 1937, *ibid.*, Box 562; Alexander to Johnson, Aug. 13, 1943, and Johnson to Alexander, Aug. 17, 1943, Johnson Papers, Box 58. This last correspondence involved the Southern Regional Council, which Johnson supported, in part, through his participation in the Durham Statement, a moderate declaration of black principles proposed in October 1942, which helped establish the SRC. See, in this regard, Sosna, *In Search of the Silent South*, 117-18.

little patience with the emphasis placed on racial considerations, which, he argued, ultimately worked against the cause of true liberation. But like Du Bois, he strongly dissented from the liberal interpretation of economic and social change and from what many, including Johnson, believed were the New Deal's contributions to eliminating the conditions responsible for black oppression. Because he could neither accept the Charles Johnson–liberal definition of reform nor the Du Bois racial separatist alternative, Bunche found himself critical of almost every existing struggle for racial change and in constant search for more meaningful options to present to black organizations and their leadership. Because his enormous intellectual energies were afforded considerable expression through his work with Gunnar Myrdal's study on the "Negro Problem and American Democracy," Bunche's thoughtful summary of the ideological dilemmas confronting black thinkers in the Roosevelt era is one of the best.[52]

After receiving his Ph.D. degree in political science from Harvard University in 1934, Bunche joined Abram Harris and, later, E. Franklin Frazier at Howard University, where for a time he headed the Political Science Department. In 1936 he was a director of the Institute of Race Relations at Swarthmore College, where Charles S. Johnson had been two years earlier, and from 1938 until 1940 Bunche was chief research assistant to Gunnar Myrdal. After World War II, he was chosen senior social science analyst in the Office of Strategic Services and put in charge of research on Africa and other colonial areas, subjects he knew well from his studies at Harvard and

52. Bunche's most significant work was done for the Myrdal project: "A Brief and Tentative Analysis of Negro Leadership," "Conceptions and Ideologies of the Negro Problem," "Extended Memorandum on the Programs, Ideologies, Tactics, and Achievements of Negro Betterment and Interracial Organizations," and "The Political Status of the Negro, with Emphasis on the South and Comparative Treatment of the 'poor white,' " unpubl. memorandums for the Carnegie-Myrdal Study of the Negro in America; Schomburg Collection, NYPL, (New York, 1940). Dewey W. Grantham has edited and provided a fine introduction to one of these memorandums, "The Political Status of the Negro," published as Ralph J. Bunche, *The Political Status of the Negro in the Age of FDR* (Chicago, 1973). Other Bunche writings include the previously noted "Programs of Organizations Devoted to the Improvement of the Status of the American Negro"; "Black and White Education," *Journal of Negro Education* 5 (July 1936), 351-58; "A Critical Analysis of the Tactics and Programs of Minority Groups," *Journal of Negro Education* 4 (July 1935), 308-20; "A Critique of New Deal Social Planning As It Affects Negroes," *Journal of Negro Education* 5 (Jan. 1936), 59-65; "The Negro in the Political Life of the United States," *Journal of Negro Education* 10 (July 1941), 567-84; "Triumph—or Fiasco?" *Race* 1 (Summer 1936), 93-96.

later at Northwestern University and the London School of Economics. His government service eventually led him to a position within the State Department and then to the United Nations, where of course he achieved fame.[53]

But during the 1930s, Bunche was part of a small group of radical black intellectuals who felt both hope and fear as they viewed the future of black people. What was crucial to Bunche and to others was how the Negro and his leaders understood and responded to the circumstances of the Depression and New Deal reform; and from the beginning of the thirties, Bunche was skeptical of both old and new organizations which claimed to represent black America.

The NAACP and the Urban League, he believed, were hopelessly middle-class in their "thinking and living." That middle-class orientation alienated them from the mainstream of black America, leading them to pursue goals which were "sensational" and evoked "admiration from the Negro elite" but left the "masses of Negroes and their problem of daily bread untouched."[54] On the other hand, the more grass-roots–oriented organizations, such as the New Negro Alliance, which supported the idea of economic boycotts to force additional Negro employment, he attacked as operating in a "black groove" and offering "only racialism with no significant hope for the mass Negro population."[55] Boycotting white enterprises within the black community did provide the Negro, Bunche conceded, an "inkling of his latent economic power and an acquaintance with the recognized weapons of labor"; but is also had dangerous manifestations. If successful, such boycotts "could only result in a vicious cycle of job displacement" since they created no "new jobs." Even worse, as was true of black nationalist ideology, boycott activities widened "further the already deplorable gap between the white and black working classes . . . by boldly placing the competition for jobs on a strictly racial basis."[56] Black separatist schemes such as those of Du

53. There is a strong need for a critical biography of Bunche. For some help relating to his background and career, see *Current Biography: Who's News and Why: 1948* (New York, 1949), 78-79; J. Alvin Kugelmass, *Ralph J. Bunche: Fighter for Peace* (New York, 1952); Bardolph, *Negro Vanguard*, 366-67; Sam Pope Brewer, "Palestine Solvent," *New York Times Magazine* (Nov. 14, 1948), 20, 22; New York *Times*, Dec. 10, 1971. Grantham's introduction in Bunche, *Political Status of the Negro*, xi-xxx, is a good discussion of Bunche's association with the Myrdal project.

54. "Brief and Tentative Analysis of Negro Leadership," 25, 195; also, on NAACP, "Programs, Ideologies, Tactics," 23-203.

55. "Programs, Ideologies, Tactics," 391-92, and "Programs of Organizations Devoted to the Improvement," 542-45.

56. "Programs of Organizations Devoted to the Improvement," 543; "Critical Analysis of Tactics and Programs," 314.

Bois were even more futile. It was "absurd to assume that the Negro, deprived of the advantages of full participation in American life today, will be able to gain . . . advantages or acceptable substitutes for them by setting himself up in a black political and economic outhouse."[57]

For Bunche, the "Negro problem" was woven into the total fabric of American life, and any solution to that problem had to include a "rich comprehension of the history and the political, economic and social forces at work" in America.[58] Both black and white were victims of racial stereotypes. White racism was responsible for reinforcing the black man's minority status, a status first prescribed by slavery and later affirmed by white economic and political domination.[59] In response to the attitudes and practices of whites, black people had created their own racial myths, affecting not only their personal view of themselves but also the tactics and strategies of their organizations. For Bunche this was as true of the NAACP and the Urban League as it was of the New Negro Alliance or Du Bois' black "cooperative commonwealth." In reacting to white racial prejudice, blacks falsely assumed that all the Negro's problems were racial in nature.[60] But Bunche held that "only in the narrowly racial sense" was it possible to comprehend black people's minority status; "in every other respect" outside of race, the Afro-American population was "subject to the same divisive influences impinging upon the life of every other group in the nation."[61] The "only hope for improvement in the conditions of the masses of any American minority group," he constantly affirmed, was the "hope that can be held out for the betterment of the masses of the dominant group. . . . Their basic interests are identical and so must be their program and tactics."[62]

Such a view made Bunche receptive to the expansion of the federal government's activities. It did not, however, make him an automatic believer in the policies of Franklin Roosevelt or the assumptions which seemed to guide those policies. At the Howard University conference in May 1935, which he had helped organize

57. "Programs, Ideologies, Tactics," 8, 443, 783; on Garveyism, 393-424, esp. 411-12.

58. *Ibid.*, 773.

59. *Ibid.*, 12-13; "Critical Analysis of Tactics and Programs"; "Critique of New Deal Social Planning," *passim*.

60. "Programs of Organizations Devoted to the Improvement," 539-40; "Programs, Ideologies, Tactics," 10-17.

61. "Critical Analysis of Tactics and Programs," 310.

62. "Programs, Ideologies, Tactics," 777.

with John P. Davis, Bunche delivered a devastating attack against New Deal liberal ideology.

"For the Negro population," he stated, "the New Deal means the same thing, but more of it. Striking at no fundamental social conditions, the New Deal at best can only fix the disadvantages, the differentials, the discriminations, under which the Negro population has labored all along." The administration's economic and social planning was designed to create an untenable balance between the interests of big business and the laboring masses. The New Deal was dominated by a white middle class which sought to maintain private enterprise while they weakly attempted to curb some of the more blatant abuses of capitalism. For Bunche, there were really only two alternatives in the 1930s; either the government would take over the means of production, or it would allow private industry to run things. But he believed, as was symptomatic of middle-class thinking, that New Dealers could do neither; caught in an "intermediate position between the working masses and the finance capitalists," they struggled unsuccessfully to achieve an equilibrium between the two.[63]

The result, he argued, was that the Roosevelt administration fostered an expanded central government which weakened the independence of the laboring masses while it helped to increase the power of the capitalists. Since it feared government ownership more than private enterprise, the middle position assumed by the New Deal amounted to utilizing the "power of the state to keep the masses in check while handling the industrialists with velvet gloves." In effect, black and white working classes had "become even more dependent upon the intervention of the state in their struggle to obtain social justice from the owners and directors of industry."[64]

For blacks, the implications of such planning were clear. Under Roosevelt, the traditional determination of large landowners in the South and industrialists in the North to "keep the Negro in a servile condition and as a profitable labor supply" remained unchanged and was "indeed often heightened by the New Deal." If the government were truly concerned about the black man, Bunche maintained in 1935, it would have used the NRA to assure "blacks living wages." But this it refused to do; instead, it continued the "inferior economic status of the Negro" by legalizing occupational and geographic wage differentials. In agriculture, where the majority of blacks were em-

63. "Critique of New Deal Social Planning," 62.
64. Ibid., 61-63.

ployed, government planning was even more disastrous. The AAA left the Negro sharecropper and tenant farmer at the mercy of large-scale white farmers; and the subsistence homestead scheme was based on the assumption that the marginal farmer should not be allowed to join the other unemployed masses in urban, industrial centers. Instead, it provided that the government would control subsistence farmers by lifting them "out of the mainstream of our economic life" and laying them "upon the economic shelf to dry rot." For black Americans, already racially segregated, that would certainly ensure their economic and social isolation.[65]

The New Deal, Bunche concluded, was primarily a "great relief program" which guaranteed "at level best only a precarious livelihood of the most meager essentials for the millions of distressed workers and farmers who are on the outside of our economic life looking in." The Roosevelt administration, moreover, failed to change any of the traditional racial stereotypes held by white people; it represented no "significant shift of ideas, traditions or loyalties." "In the nature of the case," it "could at best do but little for the Negro within the existing social structure"; since blacks could not boast a meaningful middle class, they did not stand to benefit from even "some of the gains made for that class by the New Deal." In the long run, administration planning served only to "crystalize those abuses and oppressions which the exploited Negro citizenry of America have long suffered under laissez-faire capitalism, and for the same reasons as in the past."[66]

A few years later, however, Bunche began to reassess his earlier harsh analysis of the New Deal. Writing for the Myrdal project between 1938 and 1940, he noted certain features of the government's programs which he now considered more encouraging from the black perspective. Particularly helpful were the coming together of black and white in the AAA-sponsored cotton control program and the inclusion of blacks in voting on cotton referendums. "The participation of Negroes in those elections," he wrote in 1941, "and on an equal basis with whites, is of the utmost significance in the South. That such activities will tend to bring about a recognition by both white and Negro producers of parallel economic interests would seem clear."[67] Other benefits he saw deriving from the administration were low-income housing, black farmers' participation in the Tenant Purchase program, social security, and wage-and-hour legis-

65. *Ibid.*, 61-64.
66. *Ibid.*, 65, 60, 65.
67. "Negro in the Political Life," 577; "Political Status of the Negro," 1052.

lation. He interpreted the Supreme Court's decisions upholding the Wagner Labor Relations Act, the principle of social security, and the Fair Labor Standards law as doing "more to better the conditions of the Negro than the broadest conceivable decision of his equal rights."[68]

He also saw more favorably the activities of black New Deal advisers, whose presence he now regarded as recognition of the "disastrous effects of the early legislation upon the Negro." Although aware of their limited power and influence, he nevertheless believed that it was "doubtful whether hundreds of thousands of dollars and many services would have gone to Negro citizens" without them. He went so far as to argue that the New Deal's efforts represented the "first feeble steps in a desirable direction—the full participation of the Negro into administrative government."[69] In 1941 he claimed that the Roosevelt administration had given for the "first time . . . broad recognition to the existence of the Negro as a national problem and undertook to give specific consideration to this fact in many ways, though the basic evils remain untouched."[70]

There were a number of reasons for Bunche's more favorable assessment of the New Deal in the late 1930s and early 1940s. First, in the process of researching the "Negro problem" for the Myrdal study, he obviously felt that the administration had in effect modified some of the "disastrous" policies connected with the NRA and AAA. He considered New Deal support of organized labor, low-income housing, minimum hours and wages, and the Farm Security Administration to be indications of a more enlightened planning. None of these policies went far enough in removing the "basic evils" symbolized by millions of still unemployed blacks; but they did signify a shift from the early thirties and helped to pave the way for Negroes to join the ranks of organized labor and to begin the process of achieving their economic and political freedom.

The coming of World War II strongly affected Bunche's views. Like Lester Granger of the Urban League and the NAACP's Walter White, he saw Nazi Germany and her allies as a direct threat to black Americans. Fascism, at home or abroad, he warned, was a real issue for the Afro-American people. "As bad as things now are, they can conceivably become far worse. . . . The American Negro will do very well indeed if he is able to hold for the time being the gains that

68. "Political Status of the Negro," 1530-31.
69. Ibid., 1455-59.
70. "Negro in the Political Life," 580.

he has thus far made under American Democracy."[71] He believed that failure to check Germany would increase the possibilities for fascism in the United States. He had little doubt that an American-style fascism would be violently anti-black; under it, black people would have no constitution or bill of rights—the "position of the Negro would be frozen permanently as an inferior racial caste."[72]

Bunche agreed with A. Philip Randolph that the war should not deter blacks from demanding their basic rights. "The unrelenting struggle to erect a true democracy upon our constitutional foundations must go on," he maintained. "The economic security of vast millions of our population, the political and educational disabilities suffered by many, the slum areas, the disgracefully inadequate protection of the nation's health—these and many other evils must be eradicated. There can be no let-up in the crusade to make a reality of American democracy."[73] "I attended the meeting called by Phil Randolph in connection with the proposed Negro Defense March," he wrote Walter White in May, 1941, ". . . and was much impressed by the outline of the project. Something of this kind is sorely needed . . . and it will constitute a crucial test for the Negro."[74]

But he also insisted that the overriding issue was still the preservation of democracy and that nothing was of more "paramount importance to the Negro."[75] In that fight, whatever its weaknesses or shortcomings, the Roosevelt administration stood as an ally of the black man. This might mean, he indicated in 1940, that blacks could "scarcely think on the basis of what is bad and what is good; we are virtually compelled to make our choice in terms of what is less bad as against something much worse."[76] The following year, in the same essay in which he pointed to the New Deal's acknowledgment of the "Negro problem," he wrote that the future of black people rested "with the future of democracy. Negroes, in great numbers, despite the disillusioning imperfections of American democracy and its racial contradictions, now must know that every blow struck on behalf of democracy is a blow for the black man's future."[77]

71. "Programs, Ideologies, Tactics," 793. On reference to Granger and White, see Lawrence, "Negro Organizations in Crisis," 317.
72. "Programs, Ideologies, Tactics," 788-90.
73. "Negro in the Political Life," 583.
74. Bunche to White, May 1, 1941, NAACP Papers, unprocessed, File B-220.
75. "Programs, Ideologies, Tactics," 793.
76. Quoted in Lawrence, "Negro Organizations in Crisis," 317.
77. "Negro in the Political Life," 582.

The coming of the war and his more extensive research into government programs were influential, therefore, in causing Bunche to reassess the New Deal and reform liberalism; but of far greater significance was what he believed to be black people's failure to create the strategy and organization necessary to challenge the political status quo. The National Negro Congress, which he helped promote with Davis and Randolph, was a particular source of disillusionment to him. Initially, Bunche had great hopes for the Congress, believing that it offered the means for developing a coalition of black and white organizations, of "Negro and white trade unions, religious, civic and fraternal bodies" which could formulate far-reaching political, social, and economic programs. Such a movement would build on the existing black and interracial organizations; it would reach into the grass roots of the black community and awaken a "response from the Negro masses."[78] At a time when mass organizations had become "increasingly vital to the preservation of those meager advantages already won for the Negro," he noted in 1936, it was extremely important that an intense effort, like that of the NNC, be made to "unite the masses of Negroes behind a definite program."[79]

Commenting after the first NNC convention in 1936, Bunche asserted that the Congress represented the "first sincere effort to bring together on an equal plane Negro leaders, professional and white collar workers with Negro manual workers and their leaders and organizers." Even more important, despite the NNC's unwise "blanket endorsement" of interracial groups and its inclusion of the "traditional reactionary philosophy of Negro business" in its platform, the convention nevertheless "held to the incontrovertible truth that the salvation of the American Negro and the solution of all his vital problems is to be found in working-class unity and mass pressure."[80]

Despite such optimism, there was a note of skepticism in Bunche's analysis of the Negro Congress. The basic problem centered on the unity question, which he considered to be the NNC's strong point. What concerned him was whether that unity amounted to anything beyond a superficial identification with race. It remained an open question, he remarked, whether the "heterogeneous" nature of black thought could be transcended in order that black people might recognize their "mass position as workers" and their need to enlist

78. "Programs, Ideologies, Tactics," 319-20.
79. "Triumph—or Fiasco?" 93.
80. Ibid., 93-95.

"in the ranks of organized labor." He particularly disliked the "race leaders" whom he called the "false prophets" and "rabble-rousers," the black politicians, preachers, lawyers, and businessmen who headed many of the NNC's committees. In the future, he warned, it might be better to have only labor and working-class organizations represented in the Congress; but if this were actually done, he was uncertain that the Congress would then have the organizational means to reach the black masses.[81] That dilemma was never satisfactorily reconciled for him.

By 1940, when Bunche analyzed the NNC for Myrdal, it had become a very different organization, one strongly dominated by the Communist party and the industrial unions. Noting the third convention in 1940, he stated that the Congress had "dug its own grave . . . It will now be reduced to a Communist cell."[82] The NNC was no longer a viable alternative either to the New Deal or to the traditional form of black protest.

Bunche's rapid disenchantment with the NNC resulted as much from its failure to accept his ideological demands as it did from internal changes in the organization. The essential problems confronting black people, he reiterated throughout the 1930s, were primarily economic and political, not racial. The Negro's dilemma could thus be "solved only in terms of full opportunity for development and complete assimilation in the political and economic life of the nation. The Negro in America has but one fundamental objective: to obtain the full stature of American citizenship."[83] It was essential for blacks to have allies who shared their similar economic interests and aspirations; they needed to realize their working-class status and join with other workers to bring reforms which would assure every American economic and political security. The American economic system, he argued, "must afford larger measure of security for all before the Negro can hope for much greater political advancement. This it can do only as a result of some far-reaching changes in the direction of a socialized economy—at least insofar as the production of the necessities of life are concerned."[84]

Such was the substance of Bunche's thinking in the 1930s. The history of the National Negro Congress in the late thirties and his assessment of it suggest, however, some of the difficulties in his analysis. The conflicting resolutions at NNC conventions in support

81. *Ibid.*, 95-96, and "Programs, Ideologies, Tactics," 354.
82. "Programs, Ideologies, Tactics," 369.
83. "Negro in the Political Life," 581, and "Political Status of the Negro," 1521.
84. "Political Status of the Negro," 1551.

211

of black businesses, boycotts, economic cooperatives, and labor unions indicated not only diversity of leadership in the organization but diversity of economic and political interests. Black ministers and politicians frequently did not share the same concerns as black intellectuals like Bunche or labor organizers like Randolph. Yet, as Bunche well understood, to exclude these individuals from participating in the NNC would have unquestionably weakened any grass-roots black movement since it was the ministers, lodge leaders, and politicians who often commanded a mass following.

At the same time, he critized the NNC for operating on the "assumption that the common denominator of race is enough to weld together, in thought and action, the divergent segments of black America."[85] But it was apparent that it was only through the "common denominator of race" that these different elements had been brought together in the first place. Once attempts were made to deemphasize race and concentrate on class interests and specific economic programs, divisions strongly emerged. Blacks were overwhelmingly laborers, and they were disproportionately unemployed, as Bunche and others constantly pointed out; but they were also black laborers and black unemployed, and the racial differential was important in how they defined their status and how others defined it for them.

Because Bunche was concerned that the stress given to race had distorted the Negro's awareness of other needs and had led organizations like the NAACP to neglect the priority of economic change, he feared any appeal to racial consciousness. But without such an appeal, there was limited chance of achieving the unity within the black community necessary to form alliances with progressive white labor groups. It was this realization that shaped the thought of A. Philip Randolph and of W.E.B. Du Bois.

And there were serious problems in finding allies among the white working classes. Looking at organized labor in the 1930s, Bunche was not comforted. Neither the AFL nor the CIO, he noted in 1940, served "the Negro. They are both weak, ridden with factional strife and disputes, controlled by a narrow-minded bureaucracy of professional labor leaders, and more often than not, socially unintelligent." Although he felt that blacks should continue to demand entry into these organizations, he was pessimistic that anything would be achieved, given the structure of organized labor; in the leadership of

85. "Programs, Ideologies, Tactics." 354-55.

212

both the AFL and CIO were men "who harbor intensive racial prejudice."[86]

Charles S. Johnson, on the other hand, considered it naïve to assume that "abstract economic philosophies" would ever alter the importance of racial caste attitudes among working classes or their representatives. "What is influencing working relations most persistently," Johnson argued in 1936, "is not the ideology of the labor movement, or the ritual of the conventional class struggle, but the cold imperative of technological changes which tend, in the interest of the employers, to disturb the old caste alignments."[87]

Johnson's thesis, however, was an endorsement of an economic status quo, and Bunche found this impossible to accept. Therefore, to avoid the logic into which his own analysis of the labor movement led him, Bunche fell back on a romantic vision of the working class. There were basic differences between labor leaders and labor rank and file, he argued: "intensive racial prejudice" did not characterize the lower elements of the labor movement. If blacks could discard their racial pride, they might be able to convince white workers that the "Negro understands the vital lessons of labor unity and organization and can lend effective aid in the movement." Black people could then help create a "people's movement," a new labor struggle in which black and white workers would achieve greater control over industries in which they were employed and together could strive for greater economic collectivization. A black organization, "representative of the masses of Negroes and assured of their support, could play a vital role in the development of a socially intelligent, unbureaucratic, democratically controlled and politically conscious American labor movement."[88]

The "People's Movement" brought together all the various features of Bunche's thesis: grass-roots blacks allied with white working classes; racial myth and prejudice attacked through the common struggle for economic justice; a mass movement of blacks and whites building a new political base while challenging existing black and white institutions and the failures of liberal national planning. Yet such a movement, so crucial to Bunche's thought, did not appear a likely reality in the Depression or war years. The scarcity of jobs in

86. *Ibid.*, 787, 780.
87. Johnson statement in an exchange with E. Franklin Frazier on "Caste and Class in an American Industry," Johnson, *American Journal of Sociology* 40 (Sept. 1936), 254. Frazier's statement, *ibid.*, 252-53.
88. Bunche, "Programs, Ideologies, Tactics," 783.

the 1930s, which affected both skilled and unskilled, black and white, increased employment competition between the races.[89] Even when the less racially conscious CIO began tentatively to embrace blacks in their industrial unions in the late 1930s, racial tension among the workers was apparent; and in the 1940s, when full employment was reached through increased defense spending and Negroes were able to break into the labor movement in even greater numbers, strong racial antagonisms among rank and file members persisted.[90] It was not through an alliance of black and white, moreover, but more as a result of Randolph's all black MOWM, with its specific demands for Negroes, that industries and unions in the 1940s were opened to greater black participation.

The difficulties encountered by Bunche in finding a meaningful organizational expression for his ideas pointed to the inherent limitations in his brand of independent black radicalism. Absorbed in the predominant economic concerns of the 1930s, he strove to direct black protest away from a purely racial explanation of the black condition, and he tried to link up the "Negro problem" with the larger social and economic ills confronting American society. Like so many thinkers in the period, black and white, he sought an expanded base from which to attack the historic and contemporary oppression of his people. With his emphasis on class rather than racial factors, he personified a neo-Marxist disposition popular among many intellectuals in the Depression era.

Yet as a black man deeply aware of the Negro's historical experience, and as a political pragmatist concerned with achieving immediate benefits, Bunche refrained from embracing the frequently mechanistic solutions espoused by a number of American Marxists.

89. Job scarcity and competition made it difficult to accomplish either the working-class solidarity that Bunche envisioned or the economic objectives conceived by the New Deal under the NRA; see Wolters, *Negroes and the Great Depression*, 83-209, *passim*, and 214.

90. See, for example, Marc Karson and Ronald Radosh, "The American Federation of Labor and the Negro Worker, 1894-1949," and Sumner M. Rosen, "The CIO Era, 1935-1955," in Julius Jacobson, ed., *The Negro and the American Labor Movement* (New York, 1968), 155-208. Also Alexander Saxton, "Race and the House of Labor," in Gary B. Nash and Richard Weiss, eds., *The Great Fear: Race in the Mind of America* (New York, 1970), 98-120. As Harvard Sitkoff argues in "Emergence of Civil Rights as a National Issue," ch. 7, it was true that the struggles of the 1930s and 1940s which blacks waged against labor union discrimination and, particularly, the more open-door racial policy of the CIO paved the way for a more interracially oriented organized labor movement. But in the 1930s and even the 1940s, despite the gains made, the labor union movement was not at the point of forging a black-white workers alliance in the manner Bunche believed was necessary.

Wanting to rid blacks of the limits imposed by racial determinism as an explanation for their oppression, he was not ready to substitute an economic or class determinism in its place. He tried instead to free the discussion of the "Negro problem" from the mythology of race. Race was an emotional, irrational attitude, he maintained, which prevented blacks and whites from facing their common economic and political powerlessness.

Charles Johnson did not accept the "race as myth" argument, but he was as anxious as Bunche to see race disappear from the minds of Negroes and whites. For Johnson, concern over race constituted the major obstacle in achieving the full acceptance of blacks in American life.

But the rationalist approach of Johnson and Bunche had, for W.E.B. Du Bois, its own serious shortcoming. As Du Bois tried to argue, such an analysis overlooked the fact that human beings were seldom simply rational creatures. Myth frequently guided behavior; people often operated emotionally, even when confronted with the obvious irrationality and stupidity of their actions. Thus, to Du Bois it seemed unrealistic to assume that unity among black Americans might be achieved in the struggle for economic, social, and political justice without the element of race entering into that struggle, if not dominating it. It was also politically naïve, since in many instances the common bond of race alone brought blacks together. Class distinctions divided them; economic and political aspirations fostered interpersonal competition.

Charles S. Johnson, of course, did not consider a unified race movement necessary for blacks to secure equal opportunity as long as there existed, as he believed there did, strong white support for the Negro's cause. Bunche, on the other hand, doubted the commitment of whites, at least in the early 1930s, and questioned the wisdom of liberal reformism itself; yet his unwillingness to criticize the New Deal's policies on the grounds of their racial implications ultimately placed him considerably closer to the mainstream of white liberal thought than he recognized at the time.

With the majority of white interracialists, he shared the view that the ultimate integration of black people into America would result primarily from broadly conceived economic and social programs rather than from racially minded civil rights legislation. Though he did not accept the opinion of a Harold Ickes or Eleanor Roosevelt in the 1930s that the New Deal was providing those programs, he did share their assumption, which was crucial, that the group needs of blacks were inextricably tied up with the dominant needs of the total society, and that, finally, only the federal government had the power to provide for those needs. Thus, he was willing to argue that any special recognition afforded blacks because of their racial condition other than assuring them equal opportunity, seriously endangered the Negro's chances of achieving lasting economic justice in America. "The Negro citizen," he stated, had "long since learned that 'special' treatment for him implies differentiation on a racial basis and inevitably connotes inferior status."[91]

Ultimately, the difference between a black New Deal critic like Bunche and the Roosevelt administration rested on the single question of whether administration reforms could overcome the historic oppression of Negro Americans. In 1935, Bunche emphatically asserted that the government's reforms failed to meet the necessary requirements of black people; by the late 1930s and early 1940s, however, he was less certain. His transition from antagonist to qualified advocate of the administration symbolized not only the attraction New Deal policies held but the weakness of those who desired to foster meaningful alternatives to their obvious shortcomings. In 1939, Bunche set forth a thirteen-point program in which he emphasized again the economic and nonracial aspects of the black struggle. "Once our economic difficulties are corrected," he concluded, "in large measure there would then be hope for the possibility of measures looking toward a fundamental improvement in race relations and in the status of the Negro people."[92] That basic belief, instead of distinguishing Bunche as a critic of the New Deal's racial philosophy, untimately placed him in the same ideological camp, and in the long run it became extremely difficult to establish any real alternative position.

The racial and class debate which Bunche, Charles S. Johnson, and W.E.B. Du Bois, among others, participated in during the Roosevelt era never produced the kind of "social perspective" Bunche considered essential for a successful black movement. But from the beginning, the experience of Afro-Americans had been shaped by the twin forces of racial and economic oppression. Given the critical nature of the Depression and the global war, it was too much to

91. Bunche, "Political Status of the Negro," 1521.
92. "Programs of Organizations Devoted to the Improvement," 549. Blacks must recognize, Bunche stated, "that under oppressive conditions, identity of economic interest can overcome racial prejudices and that black and white unity is possible even in the deepest South," *ibid.*, 549. That was almost a summary of the liberal racial philosophy of the New Deal.

expect that either black or white thinkers would unravel such a complex interrelationship. Nevertheless, the 1930s and 1940s clearly indicated how crucial an interpretation of racial and class concerns was in determining government policy and the strategies and goals black leaders and organizations pursued.

NINE

Looking Backward

AN AMBIVALENT LEGACY

Henry Lee Moon, a member of the national staff of the NAACP and a former New Deal adviser, commented in 1948 that under Franklin D. Roosevelt's guidance the federal government had "ceased to be an abstraction enshrined in remote Washington." Instead, he said, government had been "brought to the threshold of practically every home in America. Government was no longer merely the concern of the people. It assumed as a national responsibility the welfare and security of the people." Because the New Deal was "broad-based and humanitarian, it recognized the disadvantaged Negro minority as an integral part of the American people. At no time since the curtain had dropped on the Reconstruction drama had government focused as much attention upon the Negro's basic needs as did the New Deal." And, Moon concluded, the "Negro masses recognized that this new concept of government provided a means by which they could accelerate their progress toward full and unqualified citizenship. Accordingly, they voted repeatedly to retain and strengthen the New Deal."[1]

Henry Lee Moon was not always an uncritical supporter of the Roosevelt administration.[2] Yet his praise in 1948 represents a view of the administration's contribution to improving the life of black Americans and the relations between black and white which is still popular. Central to that interpretation is the premise that some of the most pressing needs of black people were recognized by many high government officials in the 1930s and 1940s; as a result, these needs were included for the first time since the 1860s and 1870s in the broad thrust of a major reform effort. Such inclusion did not mean that by the 1940s blacks had won their "full and unqualified citizenship," but it did signify to Moon and others that their status in American society had been dramatically altered through the development of the "welfare state," which owed its existence both to

1. Moon, *Balance of Power*, 21.
2. In his previously mentioned "Racial Aspects of Federal Public Relations Programs," written in 1943, Moon showed far more disapproval of the Roosevelt administration, though he still found much to commend in its importance to blacks.

the domestic thirties and the war years. In addition, an economic as well as a political base had been established which, in Gunnar Myrdal's words, gave black people a "broader and more variegated front to defend and from which to push forward."[3]

Myrdal's classic work *An American Dilemma,* published in 1944, provides the most comprehensive historical and theoretical justification of this thesis. Though the Myrdal project was immense and not simply a study of the New Deal, it began in 1938 and continued through 1943, and much of the material on blacks and on race relations was formulated from an analysis of the Roosevelt years. As did Moon four years later, Myrdal concluded that the "great import of the New Deal to the Negro" was that, for the first time in the nation's history, the federal government had done "something substantial in a social way without excluding the Negro." Until the 1930s, he wrote, "the practical Negro problem involved civil rights, education, charity and little more." But because of the New Deal's response to the Depression, that problem was redefined "in pace with public policy in the 'new welfare state,' " and thus came to include not only civil rights but also "housing, nutrition, medicine, education, relief and social security, wages and hours, working conditions, child and woman labor."[4]

Myrdal's optimistic assessment of the Roosevelt administration and the basis for much of his analysis and the conclusions he reached in *An American Dilemma* rested on his "principle of cumulation." According to the Swedish social scientist, the "Negro problem" could be understood as emanating from a "vicious circle" of prejudice and oppression, or what he preferred to call the process of "cumulation." From the beginning, the black American's status had been determined by an interdependency of two factors: white prejudice with its accompanying discrimination and the depressed level of black "standards of living, health, education, manners and morals." White prejudice was initially responsible for fostering the

3. Myrdal, *An American Dilemma,* I, 74. For the views of others who have shared the Myrdal and Moon sense of the welfare state's significance to blacks but have also criticized certain features of the New Deal's relationship to Negro Americans, see Leslie H. Fishel, Jr., "The Negro in the New Deal Era," *Wisconsin Magazine of History* 48 (Winter 1964-65), 115-17; Schlesinger, *Politics of Upheaval*, 432-34; J. Saunders Redding, *The Lonesome Road* (Garden City, N.Y., 1958), 260, 269-70; August Meier and Elliott Rudwick, *From Plantation to Ghetto: An Interpretive History of American Negroes* (3d ed., New York, 1974), 404-13; and discussion by Bernard Sternsher in Sternsher, ed., *The Negro in Depression and War: Prelude to Revolution, 1930-1945* (Chicago, 1969), 3-6, 45-52.

4. Myrdal, *An American Dilemma,* I, 74.

low standard of existence for Negroes, but those standards then operated as reinforcements to white America's prejudiced view of blacks as inferior human beings. "White prejudice and Negro standards," he noted, "thus mutually 'cause' each other." Traditionally, since the two factors remained basically unchanged, they appeared "to balance each other." But, Myrdal asserted, this process of static "accommodation" need not continue, since if either of the factors changed, it would "cause a change in the other factor, too, and start a process of interaction where the change in one factor will continuously be supported by the reaction of the other." Any increase in white prejudice, for instance, would thus have the added effect of worsening black conditions in the country.[5]

On the other hand—and here is where the New Deal shaped Myrdal's optimism—a favorable change in either white prejudice or in Negro standards would inevitably lead to a raising of the status of Afro-Americans and a lessening of conflict between the two races. To Myrdal, then, the power embodied in the federal government and the willingness of the Roosevelt administration to use that power to improve the economic and social conditions of the American people, including blacks, were of singular importance. According to the "cumulative causation" principle, even if the government did not directly attack white prejudice by inspiring changes within the black community through federal programs of economic and social assistance, white racism would be weakened since its justification would diminish as blacks improved their level of existence.[6]

In less precise theoretical terms, the Myrdal "principle" embodied, with a few variations, the racial assumptions held by white race liberals and a number of blacks during the 1930s and 1940s, assumptions which strongly determined their approach to race issues. The similarity of thought between Myrdal and many of the individuals discussed in this book may have also derived from the fact that quite a few black and white reformers were directly involved either as consultants or as staff members in helping Myrdal to compile material and formulate conclusions on the "Negro problem."[7]

5. *Ibid.*, 75-76.
6. For an extended discussion and description of the "cumulative causation" theory, see *An American Dilemma*, II, appendix III, 1065-70.
7. These include Ralph J. Bunche, a senior research assistant, and W.E.B. Du Bois, Charles S. Johnson, Eugene Kinckle Jones, Walter White, Will Alexander, Edwin Embree, and Clark Foreman, among many others; see Myrdal, *An American Dilemma*, I, liii, for full listing of individuals consulted or serving on his staff. Harold

To what extent were they right in their evaluation of black progress during the Roosevelt era? Certainly there is considerable evidence to indicate that as a result of the Depression and war years the
condition of black people was changed, and a more favorable climate
was established for Negroes and their white allies to press the cause
of racial justice and equality. The spirit of reform generated during
the thirties and the ideals associated with the national defense effort
of the forties clearly helped release energies and provided for the
expression of new ideas and movements aimed at bringing racial
improvement to America.[8]

In the long run, this may have constituted the most significant
contribution of the Roosevelt era, since in the postwar period it was
considerably more difficult to keep the "Negro problem" hidden or
to isolate racial issues from the broader questions which affected the
American people. Inspired, in part, by the examples of white New
Dealers like Harold Ickes, Eleanor Roosevelt, Will Alexander,
Clark Foreman, and a few others, race equality assumed after 1945 a
more central place in liberal ideology. Prior to the New Deal, the
"Negro problem" was never a central consideration of white reformers or reform philosophers.[9] Within the black community new

L. Ickes was also contacted by Bunche as to Ickes' contribution to race relations; see
Ralph J. Bunche to Ickes, Sept. 25, 1939, Records of the Office of the Secretary of
Interior, NARG 48.

8. The most comprehensive and detailed discussion of the 1930s, the New Deal,
and how the environment of the times encouraged civil rights activities then and in the
years to come is Harvard Sitkoff's "Emergence of Civil Rights as a National Issue." See
also Maskin, "Black Education and the New Deal,"; Donald Ross, "The Role of Blacks
in the Federal Theatre, 1935–1939," *Journal of Negro History* 59 (Jan. 1974), 38-50;
and Robert K. Carr, *Federal Protection of Civil Rights: Quest for a Sword* (Ithaca, N.Y.,
1947), 163-64, in which Carr argues that President Roosevelt, at least in the early
1940s, gave support to the Civil Rights Section (CRS) of the Justice Department in
prosecuting lynching cases involving blacks. On the importance of the Roosevelt
years and the forties see Dalifume, " 'Forgotten Years' of the Negro Revolution,"
90-106. For a general discussion of gains blacks achieved during World War II, see
Neil A. Wynn, *The Afro-American and the Second World War* (New York, 1975).
Reference to "new" ideas and movements should perhaps be placed in quotes, since
the struggle for black equality in both the white and black communities has always
relied on past generations. What was new, of course, about the 1930s and 1940s was
the general circumstances affecting white and black activities.

9. As was suggested earlier, few white reformers showed concern over the problems of blacks or with the cause of racial prejudice in the early twentieth century. For
assessments of progressivism and civil rights issues see Dewey W. Grantham, "The
Progressive Movement and the Negro," *South Atlantic Quarterly* 54 (Oct. 1955),
461-77; Gilbert Osofsky, "Progressivism and the Negro: New York, 1900-1915,"
American Quarterly 16 (Summer 1964), 153-68; Nancy J. Weiss, "The Negro and the

organizations took root, employing tactics and developing strategies which were later utilized in the "Negro revolt" of the 1950s and 1960s. Older organizations underwent transformation, and some, notably the NAACP and the National Urban League in the forties, saw their memberships and activities considerably increased.[10] Black masses also found assistance for their housing, labor, educational, and health needs in the New Deal welfare programs. And as a result of Supreme Court decisions, a growing awareness of their political potential, and support given them by white liberals, black people increased their influence within American politics, especially, of course, within the Democratic party "coalition." One writer who has argued the significance of these and other events to blacks concludes that the "sprouts of hope" produced during the Roosevelt years "prepared the ground for the struggle to follow."[11]

But, in retrospect, the "ground" established in the 1930s and 1940s contained a number of soft areas which, despite the enormous progress black Americans have made since the late 1940s, continue to be sources of some difficulty. Moreover, the degree of material success blacks achieved between 1932 and 1945 should not be exaggerated. By 1940, whether the indices were unemployment, relief, or income, it was obvious that Negroes were still disproportionately isolated from the mainstream of the nation's economic

---

New Freedom: Fighting Wilsonian Segregation," *Political Science Quarterly* 84 (Mar. 1969), 61-69; Howard W. Allen, Aage R. Clausen, and Jerome M. Clubb, "Political Reform and Negro Rights in the Senate, 1909-1915," *Journal of Southern History* 27 (May 1971), 191-212. In the Truman years, civil rights became a more acceptable part of liberal thought, a fact clearly symbolized by the battle over the Democratic party's plank on civil rights at its 1948 convention. More than anyone else, the late Hubert H. Humphrey embodied in his thought and activities the postwar liberal commitment to black rights and New Deal liberalism. On the Truman years and black concerns, see William C. Berman, *The Politics of Civil Rights in the Truman Administration* (Columbus, Ohio, 1970), and Barton J. Bernstein, "The Ambiguous Legacy: The Truman Administration and Civil Rights," in Bernstein, ed., *Politics and Policies of the Tcuman Administration* (Chicago, 1970), 269-314.

10. See Parris and Brooks, *Blacks in the City*, chs. 28-31, *passim*; Weiss, *National Urban League*, 303-9; Lawrence, "Negro Organizations in Crisis," 375-77. Lawrence states that the NAACP increased its membership sixfold during the war years. Also showing some revival were the National Negro Business League and the National Council of Negro Women; Lawrence, 378.

11. Sitkoff, "Emergence of Civil Rights as a National Issue," 403. For an interesting discussion of blacks and the "Roosevelt coalition," see Samuel Lubell, *The Future of American Politics* (Garden City, N.Y., 1956), esp 86-105.

life.[12] One student of the period has concluded that "it is probably safe to say that the Negro population was less an integral part of the basic American economy in 1940 than at any time since the invention of the cotton gin."[13] Black New Dealer Robert Weaver noted in 1946 that it "was generally conceded that the Negro was losing his quest for economic security and occupational advancement"; when the "defense program was launched the Negro had long been haunted by unemployment."[14] Black job opportunities did, of course, increase considerably during the boom years of World War II, but since 1945 the high incidence of black unemployment and relief and the low level of black incomes have continued to be daily facts of Afro-American life.[15]

Many of these later conditions were clearly apparent in the Roosevelt years. One of the most comprehensive analyses regarding the impact of federal policies on the black population came out in conferences organized in 1937 and 1939 by black New Dealer Mary McLeod Bethune and sponsored by the National Youth Administration. Planned around the theme of the "Fundamental Problems of the Negro and Negro Youth," the conferences included a fairly broad cross section of black leaders and black and civil rights organizations. Though the general membership tended to reflect the more moderate segments of Negro America, many of those attending and taking part in conference proposals were "militants" like John P.

12. Unemployment and relief figures vary tremendously, but for a general discussion of both as well as black income to 1942, see Sterner, *The Negro's Share*, chs. 2, 3, and 5. Myrdal noted in 1944 that public relief had "become one of the major Negro occupations; all through the thirties it was surpassed only by agriculture and, possibly, by domestic service," Myrdal, *An American Dilemma*, I, 353-54; see also Lawrence, "Negro Organizations in Crisis," 200. Lawrence quotes from the U.S. 16th Census, *The Labor Force: Employment and Personal Characteristics* (1943), indicating that as of March 1940, 26.6 percent of black urban males of working age were unemployed compared with 16.1 percent of the total male labor force in the cities; Lawrence 308.

13. Lawrence, "Negro Organizations in Crisis," 200.

14. Weaver, *Negro Labor*, 15.

15. For some illuminating analyses of black unemployment, relief, and income statistics through the mid-1960s, see Louis A. Ferman, Joyce L. Kornbluh, and J.A. Miller, eds., *Negroes and Jobs: A Book of Readings* (Ann Arbor, Mich., 1968); Leonard Broom and Norval D. Glenn, *Transformation of the Negro American* (New York, 1967), 105-56; Rashi Fein, "An Economic and Social Profile of the Negro American," and Daniel Patrick Moynihan, "Employment, Income, and the Ordeal of the Negro Family," in Talcott Parsons and Kenneth B. Clark, eds., *The Negro American* (Boston, 1967), 102-59. For discussion and bibliographic references to other studies on blacks' economic status and housing conditions in recent years, see James M. McPherson et al., eds., *Blacks in America: Bibliographical Essays* (New York, 1971), 340-64.

Davis, A. Philip Randolph, and Ralph J. Bunche. They joined with New Deal advisers like Bethune, Robert Weaver, and other black officials, with former New Dealers Forrester Washington and Robert Vann, and with established figures like Walter White and Lester Granger of the Urban League to provide an extensive evaluation of federal programs and to offer a number of recommendations for increased government activity on behalf of the black minority.[16]

In both 1937 and 1939 conferees praised the efforts made up to that time by the administration, and they especially applauded the policies of the PWA, USHA, and NYA.[17] Yet the general and unmistakable tone of this moderate body was critical of the federal government's role in changing those "fundamental" conditions confronting the black population. The 1937 conference noted four central problems which still faced the majority of blacks: unemployment and the lack of economic security; inadequate educational and recreation facilities; poor health and housing; and fear of mob violence, and the "lack of protection under the law."[18] In her letter to the President reporting on the 1937 conference's findings, Mary Bethune noted that America had opened "wide the door of opportunity to the youth of the world" but had slammed it "shut in the faces of its Negro citizenry." The "great masses of Negro youth," she stated, "are offered only one-fifteenth the educational opportunity of the average American child. The great masses of Negro workers are depressed and unprotected in the lowest levels of agricultural and domestic service while the black workers in industry are generally barred from the unions and grossly discriminated against. Their housing and living conditions are sordid and unhealthy; they live in constant terror of the lynch mob, shorn of their constitutionally guaranteed right of suffrage, and humiliated by the denial of civil liberties."[19]

16. The first conference took place Jan. 6-8, 1937, and the following one Jan. 12-14, 1939. Both conferences held the majority of their general sessions in the Department of Labor's auditorium. Ralph Bunche's "Political Status of the Negro," 1450-51, analyzes the general make-up of the meetings. Both Davis and Randolph served in 1937 and 1939 on the "Economic and Social Security" committee.

17. See Mary McLeod Bethune to FDR, Jan. 1937, in *Conference on the Problems of the Negro* Report, 1937; Bethune to FDR, Jan. 1939, in *Proceedings of Second Conference*, 1939.

18. *Conference on the Problems of the Negro* Report, 1937, 6.

19. Bethune to FDR, Jan. 1937, *Conference on the Problems of the Negro* Report, 1937.

Two years later, summing up the 1939 conference's investigations involving black gains made since she had submitted her first report, Bethune concluded that although some recommendations had been realized, there was still "much—very much—to be done." Cited as essential to improving the status of Afro-Americans were federal legislation outlawing lynching; elimination of discrimination in the federal civil service; unrestricted use of the ballot; continuation of an adequate, federally financed work relief program; expansion of low-rent housing; extension of social security coverage to agricultural and domestic workers; participation of blacks in the FHA; additional black appointments to all federal policy-making bodies; full involvement in the apprenticeship training and vocational guidance programs; creation of a national health program; and continuation and extension of the CCC and the NYA.[20]

In 1942, a conference organized by the National Urban League on "Problems of Negroes in a World at War" cited many of the same concerns and offered demands similar to those presented in 1937 and 1939. At that conference were also individuals and organizations who had participated in the NYA meetings and who, since the early days of the depression, had been engaged in civil rights concerns.[21] And, as earlier, feelings of both gratitude and despair were directed at the Roosevelt administration in 1942. Bethune's report to FDR in 1939 stated that it was not in a spirit of "complaint or carping criticism" that black leaders made their requests but in "calm and sober analysis of our critical situation" and with the support that "12,000,000 Negroes in the United States" offered the "National Administration in its recognized determination to give to Negroes equality of opportunity, with all other loyal American citizens."[22]

Yet following the resurgence of political conservatism and the outbreak of World War II, there was little inclination or will on the part of Roosevelt and his administration to act on the demands blacks made in 1939 or 1942. Despite what the National Youth Administration conference's 1939 statement suggested, it remained

20. *Proceedings of Second Conference*, 1939, 32–33.
21. *Report on the Conference of National Organizations* on "Problems of Negroes in a World at War," Jan. 10, 1942, NUL Publication, NUL Papers, National Defense Program File, Ms. Div., LC, Ser. 6, Box 13. Some of those attending the conference, held at the Harlem YMCA, were Lester Granger, Walter White, William Hastie, Robert Weaver, Dr. M.O. Bousfield (of the Rosenwald Fund and Urban League), and Mary McLeod Bethune. Organizations and participants are included following p. 11.
22. Bethune to FDR, Jan. 1939, *Proceedings of Second Conference*, 1939.

uncertain just how committed the government was to giving "Negroes equality of opportunity with all other loyal American citizens." The critical issue black leaders faced then—and had faced from the start—was how they might force a government that had provided some benefits and seen fit to include their people in some reform programs to maintain and expand its commitment, given the continued problems blacks confronted.

It was, in effect, the Negro's inclusion—and the nature of that inclusion—in the framework of New Deal liberalism of the 1930s that complicated their task. The redefining of the "Negro problem" within the context of the federal welfare state both expanded and limited the manner in which blacks were able to pursue the goal of "equality of opportunity." Taken as a whole, administration policies from 1933 to 1945 amounted to a tremendous increase in federal authority and influence in the daily lives of the average American citizen, black and white. The partial incorporation of blacks into the general welfare reforms produced, as Myrdal and others have noted, a greater awareness regarding black needs than had previously existed. The potential power of the government to reverse the traditional oppression and exploitation experienced by black people was therefore great. But as William Hastie indicated in 1939, and as Robert Vann and Forrester Washington among others had pointed out earlier, an expanded federal authority also created numerous additional problems for the black minority, problems which involved not only their immediate and future condition in the 1930s and 1940s, but the very nature of their leadership and organizations in the Negro community.

Realizing the necessity, as well as the potential value, of expanded federal activity, black leaders were concerned to find how that activity might best enhance the welfare of their people. There were, in effect, few precedents to help them in this endeavor, and their challenge was made even more difficult by the lack of economic and political power black people possessed, the lack of unity and cohesion within the black community, and the lack of any clear ideological perspective in which they might judge and determine the actual meaning of the many government programs which emerged after 1933.

What all Negro groups sought, of course, was a voice strong enough to assure them some control over the decision-making processes within the federal system. Some, like those active in the NNC and the MOWM, believed it necessary to create a mass movement among all black peoples and form alliances with sympathetic white organizations that would be comprehensive enough to match the expansive influence of the federal government. But that was never realized, primarily because of the difficulty of overcoming divisions within the black community and because it was hard to sustain such a mass movement except when specific issues were present, such as lynching or discrimination in defense industries and the armed forces. Other groups tried through more modest means to build pressure groups in local communities or, as in the case of the NAACP, to apply pressure on highly placed government and congressional figures. But, as the black organizers realized, such an approach had only limited value when there existed little real power to back up that vocal pressure. Still others saw the placing of Negroes within the government as a major means of ensuring greater administration accountability to the black population. Again, however, although certain beneficial results were achieved, black New Dealers were primarily dependent on the authority of their white superiors, who might or might not be willing to follow their suggestions and to act upon their proposals.[23]

23. The issue of black leadership, particularly the question of whether the lack of unity among leaders and organizations is an asset or a liability in the quest for black liberation, can be argued from different vantage points. Herbert Garfinkel maintains that the tendency for minority groups like blacks to seek out a single leader and a single mass movement has been a weakness. "There has been too great an inferiority complex among Negroes," he writes, "with respect to their leadership. A decided feeling persists that there is more schism in the Negro community than elsewhere. This reflects the view that there should be but one Negro organization leading the protest battle to which everyone can give wholehearted support, that anything less is but petty bickering. Presumably, if only the leader could be found to bring this about all would be well. . . . The idea that there would necessarily be a gain from having a single organization is predicated on an assumption which is questionable. The assumption is that there is a single path to racial advancement." Garfinkel, *When Negroes March*, 183. Similarly, Gilbert Osofsky notes a "greater diffusion of effective leadership" as a result of the thirties' experience of blacks; Osofsky, ed., *The Burden of Race: A Documentary History of Negro-White Relations in America* (New York, 1967). E. Franklin Frazier saw the 1930s and 1940s as having produced what he called a "functional leadership," rooted in the growing urbanization of blacks and away from a single black leader; Frazier, *The Negro in the United States* (New York, 1949), 548. The key consideration, however, is not whether a "functional," "diffused," or competitive leadership is more desirable than a single mass leader and movement; what is of concern is how leaders and organizations either singly or in unity can further the Negro's struggle for power, influence, and participation in the existing political, social, and economic institutions. During much of the 1930s and early 1940s, the absence of unified struggle or basic agreement on objectives involving the federal

Toward the end of the Roosevelt era, another attempt was made to build what Robert Vann in particular had urged earlier, an independent black political force. In 1944, urged on by A. Philip Randolph, a "National Non-Partisan" political conference was called, and in the same year a statement was issued entitled a "Declaration by Negro Voters" which included among its signers Randolph, Mary McLeod Bethune, Walter White, Thurgood Marshall, Rayford Logan, Adam Clayton Powell, Jr., and Max Yergan of the NNC. The "Declaration" asserted that the black man's vote could not "be purchased by distributing money to and through party hacks," nor could it "be won by pointing to jobs given to a few individuals." Recognizing that Negroes had generally supported the Democrats since the mid-1930s, the document's signers now declared that their vote no longer belonged "to any one political party," and they urged blacks to vote for individuals in both parties who supported the cause of racial justice.[24] Supporting such a stand for political independence, a columnist for the Chicago *Defender* concluded that "no Negro under 25" had any "real recollection of the awful Hoover Administration, and so F.D.R.'s reforms don't mean a thing to them."[25]

Yet such a view was indeed premature. Many blacks still seemed to recall those years under Hoover and remember PWA, WPA, CCC, and NYA reforms, and in case they might forget, Democratic party political hopefuls, as well as veterans of the New Deal like Harold Ickes and Henry Wallace, spent considerable time in 1944 within

---

government and the Roosevelt administration limited blacks in pressuring the administration, the labor movement, and the Democratic party. If the lack of unity and internal black competition gives the impression of divisions within the black community, it does little to further the goal of forcing concessions from established power groups. If there is general agreement on objectives, competition among groups can, of course, be healthy and helpful to all concerned. But it depends on the circumstances and the conditions of the time. In effect, the nationalizing of power in Washington reinforced to some degree black people's feelings that what was required was a national movement and a national leader; for a time Martin Luther King, Jr., fulfilled that hope during the late 1950s and early 1960s.

24. Reference to Randolph's role in calling the conference noted in New York *Times*, Apr. 30, 1944, and Chicago *Defender*, June 24, 1944. Statements from "National Non-Partisan Conference" from "Declaration by Negro Voters," *Crisis*, 16-17. Walter White wrote to Eleanor Roosevelt that he "was immensely impressed with the unanimity of opinion among the organization representatives. There was no disagreement on principle and little on the form of presentation." White to ER, June 20, 1944, ER Papers, Box 1751.

25. Charley Cherokee, "National Grapevine," Chicago *Defender*, June 24, 1944.

the black community refreshing their memories.[26] Although the 1944 Democratic plank on civil rights was dramatically weaker than that of 1940 (Walter White called it a "mouse of evasion") and the Republican party in 1944 issued a strong statement calling for a permanent FEPC, repeal of poll taxes, and even anti-lynching legislation, and despite the efforts of the "Non-Partisan" political organizers, the majority of black voters backed Roosevelt's bid for a fourth term and supported Democratic party candidates for the most part. One of those helping to ensure a Democratic victory was Mary McLeod Bethune, who had been one of the original signers of the "Declaration by Negro Voters."[27]

It has been always easier to declare independence than actually to realize it. What made it so much more difficult for blacks during the 1930s and 1940s and the years that followed was their own ambivalence toward independence when it represented a possible break with the Roosevelt administration, the Democratic party, and the federal government. Few black leaders were prepared to surrender what Franklin D. Roosevelt's leadership and the prodding of race liberals like Harold L. Ickes, Eleanor Roosevelt, and others had helped them to gain—that is, the inclusion of the black rights struggle within the orbit of liberal reformism. They were not ready to forget that before the 1930s the national government, especially the executive branch, played only a minimal role in giving either com-

26. Both Ickes and Wallace made speeches in Harlem during the 1944 campaign urging blacks to support Roosevelt and the Democratic party in the coming election; see New York *Times*, Oct. 2, Nov. 2, 1944. Clark Foreman took time off from his duties as a teacher at Black Mountain College and as head of the SCHF to join the staff of the CIO's Political Action Committee (PAC). PAC worked closely with blacks like Bethune and Weaver to achieve FDR's reelection; see New York *Times*, June 25, 1944, and Moon, *Balance of Power*, 34-35.

27. On the Democratic planks relevant to blacks in 1940 and 1944, see discussion in Moon, *Balance of Power*, 31-34; and on the 1944 Democratic convention and civil rights, New York *Times*, July 19, 20, 21, 23, 1944. For reference to the Republican statement on civil rights, New York *Times*, July 6, 1944, and Donald R. McCoy, *Landon of Kansas* (Lincoln, Neb., 1966), 507. The complete platforms of the Democratic and Republican parties in 1940 and 1944 can be found and compared in Kirk H. Porter and Donald Bruce Johnson, eds., *National Party Platforms*, 1840-1956 (Urbana, Ill., 1956), 381-87, 389-94, 402-4, 407-13. For discussion of Alf Landon and the "Negro problem," see McCoy, 45, 98, 103-5, 240, 277, 297, 311-12, 332-33, 420, 447, 507, 510. Walter White's comment quoted in New York *Times*, July 22, 1944; see also the previously noted White to ER, July 7, 1944, Aug. 9, 1944, ER Papers, Box 1751, on his political feelings in 1944. Besides Bethune, other prominent blacks working for Roosevelt's reelection included Hastie, Weaver, and Du Bois; Moon, *Balance of Power*, 35.

fort or direction to the Negro's pursuit for justice in America. Indeed, as Henry Lee Moon indicated, the relationship between blacks and the federal government since Reconstruction had often been an antagonistic one (with a few exceptions), even in times of national reform.

After 1930, it was different. When "looked upon from the practical and political viewpoints," Myrdal pointed out in 1944, "the contrast between the present situation and the one prior to the New Deal is striking." The striking fact was that from the 1930s on, the federal government with its "enormous influence" became the primary factor in the civil rights struggle. The "whole configuration of the Negro problem" had changed, Myrdal wrote, and he was right.[28] After 1933, whatever the strategic or ideological debate, at whatever level within the black community, the government in Washington and its policies assumed major consideration.

But the new "configuration" was shaped not simply by the expansion of federal power but also by the particular manner in which that power was exercised for the betterment of Negroes and other American citizens. Here the assumptions made and the approach pursued by white race liberals are of prime importance. More than any others during the 1930s and 1940s, this handful of interracialists, largely isolated from the mainstream of American power and influence prior to 1932, tied their racial goals to the rising star of the New Deal. They were the New Deal's most vocal and articulate spokespersons for race justice; they provided the public rationale for the administration's policies to black Americans, a link between the government and the black community, and advice and counsel to Negroes both within and outside the New Deal. Whatever racial philosophy can be discerned in the Roosevelt administration's reform policies can be attributed to these individuals.[29]

Their desire to see race removed as a source of antagonism and conflict between black and white and their need to identify with a broad movement for change in American life assured their outspoken advocacy of New Deal reformism. From the start, the "solution" to the "Negro problem" for a Harold Ickes or an Eleanor Roosevelt, and especially for southern race liberals, was understood to go hand in hand with the successful development of administration reform and recovery. Committed to assuring blacks a "square deal," con-

28. Myrdal, *An American Dilemma*, I, 74.

29. Wolters, *Negroes and the Great Depression*, Part I, *passim*; Sosna, *In Search of the Silent South*, ch. 4; Sitkoff, "Emergence of Civil Rights As a National Issue," ch. 3; Kifer, "The Negro Under the New Deal," 272-80.

cerned with the special disabilities of the Negro minority, and opposed to any form of discrimination, they stood as friends of all the oppressed. Either as government officials or supporters of the government, they worked to include blacks wherever possible, both in the administration and in its reforms. These liberals were far ahead of the majority of their colleagues, the Congress, the President, and the nation in expressing a fundamental concern for race justice. Whatever their faults or the limits of their leadership, they deserved the respect and admiration which often came their way.[30]

Yet it is hard to escape the conclusion that, finally, most white interracialists were concerned more for the future of liberal reform than for the black American. In their minds, of course, the two were inseparable, but that determination came less from a considered analysis of America's race situation or the needs of black people than from their own hopes and fears. Some of the fears which shaped their understanding of issues were well founded: race violence was not only possible, it was frequently a reality in their time; the depth of white racist hostility toward Negroes was indeed strong, especially in the South, and it existed elsewhere in the country and in the Roosevelt administration itself. The wish, therefore, to pursue policies that might avoid open racial conflict sprang from legitimate concerns; but too often those concerns governed white liberal behavior and the restrictions liberals attempted to impose on the activities of blacks and others in the struggle for justice. And, as Peter Kellogg indicates in his study of northern liberal race thought, there were strong political considerations involved in the pursuit of a racial harmony strategy as well: the need to maintain the Democratic coalition and the worry that liberalism might be dragged down under the weight of racial discord.[31]

In a practical sense, politics naturally affected the options available to racial liberals. As Franklin Roosevelt often told blacks like Mary McLeod Bethune and Walter White, the administration had to work with a Congress in which southern racists controlled key positions in the legislative process; reform programs had to acknowledge the

---

30. As noted earlier, the absence of any clear view on the race issue and black rights among prominent northern liberals, many of whom were critical of the New Deal for being too moderate in its economic reforms, simply added to the strength of those liberal interracialists in the government as well as their prominence in the fight for black rights; see Kellogg, "Northern Liberals and Black America," *passim*, esp. 427-35.

31. *Ibid.*, 33-84, 427-35. Also see Sosna, *In Search of the Silent South*, chs. 4-6.

prevailing attitudes of trade unionists, of industrial managers, of state and local officials, and of the population as a whole.[32]

But politics and race fears threatened as well the hopes inspired by liberal belief that black life would improve measurably under the aegis of the New Deal. Racial attitudes would change, they argued, as federal programs of economic and social aid increased opportunities for blacks; the "Negro problem" was fundamentally a class problem and treated best by economic reform. Yet that philosophy was not designed to deal directly with existing racial attitudes, which constantly frustrated reform programs and the good intentions of New Dealers. In effect, the philosophy avoided confronting racial attitudes. Thus, by perceiving the "solution" to the "Negro problem" in primarily economic and not racial terms (or a combination of both), race liberals accepted what Lillian Smith called the "patterns" of white bigotry and prejudice, allowing those patterns to go largely unchallenged either by the federal government or by those who had a stake in the continued oppression of black people.

Failing to acknowledge the intensity with which anti-black attitudes had been fundamentally ingrained in the entire institutional structure of American life, the race liberals weakened their efforts, as Smith pointed out. Such a failure also weakened Gunnar Myrdal's analysis of the "Negro problem" and the optimistic conclusions his study reached in 1944. Carl N. Degler noted twenty-five years after publication of *An American Dilemma* that "throughout his book Myrdal made it clear that he saw prejudice as an idea; if that idea could be altered or destroyed by education then prejudice and discrimination would disappear. Thus, at the end of his study he observed: 'The important changes in the Negro problem do not consist of, or have close relations with, "social trends" in the narrower meaning of the term, but were made up in people's beliefs and valuations.' The change in short would take place in people's minds."[33] That change would ultimately occur, Myrdal and the New Deal liberals believed, when the class status of black people was raised, when black economic and social inferiority no longer provided a convenient rationale for white prejudice, and when whites were directly confronted with the inherent contradiction in their

32. Bethune, "My Secret Talks," 42-51; White, *A Man Called White*, 169-70; Morrison, "The Secret Papers of FDR," 3-13.

33. Carl N. Degler, "The Negro in America—Where Myrdal Went Wrong," *The New York Times Magazine* (Dec. 7, 1969), 154.

profession of "democracy" and their irrational denial of democracy's basic rights to the black minority.[34]

But Myrdal's and liberal New Dealers' analysis of racial attitudes was based on a limited reading of the intensity of those attitudes. Degler has argued that Myrdal's model ignored "the fact that one of the sources of prejudice and discrimination is competition for social status. It is axiomatic that one of the reasons why many whites insist upon caste positions for blacks is that it places a social floor beneath the whites; it provides status through color if not by class." In fact, Degler concludes, what is now known "about the relationship between social mobility and prejudice historically contradicts the Myrdal assumption that as Negroes rise economically they will be more readily accepted by whites."[35]

Another assumption in *An American Dilemma* helps to illuminate the thought and activities of liberal whites and blacks in the thirties and forties. "The Negro problem," Myrdal wrote in his introduction, "is an integral part of, or a special phase of, the whole complex of problems in the larger American civilization. It cannot be treated in isolation."[36] Basic to that understanding and to the ideas expressed throughout the period by liberals and the majority of blacks, moderate as well as radical, was the belief in an existing common culture, one shared equally by Negro and white. As sociologist Stanford M. Lyman notes, "To Myrdal, blacks and whites agree on the elements of the core culture but disagree only on their priorities. The idea of a separate black culture or a subculture developed in isolation" was "not taken seriously by Myrdal."[37] Neither, with the notable exception of W.E.B. Du Bois, was it taken seriously by most black and white thinkers and activists during the Roosevelt era.

Affirmation of a common, unified culture, then, went together with the class thesis, with the argument for similar economic interests, and with the solution liberal whites offered to the American

---

34. Myrdal, *An American Dilemma*, I, 75-76.

35. Degler, "The Negro in America," 156. For a similar attack on the failure of liberal thought in respect to the question of race, see Leonard J. Fein, "The Limits of Liberalism," *Saturday Review* 53 (June 20, 1970), 83-84.

36. Myrdal, *An American Dilemma*, I, lxxvii.

37. Stanford M. Lyman, *The Black American in Sociological Thought: A Failure of Perspective* (New York, 1972), 117. Lyman's entire essay on Myrdal is well worth reading. See *ibid.*, 99-120. For an early attack on Myrdal's cultural assumptions, see Ralph Ellison, "An American Dilemma: A Review," in Ellison, *Shadow and Act* (New York, 1964), 303-17. Ellison wrote his review in 1943.

racial dilemma. The "Negro problem" would be eliminated as it merged into the other problems the welfare state was attacking and as black people began to be viewed as part of the larger class which, as Harold Ickes put it, "the New Democracy was designed to aid." The result, whether intended or not, was that blacks were seen primarily as reactors to rather than initiators of the forces of the dominant culture, including the forces shaping the "New Democracy." Seldom doubting the commonality of their interests, cultural and economic, liberals assumed that change would be slow but inevitable; thus, black people were cautioned not to force race issues which would only have the effect of endangering progress already achieved.[38]

In the end, the "configuration," a framework in which the battle for race equality was fought out, erected during the Roosevelt era, was filled with its own ambivalence. The ambivalence of blacks derived from their acceptance of benefits won from a government showing sympathy for their plight and a willingness to embrace them in its general reforms, but one which also exacted a certain dependence that complicated, if it did not render impossible, the quest for self-determination. For whites, ambivalence came from racial assumptions, shaped by past and present experience, and an intense loyalty to reform liberalism that encouraged them to work for improvements in black life but not to attack the racial as well as the political patterns of American society which frequently compromised their interracial hopes and their reform goals.

Since liberal whites held the power during the Roosevelt years,

38. Ralph Bunche's criticism of the role of whites in interracial movements has application to white liberals in the New Deal as well as those who operated outside the government. Bunche wrote that "in the very nature of race relations in this country, the white members of the interracial groups must take upon themselves the responsibility for fixing the measures of value in inter-group relationships. It is not merely a question of *how much* the Negro is to ask for or to expect, but also *how* he is to ask for it, or, indeed, whether he should *ask* for it at all, since it may often be more 'strategic' to permit his sympathetic white friends to act on his behalf. It is the whites alone who are in position to advise the Negro that it is better for him to ask for little and to anticipate something than to ask for too much and gain nothing. It is the white, also, who can lean on realism and inform the Negro that if he goes before responsible officials in the community and demands or asks for benefits, his appeals are apt to be ignored. Whereas, if his white friends appear in his behalf, he has a better chance to receive the favor. That this half-a-loaf approach of the interracialist has won local benefits of various kinds for Negroes . . . is not denied; but this is no storming of the bastions of racial prejudice nor does it even aim toward them. In its very nature it is a defeatist attitude, since it accepts the existing racial patterns while asking favors and exceptions within them." Bunche, "Programs, Ideologies, Tactics," 559-60.

their historical impact was far greater. Only when World War II forced race into the center of their consciousness and their politics, where they could no longer avoid it because neither white racists nor blacks would allow them to do so, did they begin to modify some of their previous attitudes and assumptions. But still they clung to the hope that their approach to the "Negro problem" would find vindication and, indeed, would be continued in the years to come. The ultimate legacy, however, was the persistence of black and white ambivalence itself, which ensured that the struggle for racial justice would continue to be perplexing and painful—for white as well as black.

Bibliographical Essay

The literature on the Roosevelt years is enormous and still grow-ing. Information concerning the activities and thinking of black Americans during the New Deal– World War II period is less abun-dant, but articles and monographs are now being published which are increasing our knowledge of the Afro-American experience during the "Age of Roosevelt." To list all the references used for this project would simply repeat references found in the footnotes; thus what is noted in this essay are those sources which were most helpful in shaping the direction I pursued in my analysis.

I have been primarily interested in the relationship of thought to public policies and less with the specific nature of those policies, which have been analyzed elsewhere. In this regard, I have relied on both the public statements and the written manuscript sources to develop a sense of the thinking and the concerns of both black and white. Of major importance are the collections of the Franklin D. Roosevelt Library, Hyde Park, where not only President Roosevelt's papers are located, of which the Official File and the President's Personal File were of special value, but also the Eleanor Roosevelt and Aubrey Williams papers. Mrs. Roosevelt's papers provided considerable information and leads on other individuals involved in this study, as well as offering the substance for my discussion of her thought and activity. The Williams papers were less helpful than one might have expected, given the New Dealer's relationship to many whites and blacks engaged in racial activities. Harold L. Ickes' papers for the period after 1932 (Manuscript Division, Library of Congress) were closed during the time this study was researched and written; they have been opened recently and should add considerable insight into the Interior Secretary's role in affecting racial policy in the New Deal administration. I did find helpful the Ickes papers available for the years to 1932, which pertained to his NAACP activities in Chicago during the early twenties. In the National Archives in Washington, D.C., I used the collections of the Civil Works Administration, the Federal Emergency Relief Administration, the Interior Department (Official Files of the Secretary), and the National Youth Administra-tion and its Division of Negro Affairs. These excellent sources

236

include the correspondence of New Deal officials like Harold Ickes, Clark Foreman, and Aubrey Williams, as well as the communications of a number of black government advisers.

The papers of the National Assocation for the Advancement of Colored People, Manuscript Division, Library of Congress, are basic to understanding the NAACP's role during the 1930s and 1940s, as well as for the information they supply on individuals like Walter White and other NAACP officials and their correspondence with black and white leaders. The National Urban League Papers, also in the Manuscript Division, Library of Congress, were less helpful for my purposes, though they did provide some worthwhile information on the League and some of its leading figures. The Julius Rosenwald Fund Archives and the Charles S. Johnson Papers, housed at Fisk University, were of major value in writing about Edwin R. Embree, Will Alexander, Clark Foreman, and Johnson, among others. Both collections are also available on microfilm at the Amistad Research Center, Dillard University, and I studied them at both locations. Disappointing were the Mary McLeod Bethune Papers at the Amistad Research Center, which consisted essentially of Bethune speeches, most of which were already in print. The National Negro Congress Papers, Schomburg Collection, New York Public Library, Harlem branch, were indispensable in learning about John P. Davis' activities and thought and in providing important documents relevant to the Joint Committee on National Recovery and the Congress itself. There is also a large section devoted to Davis, the Joint Committee, and the NAACP-NNC relationship in the NAACP Papers. The unpublished memorandums of Ralph J. Bunche prepared for the Carnegie-Myrdal Study of the Negro in America, which are in the Schomburg Collection, Harlem branch, New York Public Library (but which I read on microfilm at the University of Illinois Library, Urbana-Champaign), were invaluable for an understanding of Bunche's ideas and for comprehending black organizations and racial thought thoughout the 1930s. The most helpful here were Bunche's "Extended Memorandum on the Programs, Ideologies, Tactics and Achievements of Negro Betterment and Interracial Organizations" and "The Political Status of the Negro with Emphasis on the South and Comparative Treatment of the 'poor white.' "

Providing additional information on the thinking of some individuals were the personal interviews collected by the Columbia University Oral History Project. Those used were: "The Reminiscences of Will W. Alexander (1952), 3 vols.; Norman Thomas (1949, 1950, 1966), 3 vols.; George S. Schuyler (1960); and Roy

Wilkins (1960). There are also a number of biographies of black and white figures that are of varying quality and usefulness. Some of the best include: Andrew Buni, *Robert L. Vann and the Pittsburgh Courier* (Pittsburgh: Univ. of Pittsburgh Press, 1974); Joseph P. Lash, *Eleanor and Franklin: The Story of Their Relationship Based on Eleanor Roosevelt's Private Papers* (New York: W. W. Norton, 1971); Francis L. Broderick, *W.E.B. Du Bois: Negro Leader in a Time of Crisis* (Stanford: Stanford Univ. Press, 1959). Less helpful but still of value are Edwin R. Embree, *13 Against the Odds* (New York: Viking, 1944), which includes brief biographical sketches of Bethune, Du Bois, Johnson, Randolph, and White; J. Alvin Kugelmass, *Ralph J. Bunche: Fighter for Peace* (New York: Messner, 1962); Jervis Anderson, *A. Philip Randolph: A Biographical Portrait* (New York: Harcourt Brace Jovanovich, 1973); Rackham Holt, *Mary McLeod Bethune: A Biography* (New York: Doubleday, 1964); and W.A. Swanberg, *Norman Thomas: The Last Idealist* (New York: Scribner's, 1976).

There are a few autobiographies and personal memoirs that proved meaningful. Among whites, the most interesting and suggestive was Harold L. Ickes, *The Secret Diary of Harold L. Ickes, 3* vols. (New York: Simon & Schuster, 1954). Eleanor Roosevelt's *The Autobiography of Eleanor Roosevelt* (New York: Harper and Row, 1961) is chatty and of little value in determining the First Lady's racial perspective. For blacks, the two autobiographies of W.E.B. Du Bois are informative, though one has to be careful of Du Bois' special pleading, particularly when he discusses his critics: *Dusk of Dawn: An Essay Town an Autobiography of a Race Concept* (New York: Harcourt, Brace, Co., 1940; *The Autobiography of W.E.B. Du Bois: A Soliloquy on Viewing My Life from the Last Decade of Its First Century* (New York: International Publishers, 1968). Walter White's *A Man Called White* (New York: Viking, 1948), is straightforward, but for an understanding of White's attitudes, his correspondence in the NAACP Papers and in the Eleanor Roosevelt Papers is essential.

A number of black journals and periodicals published essays by both blacks and whites discussed in this study as well as articles on important issues and events of the thirties and forties. *Crisis*, the NAACP's journal, and *Opportunity: Journal of Negro Life*, the official organ of the National Urban League, were read for the entire period. The *Journal of Negro Education*, which was published at Howard University, contained many thoughtful articles, especially by Howard intellectuals like Ralph Bunche, who used the journal as a vehicle to express their opinions on current race questions. *Race*, which lasted for only two issues (1935-36), was another source reflecting the thought of radical black intellectuals. Also useful were the *Journal of Negro History* and *Phylon*, which was founded by W.E.B. Du Bois in 1940.

Of the non-black periodicals, the *New Republic, The Nation, Saturday Review of Literature, Survey Graphic, Common Ground*, and *Common Sense* were the most valuable in publishing essays by whites and occasionally by blacks. Lillian Smith's *South Today* (formerly *North Georgia Review*) was of primary significance as a forum for Smith's writings, but it also supplied information and commentary on interracial activities in the South and elsewhere in the 1940s.

Black newspapers are an invaluable source for learning about matters of relevance to the black population: the Chicago *Defender* and the Pittsburgh *Courier* were read for the years 1932 through 1945, and of course the *Courier* was a major source for the thought of Robert L. Vann, its editor and publisher until 1940. As most historians acknowledge, the New York *Times* is an indispensable guide for following political and social events in contemporary history. The *Times* also did stories periodically on affairs affecting the black community.

There is no existing history which analyzes the racial thought of the Roosevelt years. Yet there are a number of books, articles, and unpublished works which have studied aspects of the Roosevelt administration– black American relationship and are fundamental in understanding the activities and views of many of the individuals I have written about. Every historian concerned with the New Deal's importance to blacks is indebted to Allen Kifer's pathbreaking, though still unpublished, "The Negro Under the New Deal, 1933-1941" (Ph.D. diss., Univ. of Wisconsin, 1961). Kifer's concern is essentially with the effect on Afro-Americans of government reform and recovery programs, but his dissertation offers additional insights into the thinking of race liberals like Harold Ickes, Clark Foreman, Will Alexander, and Aubrey Williams. More broadly conceived and focusing primarily on the economic features of the New Deal– black relationship but of equal importance in comprehending the nature of government programs in the 1930s is Raymond Wolters' fine *Negroes and the Great Depression* (Westport, Conn.: Greenwood Publishers, 1970). Harvard Ira Sitkoff's dissertation on "The Emergence of Civil Rights as a National Issue: The New Deal Era" (Ph.D. diss., Columbia Univ., 1975) is somewhat indiscriminate in its analysis, but it covers almost everything pertinent to civil rights matters during the 1930s, including some of the contributions made by New Dealers like Eleanor Roosevelt and Ickes. To understand the ideas of southern race liberals such as Will Alexander, Aubrey Williams, Clark Foreman, and many others, and as a guide to placing their thought and activity within the broad cultural and political context of the southern experience, Morton Sosna's *In Search of the Silent South* (New York: Columbia Univ. Press, 1977) is basic. Also of great value in this regard is George B. Tindall, *The Emergence of the New South, 1913-1945* (Baton Rouge: Louisiana State Univ. Press, 1967). For the non-southern race perspective, Peter J. Kellogg's "Northern Liberals and Black America: A History of White Attitudes, 1936-1952" (Ph.D. diss., Northwestern Univ., 1971), is a good starting point. Kellogg's interpretation of liberal race assumptions conforms to my own reading, and his dissertation is especially valuable for the understanding he provides of the racial attitudes reflected in journals like the *New Republic* and *The Nation*.

Other works helpful in understanding the thought of certain liberal interracialists or the circumstances which influenced their beliefs are Frank Friedel, *F.D.R. and the South* (Baton Rouge: Louisiana State Univ. Press, 1965); Tamara K. Hareven, *Eleanor Roosevelt: An American Conscience* (Chicago: Quadrangle, 1968); Thomas A. Krueger, *And Promises to Keep: The Southern Conference for Human Welfare, 1938-1948* (Nashville: Vanderbilt Univ. Press, 1967); Lillian Smith, *Killers of the Dream* (New York: W. W. Norton, 1949); Leslie H. Fishel, Jr., "The Negro in the New Deal Era," *Wisconsin Magazine of History* 48 (Winter 1964-1965), 111-26; M. Judd Harmon, "Some Contributions of Harold L. Ickes," *Western Political Quarterly* 7 (June 1954), 238-52; and John A. Salmond, " 'Aubrey Williams Remembers': A Note on Franklin D. Roosevelt's Attitude toward Negro Rights," *The Alabama Review* 25 (Jan. 1972), 62-77.

In addition to the above, a number of studies that have analyzed specific New Deal programs and government policies in the 1940s were important sources on both whites and blacks. These include Sidney Baldwin, *Poverty and Politics: The Rise and Decline of the Farm Security Administration* (Chapel Hill: Univ. of North Carolina Press, 1968); Louis Ruchames, *Race, Jobs and Politics: The Story* of the FEPC (New York: Columbia Univ. Press, 1953); Marc W. Kruman, "Quotas for Blacks: The Public Works Administration and the Black Construction Worker," *Labor History* 16 (Winter 1975), 37-51; Donald Ross, "The Role of Blacks in the Federal Theatre, 1935-1939," *Journal of Negro History* 59 (Jan. 1934), 38-50; John A. Salmond, "The Civilian Conservation Corps and the Negro," *Journal of American History* 52 (June 1965), 75-88; Christopher G. Wye, "The

New Deal and the Negro Community: Toward a Broader Conceptualization," *Journal of American History* 59 (Dec. 1972), 621-39; Melvin Ruebin Maskin, "Black Education and the New Deal" (Ph.D. diss., New York Univ., 1973); and George Phillip Rawick, "The New Deal and Youth: The Civilian Conservation Corps, The National Youth Administration and The American Youth Congress" (Ph.D. diss., Univ. of Wisconsin, 1957).

Two books which are critically important for the penetrating analysis they provide of political and cultural thought during the 1930s and for the comparison they offer of the reform and racial assumptions of pro– New Deal liberals and liberal-left critics of the Roosevelt administration are R. Alan Lawson, *The Failure of Independent Liberalism (1930-1941)* (New York: Capricorn, 1971), and Richard H. Pells, *Radical Visions and American Dreams: Culture and Social Thought in the Depression Years* (New York: Harper and Row, 1973).

As in the case of liberal whites, there is no general history that examines black political and social thought during the 1930s and 1940s, but there are a number of specialized studies which offer important insights into Afro-American protest activity and the attitudes of a number of prominent black leaders. For a background to the thirties and forties, one should consult August Meier, *Negro Thought in America, 1880-1915* (Ann Arbor: Univ. of Michigan Press, 1963), Nathan Irvin Huggins, *Harlem Renaissance* (New York: Oxford Univ. Press, 1971), and S.P. Fullinwider, *The Mind and Mood of Black America: Twentieth Century Thought* (Homewood, Ill.: Dorsey Press, 1969). Fullinwider's study carries its discussion of black thinkers like W.E.B. Du Bois, E. Franklin Frazier, and Charles S. Johnson into the 1930s, but a book that concentrates on these individuals, as well as others discussed in my study, is James O. Young, *Black Writers of the Thirties* (Baton Rouge: Louisiana State Univ. Press, 1973). Besides Young, Ralph J. Bunche's Carnegie-Myrdal memorandums and his various articles are, of course, basic to evaluating black thought and political activity in the thirties.

Despite some of my criticisms of it, Myrdal's *An American Dilemma: The Negro Problem and Modern Democracy*, 2 vols. (2d ed.; New York: Harper and Row, 1962), is the starting point for gaining a sense of black life in and prior to the New Deal years. On the political activities and internal struggles of the NAACP, the National Urban League, the National Negro Congress, and the March on Washington Movement, the following are important: Wolters, *Negroes and the Great Depression*, for discussion of the NAACP and the

NNC; Guichard Parris and Lester Brooks, *Blacks in the City: A History of the National Urban League* (Boston: Little, Brown and Co., 1971); B. Joyce Ross, *J.E. Spingarn and the Rise of the NAACP, 1911-1939* (New York: Atheneum, 1972); Nancy J. Weiss, *The National Urban League, 1910-1940* (New York: Oxford Univ. Press, 1974); August Meier and Elliott Rudwick, eds., *Along the Color Line: Explorations in the Black Experience* (Urbana, Ill.: Univ. of Illinois Press, 1976), for essays on the NAACP; Lawrence S. Wittner, "The National Negro Congress: A Reassessment," *American Quarterly* 22 (Winter 1970), 883-901; Herbert Garfinkel, *When Negroes March: The March on Washington Movement in the Organizational Policies for FEPC* (Glencoe, Ill.: The Free Press, 1959); Richard M. Dalfiume, *Fighting on Two Fronts: Desegregation of the Armed Forces, 1939-1953* (Columbia, Mo.: Univ. of Missouri Press, 1969) and "The 'Forgotten Years' of the Negro Revolution," *The Journal of American History* 55 (June 1968), 90-106.

On black New Dealers, B. Joyce Ross, "Mary McLeod Bethune and the National Youth Administration: A Case Study of Power Relationships in the Black Cabinet of Franklin D. Roosevelt," *Journal of Negro History* 60 (Jan. 1975), 1-28, is a thoughtful and significant study. Also helpful is Jane R. Motz, "The Black Cabinet: Negroes in the Administration of Franklin D. Roosevelt" (M.A. thesis, Univ. of Delaware, 1964).

Other studies which relate to the black experience of the 1930s and 1940s and provide a context for understanding black American concerns are Dan T. Carter, *Scottsboro: A Tragedy of the American South* (Baton Rouge: Louisiana State Univ. Press, 1969); Harold Cruse, *The Crisis of the Negro Intellectual: From Its Origins to the Present* (New York: Morrow, 1967); Wilson Record, *The Negro and the Communist Party* (Chapel Hill: Univ. of North Carolina Press, 1951).

Finally, Arthur M. Schlesinger, Jr.'s three-volume work *The Age of Roosevelt* (Boston: Houghton Mifflin, 1957-1960), and especially his last volume, *The Politics of Upheaval* (1960), should be read for a general understanding of the New Deal years and the Roosevelt administration. The best one-volume study remains William E. Leuchtenburg, *Franklin D. Roosevelt and the New Deal, 1932-1940* (New York: Harper and Row, 1963). For the war years, see James MacGregor Burns, *Roosevelt: The Soldier of Freedom* (New York: Harcourt Brace Jovanovich, 1970). Besides the Myrdal study, there are two general histories of the black American experience of merit, August Meier and Elliott Rudwick, *From Plantation to Ghetto: An*

Interpretive History of American Negroes (3d ed.; New York: Hill and Wang, 1976), and John Hope Franklin, *From Slavery to Freedom: A History of American Negroes* (4th ed.; New York: Knopf, 1974).

Index

Abbott, Robert S., 23
Addams, Jane, 18
"Adviser on the Economic Status of the Negro." 13, 16– 17; controversy over, 18– 20; *See also* Clark Foreman
Agricultural Adjustment Administration (AAA), 24, 43, 141– 42, 159, 163, 178, 207, 208
Agriculture Department, U.S., 202
Alexander, Will W., ix, xi, 8– 12, 16– 17, 49– 62, 83, 90, 105, 158, 196; activities in the twenties, 8-11; friendship with Edwin Embree and Charles Johnson, 14, 14n5, 49– 50, 200, 202; attraction to Franklin Roosevelt and New Deal, 14– 15; secures Clark Foreman's position in New Deal, 16– 17; relies on Foreman for information, 37, 37n70; "pivotal figure" among southern race liberals, 49-50; heads FSA, 51– 52; and with OPM, 53, 110; southern liberal race perspective, 52– 55; on race stereotypes and consciousness, 56– 60; impact of World War II on, 53– 54, 95– 96; on segregation, 52, 54, 56– 57, 59, 60– 61, 60n35, 62; class and labor status of blacks, 55-56, 61; and qualities of black leadership, 58– 59, 82, 122; New Deal importance to blacks, 57, 59-62; contribution to liberal race thought, 61-62, 73– 74, 75, 221; recommends Forrester Washington, 139; cooperation with Walter White, 182, 185

Amalgamated Clothing Workers Union, 196
Amenia Conference (1933), 15, 104– 05, 106, 192
American Council of Education, 57
American Federation of Labor (AFL), 99, 123, 141, 212-13
American Federationist, 124
American Friends Service Committee, 9
An American Dilemma, x: discussed, 219– 20, 232-33
Anderson, Marian, 21, 82
Atlanta, Ga.: housing project, 23, 35
Atlanta School of Social Work, 139

Bagnall, Robert, 18
Bailey, Sen. Josiah W., 33
Bankhead-Jones Farm Tenant Act, 50, 163
Bardolph, Richard, 107
Berea College, 13
Bethune, Mary McLeod, xii, 37, 110– 21, 131, 165; friendship with Eleanor Roosevelt, 77, 79, 82, 111– 12, 182; shares views of white liberals, 111, 120; background, 110-11; accessibility to President Roosevelt, 112, 231; praises President, 119; supports New Deal, 113-15, 119-21; and Office of Negro Affairs, 115, 116– 17; influence, 110, 112– 13, 134, 146, 147, 148; frustrations, 116– 19; on strong government and black involvement, 113– 15; and "New Negro," 120– 21; organizes conferences on "Problems of Negro," 112, 119,

244

Twentieth-Century America Series

DEWEY W. GRANTHAM, GENERAL EDITOR

Each volume in this series focuses on some aspect of the politics of social change in recent American history, utilizing new approaches to clarify the response of Americans to the dislocating forces of our own day—economic, technological, racial, demographic, and administrative. Volumes published are:

The Reaffirmation of Republicanism: Eisenhower and the Eighty-third Congress by Gary W. Reichard
The Crisis of Conservative Virginia: The Byrd Organization and the Politics of Massive Resistance by James W. Ely, Jr.
Black Tennesseans, 1900-1930 by Lester C. Lamon
Political Power in Birmingham, 1871-1921 by Carl V. Harris
The Challenge to Urban Liberalism: Federal-City Relations during World War II by Philip J. Funigiello
Testing the Roosevelt Coalition: Connecticut Society and Politics in the Era of World War II by John W. Jeffries
Black Americans in the Roosevelt Era: Liberalism and Race by John B. Kirby